STRATEGIC PROJECT MANAGEMENT TRANSFORMATION

Delivering Maximum ROI & Sustainable Business Value

MARC RESCH, PMP

Copyright ©2011 by Marc Resch

ISBN: 978-1-60427-064-8

Printed and bound in the U.S.A. Printed on acid-free paper

10 9 8 7 6 5 4 3 2 1

Library of Congress Cataloging-in-Publication Data

Resch, Marc, 1968–
Strategic project management transformation : delivering maximum ROI &
sustainable business value / by Marc Resch.
    p. cm.
  Includes index.
  ISBN 978-1-60427-064-8 (hardcover : alk. paper)
1. Project management. 2. Strategic planning. I. Title.
  HD69.P75R47 2011
  658.4'012—dc22
                                                              2011015498

Phone: (954) 727-9333
Fax: (561) 892-0700
Web: www.jrosspub.com

Contents

Acknowledgments

I would like to acknowledge and thank Bill Vignes for his tremendous contributions to this book. Bill not only volunteered his personal time to review and provide valuable insight and input, but also coached me throughout the entire process, which made it truly fulfilling and rewarding. A better coach can't be found anywhere! I would also like to thank Sunny van der Berg for her superhero formatting skills and for assisting me with numerous aspects of this book. Finally, I'd like to thank my editor and publisher Drew Gierman of J. Ross Publishing for his professionalism and for encouraging and assisting me throughout all phases of this project.

Preface

Why This Book and Why Now?

You can't read any project management publication or business trade journal these days without seeing references to the astronomically high failure rates for projects. It's common to see project failure rates reported as high as 60, 70, and even up to 85%! These failed projects, consequently, result in *billions* of dollars of wasted money. It's also common to see business leaders commiserating around water coolers about their out-of-control project costs and the negligible business value that results from all this spending. It pains me to see such staggering statistics and discontent from corporate leaders because I know it's not due to the lack of effort or competence of project professionals around the world. There is something inherently flawed in the way projects are being managed and executed at *all levels* of organizations to have so many of them result in failure. These flawed approaches have to stop if we are to prevent this disturbing trend.

I don't lend much credence to all of those alarming statistics regarding the costs and percentages of failed projects, and I won't definitively quote any of them in this book. But one thing is for sure, there are *a lot* of project failures occurring out there and that is not good. We need to stop wasting our valuable time, money, and efforts on failed projects. There are too many skilled and dedicated project and business professionals to allow this trend to continue.

Why do so many projects fail? Quite simply, it's because they don't deliver the financial value or business benefits they are set out to deliver. At best they deliver a fraction of their targeted business outcomes. What's truly unfortunate is that project professionals often execute these projects flawlessly and receive sign-off and approval from satisfied stakeholders, and yet these projects still don't deliver the expected results. A strong emphasis is placed on project delivery, but the focus on value attainment is seriously lacking.

The transformation from project management to *strategic* project management is long overdue. All levels of organizations must embrace this transformation if they are to turn their project failures into project successes. Project investments can only be successful when they deliver their expected business returns. By embracing and implementing business-focused, value-driven project processes and techniques, organizations can consistently achieve optimal and sustainable business returns from their project investments. This book shows how organizations and individuals can make this transformation.

Who Is the Target Audience for This Book?

Projects are financial and strategic investments implemented to produce maximum financial returns and beneficial change so that organizations maintain or increase their competitiveness in the marketplace. Projects are instrumental for a company's long-term success and possibly their survival. It is imperative, therefore, that corporations achieve, and even exceed, the desired results from their project investments. To achieve these strategic results, all levels throughout the organization must play active roles in project selection, execution, and value attainment efforts. With any project, important decisions are made, funding is provided, resources are allocated, change is implemented, resistance is overcome, and behaviors are modified. It takes more than just the project manager and core project team to perform these critical activities; it also requires active involvement from practically all areas of the business. For this reason, the target audience for this book is anyone involved in the end-to-end delivery of project investments—from project ideation to value attainment. We are embarking on an organizational transformation, not just a project management one.

Professional Development Game Plan for Success

Organizational transformation begins with individuals, and this means you! At the conclusion of each chapter you will find the Professional Development Game Plan for Success. Warren Buffet, a man who knows a thing or two about investments, says, "The most important investment you can make is in yourself." To transform ourselves and those around us into business-focused, value-driven project professionals, we need to invest in our professional development to enhance our knowledge and capabilities in key areas of project value management. Irrespective of your title or role within your organization, you, undoubtedly, have some involvement, authority, influence, decision-making abilities, or input into one or several projects. By following the Professional Game Plan for Success at the end of each chapter, you will enhance your knowledge and capabilities considerably in value attainment processes and techniques and, as a result, will be able to positively impact your organization and the outcomes of all of your project investments.

They say that knowledge is power, but knowledge with action is even more powerful. For this reason, you will not only be learning, but you will be taking action as you navigate the Professional Development Game Plan for Success. I will be asking you thought-provoking questions to stimulate your mind and to help you determine your appropriate courses of action. I highly encourage you to take the exercises seriously and put forth the effort to learn from them and apply them to your jobs. Too often we read books and immediately forget what we just read. The Game Plan for Success will prevent this from occurring. I will be asking you to revisit and scrutinize some of your prior project deliverables to solidify what you've learned in the chapter. I will also be asking you to develop strategies and action plans for your current or future projects based on the lessons that you learned from the chapter and your prior projects. *I can't overemphasize the importance of writing down your findings, conclusions, and action plans!* Writing down this information will set your development efforts in motion and will create the roadmap to your eventual success.

You can record your information however you see fit, but we've provided a downloadable, easy-to-use Professional Development Game Plan for Success template at www.jrosspub.com/wav for your convenience. This template is designed around the questions and action plans set forth at the end of each chapter and can guide you through the process. You can print the template and write down your information the old-fashioned way, or you can complete it on your computer. It doesn't matter as long as you do it. Let's get started. Go ahead and download this template and be on your way to becoming a business-focused, value-driven professional who delivers maximum and sustainable business value from all of your project investments!

Foreword

I've been a business development executive for consulting companies for most of my career. As such, my teams are brought in to discuss, scope, and deliver projects that lend to an organization's increased business value in some way, shape, or form. Whether it's risk mitigation, creating operational efficiencies, or focusing directly on creating a measurable strategic advantage, we always know that there's a bigger picture in mind.

What frustrates me is the number of times we engage in these high-level, strategic, business-value conversations with our customers only to find the value we're trying to drive is lost in the mire of on-time, on-budget metrics that seem to pervade the middle management layers of an organization.

Currently, as a VP and a director of a global consulting firm, I see this from yet another level. The C-level executives get it today. All divisions within an organization need to demonstrate measurable business value. Measures are taken, frameworks are adopted, and cultural transformation initiatives abound, but it still seems like something is getting lost in the translation when it gets down to individual project execution.

With this book, Marc has given every layer of a project initiative, from the chief stakeholder to a member of the implementation team, the framework, tools, baseline education, and motivation to align all lifecycle phases toward helping an organization realize every last bit of business value they can wring from their investment dollars.

I am also a trained business and personal development coach, and I am passionate about it. Developing the *who* in the equation is paramount to the *what* and the *how*, which seem to fall in place once individuals are aligned with their core beliefs and goals. This is where the greatest gains can be realized and they reverberate throughout an organization, a family, or a person's life. Within the context of the people, process, and tools analogy, Marc also adopts a strong *people* approach, helping the project professional identify areas to shift his viewpoints from a daily, task-laden existence to a focus on the greater good of the organization.

Marc understands that people are not invested in tasks. What motivates an individual changes from person to person, but one thing is universal: People have an inherent need and strive to be a part of something bigger than themselves and, in this quest, they strive to add value.

While the focused, measured, and daily tasks of any project are integral, I have been involved in only a precious few projects that were built to align a team toward a greater, singular vision. Marc's vision is to align the entire project team toward the greater good in driving true shareholder value for the organization.

There's a story about two workers who are lugging heavy lumber, concrete, and such under a blazing sun, building a structure. It's clear that one is miserable and the other seems energized. When the first one is asked, "How's it going?" the response is, "I just can't wait to get done with work so I can get home. Dragging heavy stuff around in this heat is horrible." The second one answers the same question with a resounding, "GREAT!" When pushed further for why he is so great, he offers, "I'm building a school where children are going to learn and grow!" Are you implementing a tool or helping a company grow to increase value, jobs, or putting food on your colleagues' tables? Marc is not only helping individuals get better at their jobs, but when adopted globally, he'll be adding to the productivity of world economies!

In Marc's Professional Development Game Plan for Success sections at the end of each chapter, you are encouraged to spend some time thinking about yourself and your projects, and this is the one thing most people lack in their day-to-day existence. We move forward from one task to the next barely taking the time to evaluate, assess, re-assess, or enjoy what we are doing. And when we do take the time to evaluate ourselves and our conditions, we're only asking the questions we inherently know to ask—those things wired into our brains over the last decades. The collaboration Marc brings from his vantage point of expertise adds creativity and true personal growth to the equation. We are prompted to look at things we've taken for granted, examine currently held beliefs for their validity today, and urged to consider new options that we may not have thought of before.

As is typically true of the universe (at least the one that I live in), I'm blessed to have had the honor to aid in the development of this remarkable book and to have re-connected with Marc at a time when our two distinct paths are so closely aligned.

The fact that you found this book at this time also has its reason. Read on!

Bill Vignes
Founder, FIRST AND GOAL Coaching
www.firstandgoalcoach.com

FIRST AND GOAL Coaching provides executive, organizational, and individual coaching to help our clients achieve drastic gains and create impactful shifts in the areas of: productivity revenue and profit creation, true alignment and coordination, and improved performance by implementing trusted methodologies and developing the individuals and teams integral to success.

About the Author

 Marc Resch, PMP, is president of Resch Consulting Group (www.reschgroup.com), specializing in assisting companies around the world to generate optimal and sustainable business results from their project investments. As a business process and technology strategy professional with more than 20 years in the field, Marc has helped numerous Fortune 500 companies achieve their project and business goals through value-focused, data-driven approaches. He possesses expertise in strategy development, organizational transformation, PMO design and deployment, process improvement, and technology deployment and optimization.

Marc is a member of the Project Management Institute and is active in both the New York and New Jersey chapters. He maintains a certification in the process-oriented IT Infrastructure Library and is a regular speaker at conferences and events around the world.

Resch graduated from the U.S. Military Academy at West Point, received an MBA from the University of North Carolina and an MS in Technology Management from Stevens Institute of Technology. He is an adjunct professor at Centenary College in New Jersey, teaching in the areas of business strategy, quantitative methods, and organizational leadership.

As a military officer and international business consultant, Marc spent time exploring many cultures and business practices around the world. His observations of the Netherlands and his working and social interactions with the Dutch laid the groundwork for his first book *Only in Holland, Only the Dutch* (www .onlyinholland.com) published by Rozenberg Publishers in Amsterdam.

Marc Resch currently resides in New Jersey, and he can be contacted at marc@reschgroup.com.

At J. Ross Publishing we are committed to providing today's professional with practical, hands-on tools that enhance the learning experience and give readers an opportunity to apply what they have learned. That is why we offer free ancillary materials available for download on this book and all participating Web Added Value™ publications. These online resources may include interactive versions of material that appears in the book or supplemental templates, worksheets, models, plans, case studies, proposals, spreadsheets and assessment tools, among other things. Whenever you see the WAV™ symbol in any of our publications, it means bonus materials accompany the book and are available from the Web Added Value Download Resource Center at www.jrosspub.com.

Downloads available for *Strategic Project Management Transformation: Delivering Maximum ROI & Sustainable Business Value* consist of business plan and cash flow templates and a review of the Professional Development Game Plan for Success.

1

Projects Are Strategic Investments

In the state of nature profit is the measure of right.
—Thomas Hobbes

Value Still Matters

Take a second and think about the key success criteria of any project. What are your thoughts? Did you say, "On-time and within budget, hit the deliverables, or even obtain stakeholder sign-off"? Are you surprised when I tell you that the CEO, corporate executives, and shareholders would say that you're wrong? If you said, "Business value," you're on the right track, and if you said, "Profit," you're thinking like an executive. In today's competitive environment, every dollar spent needs to be tightly tied to the bottom line: a company's overall profitability. Every project needs to be viewed as a strategic investment that demands a return. How much money did the project make the company? If the project didn't drive profit or cost savings, then why spend valuable and finite resources on it? It's become abundantly clear that projects are strategic investments, and a project that makes money for the company or ensures value continuity is a good investment; if it doesn't make the company money or provide value continuity, it is a bad one.

With shareholders' insatiable quest for profitability and returns on their investments, corporate leaders are accountable for demonstrating these returns in all areas of the business. At any given moment within an organization, the portfolio of projects can be immense, consuming invaluable corporate resources; namely time and money. It is imperative, therefore, that the utilization of time and money is well spent and that project efforts directly contribute to

1

the overall benefit of the company. This book describes the processes, techniques, and tools that project professionals can use to forecast accurately the quantifiable benefits, to guide project execution toward those benefits, to hand-off a solid value attainment plan to business operations, and, ultimately, to attain—and even exceed—the targeted business benefits.

Project professionals are now on the front lines of delivering profitability. They must view their projects as investments and treat them as such. Much like an investor expects an investment company to perform a proper and thorough analysis of its portfolio of stocks, project stakeholders expect their project teams to perform similar analyses on their portfolio of projects. Investment companies produce periodic performance reports with detailed metrics for their investors. Similarly, project teams must produce project performance reports for their stakeholders showing the business value that their projects are delivering to the company.

A paradigm shift needs to take place at the corporate and project level. How do we make the jump from *project management* to *project value management?* By the end of this book you'll have all of the tools you need to be the catalyst in this transformation.

Managers, stakeholders, project sponsors, project managers, business owners, and anyone else involved in selecting and delivering projects must now think in terms of strategic investments. Projects must have a business focus with quantifiable value metrics identified, monitored, and reported throughout the project lifecycle—and even beyond—to truly capture business value from them. This strategic approach will greatly enhance a project team's ability to guide the project decision making process and fine-tune project execution for peak performance and results.

Questions that project professionals need to ask include:

Project predeployment

- Should we invest in the project?
- How do we differentiate between competing projects?
- How do we calculate return on investment (ROI) and other business metrics?
- What can we expect to achieve, in hard numbers, if we invest in this project?
- In which projects should we invest?
- What are the important non-ROI contributing benefits?
- What are the success criteria for this project?
- How do we account for risk and uncertainty?
- How can we build an accurate business case with so much uncertainty?

Project execution and operations

- Is the project achieving its intended business objectives?
- Is the project making us money or is it on track to make us money?
- How can management help guide the execution to achieve and optimize business objectives?

- Are the key metrics being monitored and reported?
- Does management understand the metrics that are being reported?
- Are the metrics useful?
- Should we continue, modify, or even terminate the project?

Post-project

- Was the project successful? Was it a wise investment?
- Did the project contribute to the company's bottom line?
- Did the project achieve its intended benefits?

- Are we done monitoring and reporting on the key project metrics?
- What lessons learned can be garnered from this project?
- Now what?

The Fundamentals of Business Haven't Changed

The purpose of any for-profit organization, simply put, is to increase shareholder wealth. Everything that a business does should contribute to that overarching objective. Even not-for-profit organizations need to tighten their belts these days and demonstrate value in order to receive funding and keep their doors open. Certainly there are ancillary purposes of business relating to employees, customers, and the communities in which they serve, but the underlying reason that businesses operate is to make money for the shareholders.

Today's environment demands the scrutiny of every dollar spent on projects and the close evaluation of the value delivered. The executives and project teams are under ever-growing pressure to quantify and validate business benefits for their project investments. If business professionals are unable to forecast the business value of possible investments, these initiatives may not be approved, even though they may indeed be beneficial to the company. Business professionals *must* possess the knowledge and skills necessary to quantify the projected returns on all of their potential investments. Project professionals *must* be able to measure and report on the progress of their projects using quantifiable metrics in order to make informed decisions that lead to increased business value.

The need to articulate the business value of projects is not limited to companies of a certain size or vertical industry. Nearly all companies are now requiring that business metrics are clearly identified and presented to project stakeholders on a regular basis. Quantifying business value and driving a project toward attaining clearly defined business benefits require strategic skills and a solid understanding of the company's vision and objectives. Project professionals must possess a combination of business, leadership, project management, and financial skills to effectively manage their projects, optimize business value, and make money for their companies. The good news is that these skills can be acquired, and project professionals equipped with these skill sets will be able to effectively drive their projects to create business value for their companies.

All companies are faced with finite resources that must be shared throughout their organizations. Money, personnel, and equipment are resources that managers must fight for to support their projects. If managers can't forecast quantifiable business returns, they may lose out altogether or only get a portion of what they require. So how do we fight for and receive these resources? *Resources will be granted to those managers who can project and articulate quantifiable business returns in a data-supported and logical manner.* These managers, in turn, will not only get approval for their current projects, but will more than likely continue to receive project approval for their future projects because of their abilities to articulate business value more effectively than their peers.

The business world has seen many changes over the past century with regard to management styles, workforce procedures, quality control, and organizational theory. Figure 1.1 presents a timeline with some of these business concepts and initiatives over the past century.

There have been numerous and diverse management theories and approaches over the years that have altered the business landscape. Some of these theories have come and gone, and some have resurfaced decades after their inception. I've recently conducted time-motion studies on a Lean methodology project that incorporated Frederick Taylor's 19th-century time study principles. Even with the introduction and re-introduction of management philosophies and approaches, one aspect has always remained constant. Businesses need to make money, regardless of their approach, to be competitive in the marketplace and increase shareholder wealth.

The Need to Quantify Business Results

Executives, shareholders, and even regulatory agencies are carefully examining the minute details of financial statements now more than ever. The Enron, Arthur Anderson, WorldCom, and Lehman Brothers scandals—to name a few—have highlighted the devastating effects that creative accounting can have on a company, its shareholders, and even the communities in which they serve. New regulatory requirements, such as Sarbanes-Oxley, Graham-Leach, HIPAA, Basel II, and others, have been imposed on corporations, requiring even more diligence with their record keeping and financial reporting. Most

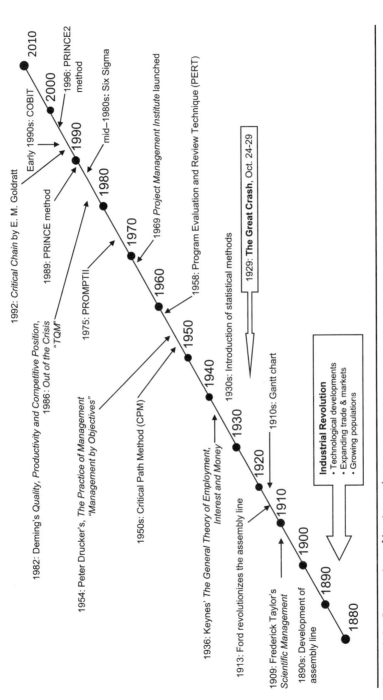

Figure 1.1 Progression of business theory

recently, the institutional banking crisis of 2009, where the government intervened and bailed out numerous banks, is leading to even more scrutiny of the accounting methods and financial reporting of corporations. With the financials under the microscope and the constant push for profitability, it's no wonder that corporate leaders are demanding to know where every penny is spent and what the returns are for each and every one of their project investments.

Many corporate leaders have adopted the mantra *no project approval without a positive ROI*. I've personally witnessed managers dismissing project ideas because project teams could not articulate the value of their proposals in business terms. That is not to say the projects were bad ideas, merely that the project teams lacked the business acumen to present their ideas using appropriate business language and metrics. This is unfortunate because some of these projects were excellent ideas and the project outputs would have been beneficial for their organizations.

Even when projects do get approved, companies struggle with effectively measuring and reporting the business benefits derived from these projects. There are many reasons why companies fail to enforce business-value measurement techniques. The most common reasons are:

- Lack of concern once the project receives funding
- Too much focus on getting the project done on-time and within budget
- Project personnel lack the skill sets to quantify business benefits
- Confusion over the benefits that contribute directly or indirectly to the ROI
- Project stakeholders are too busy
- Project planning documents and business cases rarely revisited once they are approved
- Minimal interdepartmental collaboration
- Tactical thinking with short-term focus
- Management doesn't provide top-down support

Companies that proactively identify, track, and manage key business metrics, on the other hand, are able to show positive results for their project efforts expressed in financial, business, and quantitative terms. These companies are able to make informed decisions about their projects and can guide them in the direction that yields the greatest business value. With this value-focused approach, project teams can demonstrate quantitative results expressed in business terms that stakeholders understand. Examples of quantitative business results derived from project investments include:

- Generated a net present value of $3.2 million by upgrading workflow management systems and software
- Achieved 85% ROI with the implementation of an employee resource planning system
- Reduced inventory by 75% to an all-time low

- Achieved 15% cost savings with a business process re-design project
- Cut procurement cost by 70%
- Increased labor efficiency by 65%
- Reached the payback period in only 14 months by accelerating project efforts
- Produced a single interface for managing all customer-facing activities, resulting in a 32% increase in export sales
- Achieved a 22% internal rate of return for the business transformation project
- Deployed SAP software and achieved total savings of $430 million
- Consolidated data centers and reduced information technology costs by 60%
- Increased cash flow by 13% with improved planning and production cycle times
- Deployed an automated replenishment system, resulting in a 95% forecasting accuracy with business partners

Modern Day Challenges

Most companies do an adequate job of managing their projects via the triple-constraints of time, cost, and scope. These measurements are still important and are valid measures of project success, but they are not the ultimate measurements of success. In addition to the triple constraints, project professionals need to focus on positive and negative cash flows, various ROI measurements, financial and nonfinancial benefits, and other key performance measurements. No, you won't need advanced degrees in mathematics, statistics, or even business to be able to generate optimal value from your project investments. You will need to implement strategic business processes and techniques to accurately forecast, measure, and manage key business metrics to effectively guide your project and business decisions to achieve optimized business value.

Whether at the organizational or individual level, a transformation is required to make this kind of shift, and along with change comes resistance. Long established behaviors die hard, but to implement a business-focused value management approach the shift from tactical to strategic thinking must take place. The area in which this will become most apparent is how we deal with business data. Relevant business data must be captured and analyzed to guide project decisions to create business value. There are challenges to capturing performance data as it typically is not centralized, and individuals are sometimes not as forthcoming as they should be with some of this information. While soliciting workers throughout organizations for project support, or while obtaining required business data, some of the responses that project professionals may encounter are:

- Takes too much time to gather such information.

- Too costly to get the data.
- Not my job to assist with other department initiatives.
- Who wants to know and why?
- This information is not pertinent.
- We've been doing just fine.
- I don't have the information.
- I'll get to it when I can.

Securing reliable business data for analysis is not simple. Project professionals may make valiant efforts to obtain critical project data only to end up frustrated and empty-handed because the need for such information hasn't been communicated to the various data sources. This is where executive sponsorship is paramount. When there is minimal support from the higher echelons of management for projects, little support will be given to project teams from the various departments. If a project is not a priority for members at the top, it certainly won't be a priority for the lower levels of the organizational pyramid.

Project professionals will continue to face these challenges as their roles evolve into even more strategic ones. All of these challenges, however, are not insurmountable and can be overcome with strategic leadership, diplomacy, and sound value management processes. As readers of this book, you are undoubtedly involved in some manner with the selection and delivery of projects, and you realize (or are being encouraged by your bosses to realize) the importance of showing measurable business value for your projects.

I will show you how you can incorporate strategic and quantitative business processes in your project management approach to give you an extra advantage in the competitive business world by teaching you to:

- Think strategically about projects
- Determine the business value of projects both in a quantitative and qualitative manner
- Get projects consistently approved
- Manage projects strategically throughout an *enhanced* project lifecycle using value-focused processes and techniques
- Implement sound stakeholder management processes to ensure project support and accountability
- Incorporate effective quantitative methods into the project management framework
- Identify, quantify, and report on key business and project metrics
- Make informed decisions and provide timely recommendations to senior management
- Develop value attainment programs to achieve optimal business value

- Use project data in *lessons learned* sessions to promote efficiencies for future projects
- Deploy continuous improvement processes that extend beyond project closure
- Get promoted!

Professional Development Game Plan for Success

1. When your executives spend money on projects, they expect to get profitable financial returns and other value-enabling business benefits from their investments. Are you thinking along these lines? What type of return did you plan to get from your last project investment? What did you do to maximize business returns from your project efforts? What was your main project goal? Tell the truth—was it completing your projects on-time and within budget?

   Action Plan

   a. Revisit two or three of your completed projects. Dust off the business cases and key deliverables and determine if these were worthwhile investments in your firm. If you were an investor, would you have invested your money in these projects or would you have pursued other, more profitable and beneficial project investments? Write down three to five reasons why these projects were or were not good investments in your company. (Record all of your answers after you download the Professional Development Game Plan for Success template at www.jrosspub .com/wav.)

   b. Now assess whether these projects were *treated* as financial and strategic investments in your company or simply as normal, everyday business affairs. Which quantitative performance objectives did you establish? How did you monitor and present the findings to management throughout the project lifecycle? What actions were taken based on these performance measurements to ensure optimal performance results? As an investor, what would you want to know about your project team and the steps they were taking to ensure the return on your investment? Were the project performance objectives ultimately achieved? Do you even know? If it is difficult for you to answer the questions above, it's time to make the shift to project *value* management. For each of the projects you used, write down three to five activities that should have been conducted or handled differently to ensure that the project teams treated and deployed these projects as strategic investments in the company and not merely everyday business affairs.

c. Now consider a current or future project. As a strategic, business-focused project professional, what can you do to ensure that you, and everyone around you, are viewing this project as an important financial investment in the firm? Write down three to five actions you will take, behaviors you will exhibit, or decisions you will make to ensure that the project is being viewed and treated as a strategic investment and not just something that needs to get completed on-time and within budget.

2

Strategic Planning: The Foundation for Success

There's never enough time to do it right the first time, but time enough to do it over if it's wrong!

—Unknown

Where Did the Planning Process Go?

I am astonished with how the planning process has become somewhat of a burden. Companies unwisely rush into the execution phases of their projects. With this mad dash to get things done quickly, companies skimp on the planning process to the detriment of their overall project success. Inadequate planning in the early stages of a project leads to difficult and tenuous situations for project teams as they progress through the project lifecycle, as I'm sure many of you can attest. It's no wonder so many projects fail to achieve their intended results and why project portfolios are laden with projects misaligned with corporate objectives and have low, overall value potential.

It's time to get back to the basics in many areas of project and overall business management. Just as in sports, it's critical to have an effective game plan when embarking on a project and to actively manage that game plan to achieve success. In American football, for instance, coaches conduct detailed and comprehensive planning sessions 6 days and nights every week, all for a 60-minute game that is played on Sunday. For both coaches and project professionals, requirements frequently change as unforeseen situations arise or as the competitive climate fluctuates. Game plans must be modified based

11

on these changing situations. Without a solid game plan that includes built-in contingencies, it is extremely challenging to adapt to changing situations or even to conduct project affairs in a coordinated fashion. An effective project game plan can only be established when planning is taken seriously and executed with the right participants.

I've had the great fortune of working with numerous cultures around the world and observing how certain cultural attributes are intertwined with certain business processes. In some cultures, the planning process is revered and is an integral part of the overall cultural and business climate. In such cultures, a rather lengthy planning process is carefully conducted that usually incorporates the tenets of group compromise and consensus building. The project planning stages can actually last the entire first half of the overall project lifecycle! Half of the time is spent on planning and half of the time is spent on executing and closing out the project.

I'm not suggesting that all projects should dedicate 50% of the time in the planning phases; all projects are different and have their own unique attributes. I am saying, however, that the length of the various phases of a project can be determined only with proper planning. Figure 2.1 shows examples of projects with different durations for the various lifecycle phases. As can be seen, project phases differ drastically from project to project and are dependent on the numerous project requirements and other factors. Efforts should be made to determine these timeframes at the onset of any project.

With the ever increasing need to show positive results on a quarterly basis, most companies operate in overdrive, and this overdrive mentality certainly flows down to the project level. Even with this sense of urgency to get things done quickly, project managers and their respective teams have been doing a tremendous job executing their projects and showing positive results. More often than not, these project outcomes have come as a result of sheer grit and determination—a true hero culture we can be! Even without allocating the necessary amount of time in the planning phases, project professionals have been able to navigate the many obstacles and drive their projects to completion. Many of these project professionals fought constant uphill battles and swam against strong currents, but eventually got the job done. I tip my hat to all of those determined project warriors! But as the role of the project team is expanding into a more strategic, business-focused one, it's going to take more than sheer grit and determination to get the job done and to achieve optimal business value from projects.

The Consequences of Inadequate Planning

Companies frequently initiate projects with inadequate upfront business, strategic, or financial analyses. Many times projects are initiated because, quite simply, they seem like good ideas or because their competitors are executing

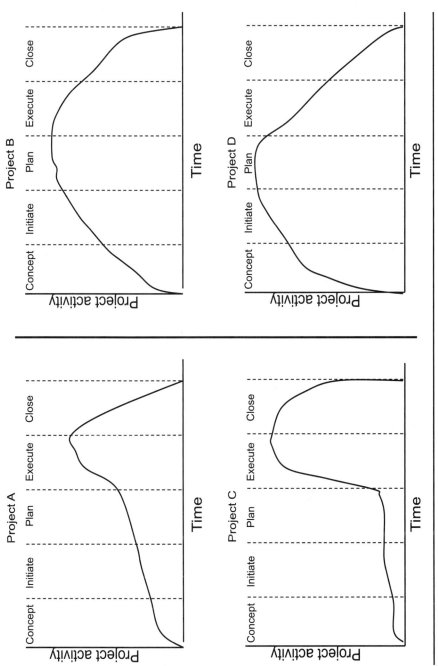

Figure 2.1 Project lifecycle timeframe examples

similar projects. I find it surprising that many companies feel pressured to implement the latest technologies even though their current technologies are supporting their business objectives just fine. As they rush to implement these new technologies, they struggle with the various nuances and glitches that are common in new technology releases or upgrades. With proper analysis up-front, many of these companies could realize that a better strategy may be to let others be the pioneers with the new technology and allow time for the glitches to be rectified. Companies always have the *do nothing* choice, and sometimes that choice is the best one.

Without adequate time allocated to planning and business analysis, project teams cannot build proper business cases and won't be able to provide justifiable reasons for their projects. Since these projects aren't treated as financial investments, they will likely fail and business benefits will not be realized. In the United States alone, the cost to companies for failed projects is estimated to be in the billions of dollars! There are other astonishing figures in the numerous trade publications stating that project failure rates can be as high as 90%. As stated in the Preface, I don't lend much credence to these exaggerated statistics; the methods for deriving these figures are often misguided and poorly executed. We can say with certainty, however, that project failure rates are extremely high and these failure rates are due in large part to inadequate planning, which is truly the foundation for project success. There are scores of reasons for the high failure rates of projects, and most of these reasons could have been avoided with proper planning (Table 2.1).

In today's global business environment, project professionals face more challenges than ever before that clearly contribute to the project failure rates. Project professionals need to be acutely aware of not only their own cultural and governmental norms and requirements, but those of other cultures around the world. A few of today's challenges in the global marketplace are:

- Vast geographical spread comprising multilingual, multicultural business environments
- Time zone differences requiring changes to the traditional workday
- Continuous organizational changes due to mergers, acquisitions, and ongoing reorganizations
- Behavioral and procedural differences across varying cultures
- Heterogeneous technology systems landscape
- Regulatory requirements in the different operating regions

Even with the additional challenges of today's global marketplace, project leaders are still responsible for the outcomes of their projects. Failed projects can be catastrophic for an organization, even if these failed projects were completed on-time and within budget. The intended results and business benefits are not accomplished and, further, failed projects often cause other unforeseen, adverse consequences, such as unmet customer needs, inefficient

Table 2.1 Reasons for failed projects

Poorly defined goals	Unclear accountability for capturing value	Business not ready for new capabilities
Limited stakeholder buy-in	Inaccurate business case	Lack of training
Rushed execution	Budget overruns	Business not ready for change
Not aligned with corporate objectives	Capabilities delivered late	Reluctance to change to new operating models
Limited accountability	Costs are underestimated to get financial approvals	Poor quality of technology launched
No value measurements in place	No systematic approach to manage scope changes	No project management methodology
Unrealistic expectations	Wrong role assignments	Changing direction mid-project
Resource limitations	Governance has no real decision-making capability	Wrong capabilities delivered
Confusion over ROI and other benefits	Performance measurements are not implemented	Closing projects before benefits are attained

use of resources, low morale, turnover, and other dire results. It is imperative, therefore, that projects are clearly defined. The success criteria has to be well thought out and established. Additionally, upfront diligent planning is conducted to satisfy business requirements and objectives.

It is simply good business to invest in those projects that yield the greatest returns and are most closely aligned with the corporate strategy. To do otherwise is a disservice to the corporate shareholders. Since nobody can predict the future with absolute certainty, proper planning, analysis, and collaboration are required to develop a solid business case to show that the project will indeed produce desirable results. Additionally, value metrics must be identified, gathered, and analyzed as the project progresses. Throughout the project's lifecycle, these are used to assess the project's effectiveness and to help guide project decisions. For many organizations such an approach poses great challenges because it requires a new way of conducting business. A paradigm shift from tactical thinking to strategic analysis must take place, and it all begins in the early planning stages of the project lifecycle.

Poorly planned projects typically negate their business value by running over budget and deriving limited benefits from their solutions. Projects that are rushed into without proper upfront planning and analysis may end up costing more money than the project saves! Money is spent, but there is little to show for the expense.

Poor planning manifests itself in several ways. One of the most common manifestations is the complete lack of communication between the project team building a new solution and the operations team that is going to manage it going forward. In my experience, failure to take into account the operational complexities is one of the most important aspects overlooked during a rushed planning phase. Too often project teams do a good job at conducting project affairs, but they don't work closely enough with the operational teams responsible for ensuring that the expected business benefits are achieved. At the project's closure, the project teams disband and the project outputs are handed over to the operational teams with little or no support. In such a scenario, the project outputs aren't understood by the operational teams, which usually results in mismanagement of the project solution, cost overruns, and unrealized benefits. Figure 2.2 shows a typical example of a project outcome with cost overruns as a result of inadequate planning. As can be seen, these project cost overruns can be significant.

Many companies end up having an inflated project portfolio because they don't treat projects as financial investments, and they execute inadequate project approval processes. Many of the projects in the portfolio, consequently, end up lingering in *open* or *green* status for extended periods of time and drain valuable resources. It's critical for companies to get a handle on all of the projects within their portfolios. One of the first things I do when embarking on any transformational project is to achieve an understanding for all of the projects that are currently in the portfolio list. In pursuing this endeavor, I usually find an inordinate number of projects that aren't even being addressed. I also find that many employees seem to take pride in the number of projects for which they are responsible, even though most of their projects linger in green status with little attention being given to them. Many of these workers even

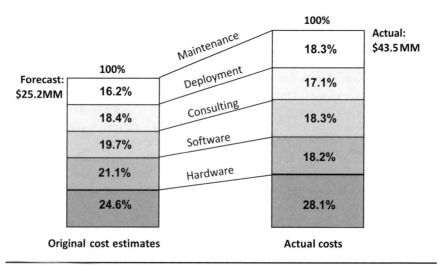

Figure 2.2   Project cost overruns

feel that having an unmanageable number of projects within their purview shows their importance to the organization and even provides for job security. *Now this is an example of tactical thinking!* This mentality of *more is better* does a disservice to the organization.

In analyzing these inflated project portfolios, most of the projects have little or no linkages to the strategic intent or the corporate objectives of the firm. Additionally, the status for these projects is usually reported as *in progress* or *on target*, even though the project completion dates have been pushed back several times. When companies take the time to capture a snapshot of all of their projects, they are oftentimes quite surprised by what they find:

- Project redundancies
- Misalignment with strategic objectives
- Incomplete business cases
- Little or no business value
- Incomplete project charters
- No management support
- Missed completion dates
- Little or no activity
- No tracking or reporting of value metrics

In many cases, the more projects that are in the portfolio, the fewer the resources to support them; this results in fewer projects being completed successfully. Quite often it makes good business sense to cut the project portfolio in half. It may sound counterintuitive, but by having fewer projects, an organization can actually complete more of them in a more efficient and cost-effective manner.

Before we go any further, let's define a project:

> *A project is a temporary endeavor; having a defined beginning and end; undertaken to meet particular goals and objectives; usually intended to bring about beneficial change or added value.*

Therefore, projects must have clearly defined start and end dates and quantifiable business objectives that are beneficial to an organization. Projects with end dates that are constantly being pushed back aren't treated as true projects and certainly don't add value to the organization. Project portfolio reviews can be quite beneficial for organizations to identify the truly important projects that bring beneficial change and to terminate the superfluous ones that merely drain valuable resources.

Project Value Alignment with Corporate Strategy

The days when project professionals merely focused on developing status reports, produced meeting agendas and minutes, created Gantt charts, and tracked project issues are long gone. Project professionals still need to know the intricacies of their projects and must still perform traditional project management duties, but they also need to see the big picture. That is, they need to be acutely aware of the business imperatives; the firm's mission, vision, strategic objectives, goals, corporate image, competitive landscape, and how their projects tie into these business imperatives. To initiate relevant projects and guide them to successful completion with quantifiable success metrics, project professionals have to possess not merely a cursory knowledge of their business landscape, but an in-depth and comprehensive understanding. It goes without saying that all business leaders within project teams, including stakeholders, steering committee members, and project advisors, need to possess this in-depth, comprehensive understanding as well.

If project benefits aren't directly related to the corporate strategic goals and objectives, they aren't actually benefits, or at least not as beneficial as they should be. True project benefits are ones that contribute directly to the overall strategic intent of the firm—the big picture. Unfortunately, many projects are aimed at alleviating immediate distress and often do not incorporate strategies that are aligned to the corporate vision. This mindset has to change as businesses are becoming more project-driven in their approach to achieving their strategic objectives.

Today's project professionals must avoid the pitfalls of losing sight of what is happening within their organizations and the environments in which they conduct business. There is a bigger picture out there, and it's the project leaders' responsibilities to find it, grasp it, and incorporate it into their overall project management approach. The good news is that it's not difficult to understand the big picture once you know where to look. Ideally, this should be completed prior to a project or during the initial stages, but it's never too late to embark on the endeavor of learning the business inside and out. I highly recommend that project leaders strive to fully understand the business, industry, and competitive landscape in which they are working because it can greatly assist in navigating project and business complexities.

There is a wealth of information out there that can be leveraged in understanding your business. Spend time perusing company websites, including the various Intranet sites if you have access. Download the annual reports for the past 3 to 5 years and get to know how the business climate has changed in those years. Look for executive presentations, town hall meeting material, steering committee documents, business plans, and other strategic, visionary material. If you can't find this material, actively seek it through management teams. In many cases, if you ask for a business plan and one doesn't exist, your company may have other, greater issues that need to be addressed. If you're lucky enough, you may even be asked to put together a business plan. Now that's a great way to get to know the business climate inside and out. In fact, why wait to be asked? Volunteering for such a worthwhile endeavor can make you an expert in your field and can go a long way in your professional development and your career.

Project professionals should also research the competition and analyze their websites and annual reports. Live quarterly earnings broadcasts can be heard by dialing into scheduled conference calls or logging onto webcasts. These sessions are not reserved exclusively for the investment community; anyone can attend. I also recommend subscribing to relevant industry-related publications and the *Wall Street Journal*. To reiterate a prevalent theme throughout this book, today's project professionals must possess the requisite business skills and must have a comprehensive knowledge of their business landscapes to be effective in their strategic roles. This knowledge will serve as a foundation for success as business-focused project professionals steer their projects in a way that aligns directly to the corporate strategic intent, contributes to the overall objectives, and brings about beneficial change for their organizations.

Too often organizations face misalignment between their strategic objectives and their approach to identifying, approving, and executing projects. Although the projects may deliver the tactical outcomes they set out to accomplish, frequently they don't contribute to the company's strategic objectives. There must be alignment between the strategic vision of the organization and the projects that are being executed. Projects that are aligned with the strategic intent of the organization and deliver business value are good investments and worthwhile projects; those that do not align are not good project investments. Figure 2.3 shows a high-level depiction of the strategic and tactical elements

Figure 2.3 Typical organizational construct

of a typical organization. Organizational behavior is driven from the top by setting the strategic direction, and projects are implemented to help steer the firm in that direction.

As shown in the figure, everything begins with the corporate mission, the *raison d'être*—the reason for being. The corporate mission drives all business activities. In support of the corporate mission, strategic objectives are developed. These objectives are usually quantifiable goals for the organization. To achieve these strategic objectives, strategic plans are identified, prioritized, and implemented. These strategic plans are usually implemented as projects, and this is where value-focused project management comes into play. The foundation of the pyramid, which is the most tactical in nature, is the day-to-day operational aspects of an organization—in other words, the *day jobs* that are performed to keep the lights on and the business running. The four areas of the organizational construct are now discussed in detail.

The Mission

Most mission statements are succinct and to the point. In effective organizations, all employees know the mission statement and can recite them verbatim. How many of us can say with certainty that we can recite our own corporate mission statements? As project professionals, we *must* know the organizational mission if we are to be successful in delivering business value from our projects. Everything flows downward from this corporate mission. If for no other reason, it's simply good business to know the mission because it ensures we are focused on the bigger picture. Some examples of corporate mission statements are illustrated in Figure 2.4. One thing they have in common is that they get to the point and clearly state the strategic intent.

- To deliver a competitive and sustainable rate of return to shareholders by developing, acquiring, and exploring for oil and gas resources vital to the world's health and welfare
- To provide the world's best communications solutions that enable businesses to excel
- To constantly improve what is essential to human progress by mastering science and technology
- To bring inspiration and innovation to every athlete in the world
- To give ordinary people the chance to buy the same things as rich people
- To increase the financial strength of families by helping them to purchase and use the value of their homes by offering honest, ethical advice and a variety of competitive mortgage products
- To give unlimited opportunity to women

Figure 2.4   Mission statement examples

Strategic Objectives

The strategic objectives translate the mission into business terms. Strategic objectives are usually tangible in nature and contribute directly to the corporate mission. They are clear and understandable; measurable and achievable; and consistent with the strategic intent. Figure 2.5 shows some examples.

Strategic Plans

The corporate objectives are achieved through the use of strategic plans. With companies being more project-based then ever before, most of these strategic plans are in the form of projects. Projects must be directly aligned to the corporate objectives and must produce quantifiable benefits that contribute to the strategic goals of the firm. They must demonstrate how their projects contribute to the mission and strategic objectives by showing alignment, monetary value, qualitative value, key performance indicators, and other relevant value attributes. Some examples of strategic plans, or projects, are given in Figure 2.6.

- Achieve $1 billion in revenues with $50 million profit
- Grow retail stores by 10%
- To be #1 or #2 in market share in every business the company operates
- Increase sales by 12%
- Gain market share by 5%
- Continue global expansion by providing service to eight additional countries
- Maintain the current cost structure
- Achieve compliance with federal, state, and local environmental mandates
- Reduce network security breaches by 10%
- Have zero injuries in the workplace

Figure 2.5 Strategic objectives examples

- Organizational restructuring
- SAP (or another major technology) implementation
- Operational support process improvement
- Data center consolidation
- Facility expansion
- Remote sales office deployment
- Infrastructure upgrade
- Product re-design
- Network security re-design
- Sales force automation tool implementation
- Corporate website re-design
- Departmental downsizing
- Outsourcing help desk

Figure 2.6 Strategic plans (projects) examples

As depicted, these initiatives are capable of having clearly defined beginning and end dates and can bring about beneficial change to organizations.

Day-to-day Operations

Day-to-day operations keep the business running. We commonly hear of these as tasks to keep the lights on. These operational tasks are usually nonproject-related and have no definitive beginning or end dates. Typical operational tasks are presented in Figure 2.7.

Project Value Alignment with Departmental Strategy

Certain projects may be difficult or impractical to align to the overarching corporate objectives, especially for larger companies. It may make more sense in these situations to focus on aligning with the applicable *departmental* strategic vision and objectives. Departmental objectives should be directly related to the overarching strategic intent of the firm. It is imperative, therefore, to fully comprehend the mission and goals of the department that is sponsoring the project. Figure 2.8 illustrates an example of the alignment between the strategic and tactical elements of an information technology division. Project professionals can add tremendous value to organizations by aligning their projects with departmental goals and objectives.

In this example, project initiatives and benefits can and must be directly linked to business objectives, whether at the corporate or departmental level. There is usually not a one-to-one relationship between one project benefit to one strategic objective and, quite often, one project benefit can lead to several strategic objectives. It is important to show clearly how projects contribute to the relevant strategic objectives. As an example, if your project is focused on improving product functionality, then you should show clearly which strategic

Day-to-day operations ▶
- Managing outsourcing, contractor, and vendor relationships
- Performing customer relationship responsibilities
- Manufacturing products or product components
- Hiring, training, motivating, and mentoring team members
- Ensuring adherence to corporate and regulatory guidelines
- Sanitizing food products for distribution
- Conducting regular sales and marketing calls
- Enforcing employee safety awareness programs
- Performing production and assembly line duties
- Conducting monthly financial reviews with investors

Figure 2.7   Operations examples

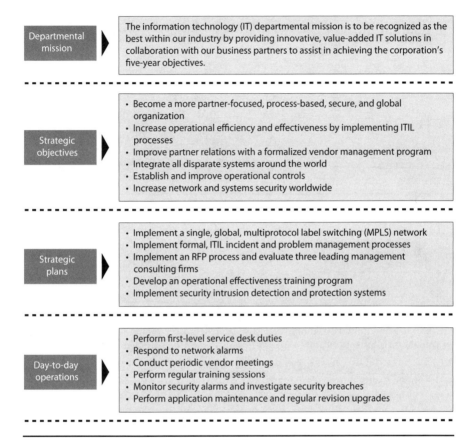

Figure 2.8 Project value alignment with departmental strategy

objectives are being met with your project. Figure 2.9 shows an example of this mapping process. Additionally, a project may have many benefits that tie back to only one strategic objective, as illustrated in Figure 2.10.

A project that can't be directly linked to strategic business objectives doesn't provide much value to the business. A project may generate a tremendous outcome, but if that outcome doesn't tie back to a strategic objective, how much value did that project really add? It is imperative, therefore, to ensure that your projects contribute to the vision and strategic objectives of the firm and that you clearly convey these contributions to business leaders. Executives and senior management crave this information because it gives them assurance that their strategic messages are being filtered down to the organization and that employees understand them.

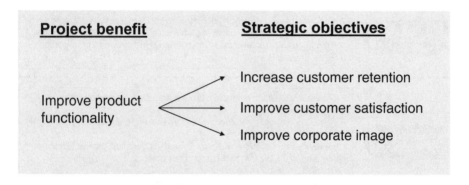

Figure 2.9   Many strategic objectives met by one project benefit

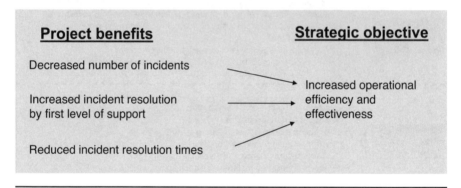

Figure 2.10   Many project benefits for one strategic objective

The Leadership Component: More Important Now

I'd like to conclude this chapter by discussing an element of importance that can't be overlooked: the leadership component to project *value* management. In this chapter we have dealt with some topics that are fairly basic in nature, but rather remarkably, are often overlooked or ineffectively executed. I want to address the leadership component because as the field of project management evolves into a more strategic, business-focused one, the requirements will become even more stringent. In forecasting business value and steering projects toward achieving that business value, project professionals will need to exhibit leadership qualities as never before. The business-focused project professional will need to work effectively with line-workers, engineers, and other staff members to gather the necessary data, synthesize that data to make it meaningful to the business, and present that information to senior-level executives, all while performing the traditional project-related activities. Sound challenging? You bet it is, but it's not impossible.

The value of a strong project leader, especially in the role of project sponsor and/or project manager, is immense. Bad project management can double, triple, or even quadruple project costs. Project leaders must deal with competing priorities, excessive workloads, fast approaching deadlines, pressure to show the business value, and constant unexpected interruptions. Business-focused project leaders need to zero in on mastering certain leadership attributes to strategically manage their projects and deliver optimal business value to their organizations. Such leadership qualities include:

- Comprehending the big picture
- Focusing on a global scale
- Maintaining a farsighted vision
- Focusing on value outcomes
- Communicating effectively at all levels
- Thinking strategically
- Being open to new ideas
- Accepting change
- Addressing risks
- Being persistent
- Being diplomatic

This list is certainly not all-inclusive, but rather addresses certain leadership attributes necessary for project leaders to compete in today's global marketplace. The project management field is clearly moving away from the management track of executing projects and is shifting rapidly to the leadership track. The discussion over the differences between managers and leaders has been going on for decades. The project manager of yesteryear clearly fell into the manager category, but we must now view the project manager role as truly that of a leader, for this role now requires a strategic business focus to bring about beneficial change that contributes to a company's bottom line.

Today's project leaders must transition from being traditional managers to that of being strategic leaders. Leaders are cognizant of the big picture at all times and focus on creating value for their organizations. Leaders focus on the overall vision and create strategies for achieving that vision. Traditional managers, conversely, are usually more analytical than visionary and focus on administering policy, creating procedures, and striving for short-term contributions. The management role is not to be undermined because policy, processes, and other management functions are essential for an organization and for projects. Table 2.2 shows some of the differences between leaders and managers. As you review the table, think of your own style and identify those areas where you may be able to step up your leadership game.

A strong leader changes the behavior of people, achieves consensus and commitment across the organization, implements change, and achieves strategic results. Project leaders need to possess, what I like to call, *adaptive*

Table 2.2 Leaders vs. managers

Leader	Manager
Seeks change	Seeks stability
Leads people	Manages work
Has followers	Has subordinates
Focused on the long-term	Focused on the short-term
Maintains a vision	Maintains objectives
Sets strategic direction	Plans details
Defines the culture	Maintains the culture
Is proactive	Is reactive
Sells ideas	Gives directives
Takes risks	Minimizes risks
Breaks rules, if appropriate	Makes rules and sticks to them
Uses conflict to generate change	Avoids conflict
Takes new approaches	Uses existing approaches
Encourages growth	Encourages the status quo
Pursues the intangible	Pursues the tangible

leadership styles to deal with the extremely situational nature of project management and business in general. Project leaders who can adapt to changing situations and personalities are more likely to be effective than those who are too rigid in their leadership styles. They need to be strong, business-focused leaders to ensure that team members remain focused, motivated, and committed to the targeted objectives; stakeholders and corporate leaders continue to support the project and make timely project decisions; and project benefits are actually realized. Achieving a positive return on investments and an optimal business value from projects relies on the decisions of corporate leaders and the actions of project and operational team members. It takes strong leadership to influence these decision makers and line-workers.

A disconcerting trend that I have witnessed over the years is the palpable disconnect between project teams and operations personnel. There is often a profound lack of communication between project teams building a solution and operations teams managing it going forward. Project team members and operations personnel usually have varying skill sets, different career paths, and contrasting business perspectives, and these differences, unnecessarily, cause internal strife that impedes progress. Project members are usually intently focused on satisfying the requirements of their projects and work feverishly to achieve that end, while operations personnel are intimately involved with keeping the business running and focused more on those activities. To exacerbate matters, many project professionals are external to the organization, many of whom are fresh out of business school with little real-world experience, whereas the operations personnel have been in the business trenches for decades. When project and operational teams are out of synch and have poor working relations, projects will, undoubtedly, encounter serious setbacks.

Operational teams are usually engrossed in day-to-day business activities, resolving issues and keeping the business running. Their time, therefore, is limited to supporting project efforts, especially since they can be asked to support multiple projects simultaneously. Project managers and team members may become frustrated with the limited availability of the operational resources because they rely on the input of these resources to support the project. Operational resources, in turn, may become frustrated with project members asking for too much of their time and taking them away from their functional duties for which they're responsible.

The varying perspectives, responsibilities, and skill sets should not be viewed as disruptive to project activities, but rather advantageous. When these differences are dealt with appropriately, they can yield tremendous benefits. Project teams are empowered to bring about change to organizations, while operations personnel have the knowledge and experience to provide input to the change process and actually make it happen. Project managers must bridge the gap between the contrasting styles and perspectives through adaptive leadership techniques. Even with the stark differences between the various team members, the project manager must ensure that everyone is focused on the long-term business objectives of the project. Achieving business value is a good thing, no matter the job function, skill sets, perspective, or where one sits within an organization.

Project leaders must be cognizant that some personnel may be willing to put their skill sets to use by putting in long hours building extraordinary presentation decks or detailed cost models, while others may be more likely to work their regular shifts providing input in a coordinated, scheduled fashion. There are certain activities that project-focused professionals can do incredibly well due to their training, skill sets, and education, and there are certain activities that operational-focused personnel can do exceptionally well due to their expansive functional and business experience. These background differences prove to be pivotal to success when embraced by project sponsors and managers. Both sides will appreciate the symbiotic relationship when project leaders are able to bring the groups together and tap into the vast skill sets within all team members. Through adaptive leadership techniques, project managers can get the pulse of team dynamics and adjust their leadership approaches accordingly to ensure optimal performance from all members of the extended project team.

I'm sure many of you have witnessed companies or project teams with an absence of strong leadership. When leadership is lacking or when traditional management methods are in place, it's inevitable that morale declines, motivation dissipates, creativity decreases, and the competitive spirit is lost. It's hard to deliver business value when teams encounter this bleak scenario. The bottom line is that project team members prefer to be led rather than to be managed, and as a value-focused project leader, you should lead rather than manage.

Professional Development Game Plan for Success

1. Planning is the cornerstone of success for any project. What is your approach toward planning? Is planning a burden to be done quickly or is it one of your most diligent project activities? How have you approached planning in your previous projects? How are you going to approach planning for your future projects?

   Action Plan

   a. Revisit two or three of your prior projects and carefully analyze the planning phase. Take a moment to list all of the formal planning activities in which your team took part. Write down five to eight activities that were executed successfully that would make your *best practice* list. What was missing? Which ones can you improve on?

   b. Complete your planning best practice list; use it, modify it, and perfect it.

2. Your projects must align to the strategic intent and corporate objectives of your firm. It is critical that all of your project efforts and activities are focused in the right direction and on the big picture. Do you know the mission of your company? What are the corporate objectives? What about your department? Do you know the mission and strategic objectives of your department? Is there a departmental business plan in place? Is it up to date? Have you read it? If you're a consultant, do you know this vital information regarding your clients?

   Action Plan

   a. Before doing any research, write down your company's or client's mission statement. Also write down all of the corporate objectives that you can remember. Having difficulties? Don't worry, you're not alone, but give it a shot anyway. See how close you can come.

b. Now go ahead and do some research. Peruse appropriate websites, business plans, and annual reports to determine the strategic intent of your firm. This simple exercise will tell you something about how knowledgeable you are about your company. Are you satisfied with the results? Write down the actual mission statement and all of the corporate objectives. *Memorize them!* Now do the same for your department. Read your departmental business plan and extract the relevant information. Write down your departmental mission statement and strategic objectives. Memorize these as well. Is the departmental business plan still timely and relevant? Does one even exist? If not, perhaps this is an area of opportunity for you. Explore your options.

3. In light of your research, are your tactical plans, that is, your projects, directly aligned to them? How do your projects contribute directly to the overall mission and strategic objectives of your firm? Which projects do not seem to have a direct line to your company's strategic intent, if any? How many projects within your portfolio are merely lingering in open status draining valuable resources and adding no value? If your answer is none, bravo!

Action Plan

a. Investigate your project portfolio. Identify three to five projects that have absolutely no correlation to your corporate or departmental mission and objectives. In other words, identify those projects that are bad investments. Record these projects and write down the actions you will take to address these project money pits. Be specific.

4. Leadership drives success in all areas of business and project management. Think about your leadership style. Do you take action and lead when appropriate? Are you more of a leader or manager? In what leadership areas would you improve?

Action Plan

a. Choose two or three facets of your leadership style and the approach that you'd like to improve on. What should you be doing that you know you are not? Be frank with yourself. Although a tremendously useful exercise, this can be rather agonizing as well. Stick with it, it will be worth it!

b. Make a list of all of the leadership resources available to you, including books, courses, mentors, peers, professional support in terms of training and coaching, and even your spouse! Which ones aren't you currently taking advantage of that you can begin to leverage? What can you do in the next two months? What can you do within the next year? Write these down!

Reference

1. Heerkens, Gary R. 2006. *The Business-Savvy Project Manager*. New York, NY: McGraw-Hill.

3

Re-defining the
Project Management
Lifecycle Approach

The height of insanity is doing things the same way and hoping for a different result.

—Benjamin Franklin

The Project-driven Organization

A project should be viewed as what? *A financial and strategic investment . . .* very good. And as an investment, a project can either yield a positive, negative, or zero return. The more diligent planning conducted during the early phases of a project will, more than likely, yield higher returns than those projects that were poorly planned. Corporate leaders are realizing that solid, business-focused project management can make their companies money and, conversely, poor project management can cost them money. For these reasons, companies are investing in project management and business-related training for their employees, managers, and even executives who are involved in projects. Corporate leaders are realizing that the identification and execution of projects can have a tremendous impact on their organizations, both positive and negative.

Before projects were viewed as strategic investments, many companies simply threw resources at business initiatives or problems under the guise of project management and hoped that those resources could achieve acceptable levels of completion. Frequently, the employees who were assigned as project managers in these scenarios weren't even project managers at all, rather they were line-managers, engineers, staff members, or some other specialized position, and they were usually unrelated to project management. Unfortunately, these *trial by fire* project managers had little or no training in project management and, in many cases, didn't even want to be in that role; however, the expectations for them to perform like a seasoned project professional remained. As anyone who has ever managed a project can attest, project management is labor intensive, highly visible, political, and it requires both specialized skills and leadership acumen. Would you pull a guy off the street to manage your retirement investments? Of course not. Companies should not simply pull anyone in to manage their project investments. Project management can mean the difference between success and failure; profitability and losses.

Executives are applying project management best practices to all parts of their organization and operating their businesses with the use of projects to achieve their strategic objectives. It has evolved into a strategic role that is helping companies navigate the many complexities of running their businesses. Engineers, specialists, and other line-workers are starting to be relieved of their part-time project management duties primarily because that role has gone from a part-time effort to a solid career path, and corporations are embracing these new careers. Project management is now considered a necessity for the long-term success of companies.

All levels of an organization, from executives to senior managers to front-line workers, are becoming involved in the execution of projects. Senior managers are intimately involved in projects, acting as project sponsors, stakeholders, and in other key roles, frequently with strict accountability to the business. These business trends indicate that companies are executing their projects in strategic alignment with corporate objectives and striving to achieve optimal business value from their project investments. Business leaders are seeking highly skilled project managers to lead their project efforts and are no longer relying on anyone who happens to have spare cycle times. Executives realize that too much is at stake to treat projects lightly. For many business professionals, this project-oriented focus may be new and untested, but to business professionals committed to the company's bottom-line results, this is a necessity.

All Projects Have a Lifecycle

All projects are one-time, temporary endeavors set forth to meet certain business objectives. These one-time endeavors usually traverse a project lifecycle and should have a clearly defined beginning and end. Some projects are short in duration, such as the implementation of a standard software package to a select group of individuals, and some are much longer, such as the deployment and consolidation of worldwide technology data centers. Short and long are relative terms, however, and certainly mean different things to different people. That standard software implementation may be extremely cumbersome for a startup company, especially if the select group of individuals includes potential investors or customers for the new company. Even the deployment and consolidation of worldwide data centers may not be viewed as a long-term project for companies specializing in this field. Regardless of the type or complexity of a project, all projects have a beginning and an end with a great deal of activity and uncertainty in between. Projects vary in size, complexity, duration, and in many other ways. Examples of projects include:

- Deploy a new technology system
- Build a new business application
- Re-design a product
- Design and implement a new business process
- Restructure the organization
- Build a bridge
- Merge two companies
- Upgrade to the newest software release

To get a better handle on all of the activity that takes place from project inception to project termination, organizations and project management practitioners have developed formal methodologies and have defined various phases of the project lifecycle. The purpose of these methodologies is to provide structure, standardization, consistency, and guidance in the management and execution of projects. There isn't one standard, ubiquitous project management lifecycle methodology that is universal for all organizations; rather, there are numerous methodologies that organizations choose to use depending on their business goals and culture. For instance, a software development company may choose a methodology more suitable to producing quality software that provides ample time for developing and testing activities, whereas a business consulting firm may choose one that is more generic and allows flexibility when managing the unique attributes of their diverse client base. In some cases, an organization may find it appropriate to develop its own project management methodology rather than choosing one of the widely accepted ones.

Project lifecycle methodologies, for the most part, aren't drastically different from one another. We know a project should have a clearly defined beginning and a clearly defined end with a great deal of activity in between. The challenge is structuring the project lifecycle to be consistent with corporate cultures and norms to effectively manage project activities for peak performance. For instance, an entrepreneurial organization that prides itself on creativity will not employ a project methodology that may be viewed as too bureaucratic or cumbersome, whereas a pharmaceutical company with stringent Food and Drug Administration requirements will want to adhere to a rigid methodology to ensure federal compliance. Figure 3.1 shows a few

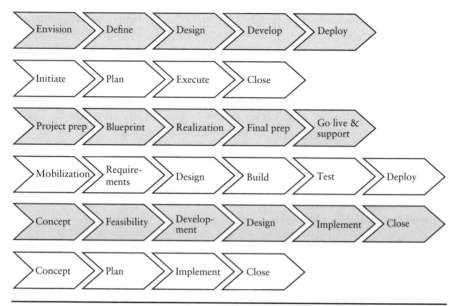

Figure 3.1   Project management lifecycle examples

examples of some of the project management lifecycle approaches that have been defined.

I have encountered and worked with countless project management methodologies for companies of all sizes across multiple industries. Based on this experience, I am able to conclude that a methodology is paramount to success if, and only if, it is accepted throughout all levels of an organization and accountability measures are in place to ensure adherence. It's best to keep the project management lifecycle methodology as simple as possible. Too often organizations adopt methodologies that are overly complex and understood by only trained project management practitioners, which only leads to confusion for the rest of the organization. In many cases, different departments within a company utilize different methodologies that, again, only lead to uncertainty and confusion. I've even observed companies that adopted the software development lifecycle approach—which is heavily focused on software development, testing, and integration—even though these companies weren't in the software development business. These companies, in view of their consistently dismal project results, would have been better off embracing different, much simpler methodologies.

One project management methodology is no better than the other; it truly depends on organizational requirements and how effectively that methodology is implemented and adopted. It is important, however, to adopt a methodology, embrace it, and ensure its consistent use across the organization. Most project management methodologies have key activities or *mandatories* that are performed throughout the project lifecycle. These key activities are usually associated with a specific project phase and, in many cases, must be completed before the project can progress to the next phase. Examples of these key activities include:

- Produce a project charter
- Define the project budget
- Develop a project schedule
- Identify resource requirements
- Obtain management sign-off approval
- Produce weekly status reports
- Track capital expenditure
- Conduct pilot testing activities
- Conduct a project closeout meeting
- Identify and document lessons learned

A project is normally initiated by a business professional who proposed an idea that could be beneficial for the organization. When there is consensus among other business leaders that the idea could indeed bring about beneficial change, a project is initiated. The project progresses along a pre-defined lifecycle until it has been completed. The project resources are then released from project obligations and business-as-usual eventually resumes. Figure 3.2 shows a high-level view of the end-to-end process of initiating and closing a project. The project management methodology depicted is a fairly standard one and incorporates key attributes of project phases of most other methodologies.

As shown in Figure 3.2, business requirements, such as the need for a process change, an enhancement to an existing product, or a restructuring of the organization, are the driving forces dictating whether or not to embark on a project investment. Once the project has traversed the various project lifecycle phases and has been officially closed, the organization resumes business-as-usual, steady-state operations with the expectation that the project delivered, or at some point in the future, will deliver business value. The key components and essential process activities for the various lifecycle phases are described, at a high level. We will build on this project lifecycle approach in subsequent sections as we delve deeper into how to effectively manage projects, not only to satisfy traditional project requirements, but to deliver optimal value and achieve lasting business benefits on a consistent basis.

Concept Phase

In the project concept phase, an individual proposes a project idea that could benefit the company in some way, solves a business problem, or addresses a specific need within the organization. If the project idea is approved, this

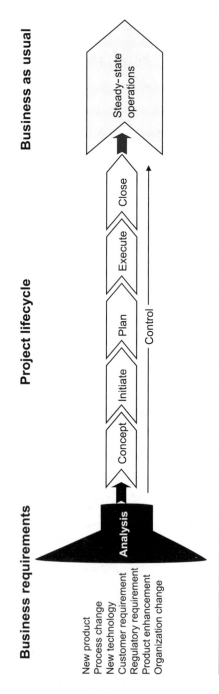

Figure 3.2   End-to-end project flow

individual usually becomes the project sponsor and maintains ownership of the project to the end. The project sponsor usually submits a project proposal that includes elements of a high-level business case to a project evaluation and selection committee. If the committee finds the idea to be a promising investment for the company, they will authorize the project sponsor to delve deeper into the details of the idea to validate its true business need.

Examples of concept phase key activities:

- Identify strategic needs for the proposed project
- Develop a high-level business case
- Develop a high-level project scope
- Analyze the impact of the proposed project
- Make a go/no go decision to progress to the next project phase

Initiation Phase

A project manager is usually assigned during the initiation phase to assist the project sponsor with the business analysis and early planning activities. The newly assigned project manager works closely with the project sponsor and, possibly, a small team to develop the key project parameters and update the business case further. The newly formed team creates a project charter that defines the scope, objectives, key participants, and desired outcome.

At the conclusion of project initiation, the project approval board evaluates the project charter that includes financial information from the business case. The charter should provide the deciding body with enough information about the merits of the proposed project to make a meaningful evaluation and decision. A determination is made as to whether the project is consistent with the organization's strategic intent and if the project budget is affordable. A decision is made to either halt the project or proceed to the project planning phase where the project really begins to gain momentum.

Examples of initiation phase key activities:

- Research potential approaches and solutions
- Update the high-level business case
- Identify a funding source
- Develop the project charter
- Assign the project team
- Secure a project budget

Planning Phase

Detailed and thorough planning begins in earnest during the planning phase. The purpose of the planning phase is to define the overall project parameters in detail and to establish the appropriate approach required to successfully manage and complete the project. In this phase, the project scope is confirmed and a detailed project management plan is developed. The plan is a pivotal starting point that serves as the foundation for all future project efforts. It includes important project elements such as a project schedule, communication plan, risk management plan, resource plan, escalation procedures, and quality plans. In the planning phase, the project funds are allocated, the project team is committed and mobilized, the project work environment is established, and project plans are developed. Planning efforts during this phase should not be taken lightly because this phase serves as the foundation for the rest of the project.

It is crucial to confirm, or re-confirm, the role of the project sponsor during this phase. Securing project sponsorship confirms commitment and accountability for the project. Additional resources may be assigned to the project team to assist with the detailed planning efforts. At the conclusion of the planning phase, the revised business case is re-evaluated and the project management plan is examined. A decision is made to either halt the project or to commit the necessary resources for the execution phase. The planning phase lays the groundwork for all future project activities and ensures that all the prerequisites for the project execution phase are in place.

Examples of planning phase key activities:

- Develop a detailed business case from the existing high-level one
- Develop a detailed project management plan
- Deploy the project team
- Define commitment levels for core and extended team members
- Develop the schedule and identify critical path elements
- Obtain acceptance of the project scope and approach from project stakeholders

For many projects, especially ones that are technical in nature, other phases must be completed before progressing to the execution phase. These phases are usually tailored for design and testing activities and are typically conducted during or after the planning phase, but before the actual execution of the project. In the design and testing phases of a project, a proposed system is usually carefully designed and tested, and a small prototype of the final product may be built and evaluated. The primary driver for these phases is to ensure that the final product will meet established specifications. Once these specifications have been met, the project can then progress to the execution phase where the final product is usually deployed into a live production environment.

Execution Phase

In the execution phase the necessary actions are performed to accomplish the project goals that were established in the previous phases. The execution phase comprises the processes and activities to complete the work defined in the project management plan. Execution involves coordinating project resources, performing work activities detailed in the various planning documents, and finalizing the product or service that the project was commissioned to deliver.

It's common to add additional resources to the project team at the beginning of this phase to address execution requirements and increased workloads. Project execution utilizes all of the plans, schedules, procedures, and templates that were prepared during prior work efforts. The conclusion of this phase arrives when the product or service is fully developed, tested, accepted, and implemented.

Examples of execution phase key activities:

- Execute the project management plan
- Initiate change control activities to implement a change to existing systems
- Test the product or service
- Deploy the product or service
- Finalize the product or service

Controlling

Controlling activities span the entire project lifecycle and include supervising all project actions that are performed to ensure the project is progressing as planned. Potential problems are proactively identified and corrective actions are taken, as needed, to control the management and execution of the project. Project performance is observed and measured regularly to identify variances from the project management plan and to take appropriate measures when the variances are too great. Uncertainties exist and unanticipated events inevitably occur with the implementation of any project. Controlling activities serve to minimize the effects of these uncertainties and unforeseen events.

Examples of controlling key activities:

- Manage the triple constraints of scope, time, and cost
- Communicate project status to appropriate stakeholders
- Manage the project team
- Maintain the project management plan
- Track milestones and deliverables
- Identify and manage interdependencies with other projects
- Track expenditure against budget
- Trigger issue management and escalation when appropriate

Closeout Phase

In the traditional closeout phase the finished product or service is presented, indicating completion of the project. Project closeout includes the formal acceptance of the project deliverables by the primary stakeholders. In this phase, the project team assesses the overall project and determines any lessons learned and best practices to be applied to future projects. Lessons learned and other project material should be stored in a centralized repository, facilitating easy access and retrieval by project members of future projects. Contract closure is necessary for settling each contract with consultants and vendors, including the resolution of any open items. Project closeout ends with administrative closeout procedures, such as providing feedback to team members, capturing key project metrics, evaluating the project budget, and releasing project resources from their project commitments.

Examples of closeout phase key activities:

- Assure project objectives have been met
- Obtain sign-off of project deliverables
- Document lessons learned
- Archive project deliverables
- Assess team performance
- Release project resources

Major Shortcomings to the Traditional Lifecycle Approach

The ultimate goal for any project should be the attainment of the intended business benefits that were documented in the business case. This goal of obtaining optimal business value from project expenditures should be the driving force for all project activities and decisions as the project traverses the various lifecycle phases. The mindset of striving for the long-term business goals greatly enhances the probability that the intended business value will be attained and that the project positively impacts the company monetarily. The business benefits that are derived from projects, however, usually occur long after the project closeout phase, and this is where the traditional project management lifecycle approach has serious shortcomings. *Project closeout activities, including project sign-off, seem to take place as a matter of course even if most, if not all, of the project benefits haven't been achieved!* This may be the single greatest reason why projects frequently fail to achieve their targeted benefits and why billions of dollars are being wasted each year on failed project initiatives.

As projects progress toward the traditional closeout phase, project team members are usually looking forward to wrapping things up so that they can get back to their regular jobs or move on to their next assignments. A massive amount of project deliverables is handed over to the project sponsor for sign-off and these deliverables are usually *dumped* on the operations teams. The operations teams, and not the project teams, are the ones responsible for utilizing the project outputs to achieve the expected business outcomes and benefits. The operations teams also have their day jobs to perform and, when these project deliverables are dumped on them, the deliverables are often dismissed, put into drawers, and business-as-usual returns rather quickly. It is unfortunate when this occurs because most of the hard work and expenditures end up being wasted. Projects fail if the intended business benefits aren't achieved, regardless of hard work, comprehensive deliverables, or effective project execution.

With project closeout occurring and project teams being disbanded before operational teams have had the opportunity to achieve the targeted business benefits, value focus is lost, accountability wanes, motivation declines, and commitment levels vanish. It's astonishing to see how little accountability and commitment there is to achieving the project objectives once the closeout phase is completed. With the traditional closeout process, key project resources are cleared of any responsibility and accountability of actually achieving the intended results, even though they've been intimately involved in the project and know all of the minute details. It's no wonder project team members, especially those members external to the organization, are so willing, and even relieved, to hand over project deliverables and to be on their merry way to their next assignments. Out of sight means out of mind!

The traditional way of managing projects utilizing the standard lifecycle approach simply doesn't work, mainly because projects are being managed to the point of administrative sign-off and not to the point of benefit attainment. A re-definition of the traditional project lifecycle approach needs to occur, and project management techniques need to be incorporated into this new definition to manage effectively projects to the point of value realization. This re-definition occurs with the use of a new, more efficient and effective methodology that we will call the *value-centric project lifecycle methodology*. The value-centric project lifecycle methodology is the wave of the future in managing projects. This methodology has the power to enable companies to consistently achieve optimal business returns for their project investments in addition to improving organizational efficiencies, increasing corporate valuations, saving struggling companies, and making careers.

The Value-centric Project Lifecycle Methodology

Projects may be executed flawlessly throughout all phases of the lifecycle, but if they don't deliver business value to organizations, then what's the point? Projects must lead to the achievement of positive business value, such as making money for the organization or achieving key strategic objectives. Project teams must never lose focus for achieving business value from their projects and must incorporate this focus into their overall approach. Business value must be measured throughout the course of the project to ensure sufficient progress is being made and to make appropriate adjustments if the project is off track. As the adage goes, you manage what you measure and if it's measured it will be managed. Most of these measurement activities, however, need to occur after the traditional project closeout phase because this is when the benefits and business value begin to emerge. It is crucial that project sponsorship and commitment remains intact until the organization has the opportunity to analyze and optimize the business results that materialize from the project efforts.

The value-centric project lifecycle methodology focuses on the long-term business value that is expected from project investments and not simply completing projects on-time and within budget. This methodology re-defines project closeout procedures to ensure projects aren't terminated until *all* of the business benefits are achieved or until the project stakeholders are satisfied with the benefits that have been or will be achieved.

Does this mean that the project lifecycle may be pushed out weeks, months, years? It certainly does. Does this mean that the same levels of commitment are required from project members throughout the extended project lifecycle? It certainly does not. This new approach ensures that accountability for results remains until those results are actually achieved. Even though the project lifecycle is extended, this approach does not add extra costs or bureaucracy to the project, but rather does the exact opposite, especially when considering how costly projects are when they don't achieve their targeted objectives. This approach incorporates efficient and effective processes and techniques to ensure that project teams are sized appropriately for each project phase. Project requirements differ from phase to phase, and the project must be staffed according to these shifting requirements and priorities. Gone are the days when large project teams are assembled at the beginning of a project, remain intact for the project duration, and make a mass exodus on project completion. The value-centric approach incorporates rationalized principles to ensure agility, efficiency, and effectiveness in project execution, all while delivering business results that endure.

Figure 3.3 presents a graphical depiction of the value-centric project lifecycle methodology. An additional phase has been added to the traditional lifecycle approach that incorporates the tenets of operational hand-off and benefit attainment. Operational staff members are usually the ones *in the trenches* who manage and execute the day-to-day aspects of the business and are fundamental in turning forecasted value into real value. With this new methodology, projects aren't officially closed until operational teams have had the necessary time to implement the project plans, track project results, fine-tune performance parameters, make strategic business decisions, and deliver positive results to the stakeholders and to the business.

With the value-centric project lifecycle methodology, project teams maintain responsibility for achieving the forecasted business results articulated in the business case. The project sponsor is still ultimately accountable to the organization for project results, but the project team remains accountable to the project sponsor until the results are achieved. Project teams will no longer

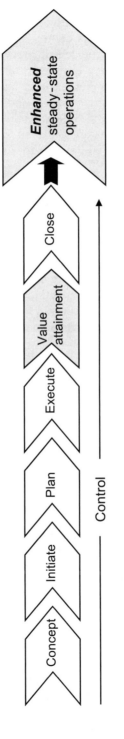

Figure 3.3 Value-centric project lifecycle methodology

merely plan to the point of administrative stakeholder sign-off, but will now have to focus their planning efforts on the longer-term to bring about the intended project benefits. The value-centric lifecycle methodology empowers project teams to focus on the long-term goals of their projects that enhance project decision making and execution. The inclusion of the value attainment phase not only brings about positive project and business results, but results that will last for the long-term since operational buy-in and acceptance is necessitated. When project benefits are achieved, organizations will no longer return to business as usual but will evolve to a more *enhanced and effective state of operations*.

The Value Attainment Phase

As we now know, optimal business value is rarely attained when projects are terminated during the traditional closeout phase. For this reason it's become necessary to enhance the traditional approach to better position ourselves to attain the business benefits articulated in the business case. We simply can't keep running our projects in this ineffective manner. The value attainment phase positions project teams and businesses for success. By incorporating this phase into the project lifecycle, project momentum doesn't stop once project solutions are deployed, but rather continues to ensure that business-value metrics are monitored and ultimately achieved. Project teams can finally see the business results from all of their project efforts come to fruition. Once the benefits have been achieved and the appropriate business-value attained, the project can progress to the closeout phase.

Decision making doesn't stop once the execution phase has been completed. If anything, some of the more important decisions will have to be made after the project money was expended and solutions were deployed. During this phase, project teams transition certain project responsibilities and deliverables to the operating organization. This transition is paramount to success because operational teams are the ones who can turn forecasted value into real value for the business. Core project teams, for the most part, cannot do this. It's imperative, therefore, to involve the appropriate stakeholders, operational team members, and other key personnel in this phase to develop thoroughly detailed and agreed-upon transition and value attainment plans. These plans ensure that project deliverables and expected outcomes are fully understood by the operational teams so that they can drive business value and bring about the desired results.

During the value attainment phase, many of the project resources can be released since most activities will now be operational in nature. In many cases it may make sense to release the entire project team except for a few key positions. These positions, furthermore, may act only in limited capacities. Many of the activities in the traditional closeout phase can even be conducted during this phase; assessing project team performance, determining lessons learned, posting project information to centralized repositories, and closing out contracts with consultants and vendors. It is critical, however, that the project is not officially closed. Most, if not all, of the business benefits haven't been achieved even with all of the hard work and valiant project efforts. Now is the time to make those valiant project efforts worthwhile by properly transitioning select responsibilities to the personnel who will make it happen.

Key activities for the value attainment phase include:

- Finalize transition and value attainment plans
- Establish a transition governance and management approach
- Specify quantified targets for achievement from the business case
- Assign accountability to individuals for business results
- Determine timeframes for achieving business benefits and outcomes
- Conduct knowledge transfer and training sessions
- Identify possible risks to achieving the intended benefits
- Develop risk mitigation plans
- Establish means of measurement for quantified targets
- Develop timely and consistent reporting mechanisms
- Capture and present key project value metrics
- Receive stakeholder input and feedback
- Make adjustments and enhancements to the project solutions to drive value
- Achieve project results

The value attainment phase is discussed in more detail in Chapter 12.

Now the Project Closeout Phase

In the traditional project closeout phase the finished product or service is presented, but the associated benefits are usually not even discussed and certainly haven't been achieved. With the value-centric project lifecycle methodology, the business value and benefits that were attained as a result of the project are carefully examined. The true success or failure of the project can now be determined with certainty. During the closeout phase, project teams can finally answer business-focused questions to determine how effective they were in achieving their intended results. The questions include:

- Were project objectives clear and translated into business terms?
- Was the business case thorough, accurate, and treated as a living document throughout the entire project lifecycle?
- Were stakeholders and project resources allocated efficiently to drive business value?

- Did the project receive top-level support throughout the lifecycle until value attainment?
- Were project communications effective and timely and did they include value metrics?
- Were value-capture mechanisms in place?
- Were the value metrics monitored and presented on a scheduled basis?
- Was accountability and ownership assigned for each project benefit?
- Did the project meet or exceed return on investment (ROI) and other financial expectations?
- Did the project meet or exceed non-ROI contributing benefits?
- Did the project outcome satisfy real business needs?
- Did the project contribute to the success and the bottom line of the company?

Traditional administrative closeout procedures also take place during this phase, such as evaluating the project budget and releasing project resources from their project commitments. But now instead of merely relying on the triple constraints of time, quality, and cost to evaluate project outcomes, project teams can present monetary business value and quantified benefits as a direct result of their project efforts. Wouldn't it be nice to close out a project and, instead of saying you completed your project on-time, within budget, and satisfied quality requirements, you can say with certainty that your project:

- Achieved a 45% ROI
- Achieved a net present value of $5.2MM
- Paid off all project costs in 1.5 years
- Achieved a 12.3% internal rate of return
- Achieved total savings of $1.92MM in 10 months
- Increased employee capacity by 22%
- Reduced inventory by 49%
- Cut procurement costs by 45%
- Increased labor efficiency by 40%
- Consolidated systems from 17 to 6
- Increased production by 22%

Professional Development Game Plan for Success

1. Organizations are becoming increasingly project-driven, and they rely on these projects to achieve their strategic goals. Regardless of your title, role, or job function within your organization, you have key responsibilities to fulfill in the execution and completion of projects. You may be serving as a project stakeholder, project sponsor, project manager, subject matter expert, or acting in some other capacity on project teams. Because of your involvement in strategic project investments,

you need to possess a solid understanding of the tenets of project management. On a scale of 1 to 5 with 5 being an expert, where are you in terms of project management? Can you readily speak to project management's key concepts? Have you been through formal training?

Action Plan

a. Assess your level of knowledge and understanding of project management. To help guide your assessment, conduct discussions with competent project managers, reference project management documentation, take a project management practice test, and analyze project management deliverables within your organization, such as project charters, Gantt charts, business cases, and risk management plans. How do you feel? If someone asked you to manage an important project starting tomorrow, are you ready? Based on your assessment, determine the appropriate actions that you can take to improve your knowledge and abilities in project management. You may consider attending formal training, taking an academic course, joining a study group, reading some books, perusing relevant websites, or even volunteering to lead a project or become part of a project team. There is nothing like on-the-job learning! Write down three to five actions that you *will* take within the next year to increase your project management acumen and improve your project management abilities.

2. Organizations achieve consistently better results when a formal project lifecycle methodology is defined and followed for all of their projects. Right now, go get a copy of your project lifecycle methodology. Was it easy to find? How would you rate it in terms of completeness? Is it clear and concise? Are there clearly defined mandatory activities for all of the project phases? Are gate reviews established not only to receive sign-off, but to encourage stakeholders to review progress, scrutinize deliverables, and offer constructive insight and feedback?

Action Plan

a. Assess your company's project lifecycle methodology. Are there gaps? Evaluate what is working well and what isn't. What project activities are consistently performed poorly, add no significant value, or are even unnecessary? Write down three to five areas that are ambiguous, poorly defined, poorly executed, lack depth, or are redundant. Fill in the blanks and complete your recommendations for improvement. Schedule some time to discuss it with your boss or team.

Reference

1. Kerzner, Harold, and Frank Saladis. 2009. *Value-Driven Project Management.* Hoboken, NJ: John Wiley.

4

Value Attainment Begins and Ends with the Business Case

Setting a goal is not the main thing. It is deciding how you will go about achieving it and staying with the plan.

—Tom Landry

The Business Case: Driving Force of the Project

The business case is one of the most important documents of any project, if not the most important. It is the primary tool used in deciding whether to invest in a project or if the company should invest in one particular project over other projects. It articulates current issues, problems, or opportunities for an organization and provides detailed information on the solutions to address the current business needs. An effective business case provides business leaders with a clear understanding of the likely outcomes that will occur when implementing a proposed solution. The costs, benefits, risks, and other key areas of the proposed solution, or solutions, are clearly defined to provide decision makers with enough information to make informed and effective decisions on whether to launch, proceed with, or even terminate a project.

To determine if a project will be a good investment, a careful analysis should be performed to discover the costs and expected benefits, with as much detail and accuracy as possible, that the project will deliver to the organization. A comprehensive study of project costs, benefits, and risks must be conducted to provide business justification for a project and to obtain an appropriate level of commitment from relevant stakeholders. A business case that articulates an in-depth understanding of the business, its issues and opportunities, and provides a compelling business justification for a project is far more likely to get approved than one that was done hastily and has limited detail. This means, however, that the best project idea to address a business need may not always be chosen if the business case for that particular idea was done inaccurately, incompletely, or was not as compelling as other business cases that were developed. Implementing suboptimal projects on a consistent basis puts an organization at a competitive disadvantage. It is crucial, therefore, that organizations give top priority to the business case development process so that they implement projects that enhance their competitive postures.

Far too often business cases are done hastily and simply list the project costs, which are usually underestimated, and the expected benefits, which are usually overestimated. The inflated benefits and minimized costs create an overly positive return on investment (ROI) for a potential project, which makes it *appear* attractive, and the decision to implement it, unfortunately, turns out to be a *no-brainer*. As these projects are implemented, stakeholders soon realize that these no-brainers end up draining their company's budgets and valuable resources and don't come close to achieving the expected benefits. Most organizations take painstaking measures to scrutinize every detail of employee expense reports and timesheets, but, ironically, many business leaders underestimate the importance of the business case and quickly read through them, if they read them at all. Business cases serve as justification for high-dollar investments and contribute directly to a company's success or failure. Business leaders must ensure that these important documents are developed with as much accuracy as possible and with input from all of the applicable areas of the business. They must also examine and scrutinize the details of the business case carefully for accuracy and completeness.

Business cases that are created consistently across an organization are indispensable in evaluating competing project ideas in an impartial manner. They offer objectivity in evaluating competing projects and prevent political influence or persuasion due to impartiality and objectivity. Far too often in the corporate world it's the most political or most vocal person who gets consistent project approval. Objective business cases prevent ineffective *awards* from occurring and ensure that the squeaky—or well-connected wheel—must *earn* the grease. The grease, of course, is project approval and the funds and resources to execute it. When business cases clearly show the expected cash flows, there will be no ambiguity in determining its true potential value.

So far we've discussed the theory of the business case, but the financial aspects begin to make the concept more concrete. Net cash flow is the heart of the financial analysis of a business case and shows the money that is expended over a period of time, as well as the money expected to come into the organization as a result of the project investment. Figure 4.1 shows a high-level depiction of the net cash flow for a project. As with any investment, money is initially spent with the expectation that more money will eventually be made than was spent. Effective project teams strive to reduce costs, increase gains, and accelerate project returns, much like the investment community.

An effective business case demonstrates net cash flows and other financial metrics, but it is not simply a financial document. While it includes financial justification for a project, the business case also includes other relevant business facts and metrics that are aligned with the strategic intent of the organization. An effective business case answers these strategic questions:

- Why is the project needed in the first place?
- What are the issues facing the organization?
- What is the recommended solution?
- How does the solution address the issues?
- What will happen if the project effort is not undertaken (the *do nothing* scenario)?
- When will the solution be deployed?
- How much money, people, and time will be needed to deliver the solution and realize the benefits?

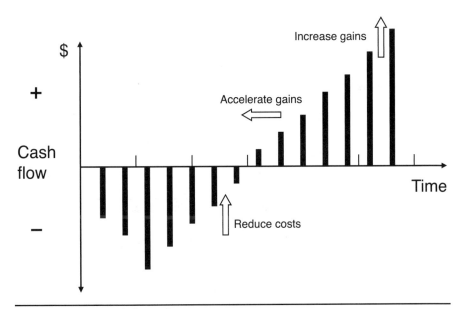

Figure 4.1   Net cash flow of a project

- How much financial value will be generated and what business benefits will be achieved?
- What parts of the business are most affected?
- How does the project contribute to the success of the company?

The business case provides a consistent message to many areas of an organization. It provides both a high-level and detailed view of the entire project and enables all departments and personnel affected by the effort to be knowledgeable about the intricacies of the project. Approaches and techniques to developing business cases are numerous and diverse. There are key components, however, that should be included in all business cases. Table 4.1 summarizes the key components that comprise effective business cases.

Table 4.1 Key components of a business case

Key business case component	Overview
Executive summary	<ul><li>High-level business needs</li><li>Summary of solution options</li><li>Recommended solution</li><li>Strategic fit within the organization</li><li>Financial results; includes costs, benefits, and net cash flow</li><li>Other qualitative and quantitative benefits</li><li>Project sponsor, project manager, key stakeholders</li><li>Overall recommendation</li></ul>
Methods and assumptions	<ul><li>Scope and boundaries of the business case</li><li>Applicable departments and personnel</li><li>Targeted time periods</li><li>Process and assumptions used in developing the business case</li></ul>
Background/ Business issue	<ul><li>Description of the current issue or opportunity</li><li>Project scope and objectives from a business perspective</li><li>Criticality of the project need</li><li>Stakeholders impacted</li><li>Departments impacted</li></ul>
Proposed solution(s)	<ul><li>Overall solution to addressing the business need</li><li>Alternative solutions</li><li>Weighted scoring comparison for competing solutions</li><li>Cash outflows and inflows</li><li>Project costs</li><li>Benefits (qualitative and quantitative)</li><li>Detailed financial analyses to include NPV, ROI, IRR, payback period, and other financial metrics, as applicable</li><li>Sensitivity analysis (best case/worst case)</li></ul>

Risk analysis	• Project risks probabilities and impact
	• Risks of not implementing the project
	• Risk mitigation plans
Contingencies and dependencies	• Project success requirements
	• Ways to achieve the project benefits
	• Departmental and individual requirements
	• Necessary decisions
	• Critical path elements
Implementation approach	• Execution plans
	• Expected outcomes
	• Timelines
	• Funding approach
	• Project management and governance strategy
	• Benefit realization responsibility
	• Resource commitments
Recommendations	• Specific recommendations
	• Specific funding requirements (reiteration)

There is an abundance of reference material that describes the numerous ways in which business cases can be structured. Many organizations do a good job of providing guidance, templates, and assistance in the development. Consequently, individuals have become quite adept at crafting top-notch business cases and proposals (although many still struggle with differentiating and incorporating ROI contributing benefits and other benefits that don't contribute directly to it. We cover this topic at length in Chapter 9). However, nearly all organizations fall short because they do not treat business cases as living documents. Throughout the project lifecycle, it is crucial to refine the details to keep it accurate as additional information becomes available. For that matter, it is typical that a business case is never referred to again once project approval has been granted. It has to become (or needs to be) the project's North Star and guide not only a project's initial perceived value and green light, but also the management of that value through implementation, completion, operations, and continuous improvement phases.

A Living Document That Drives Business Value

The initial business case should be written during the concept phase of a project and enhanced during the initiation and planning phases as key participants become involved and more information becomes available. The purpose of fine-tuning it during these early project phases is to get to a level of confidence where the project team and the stakeholders can all agree that the project will indeed generate the projected returns as specified in the document. Business leaders can more confidently approve projects or the continuation of projects with business cases that are accurate and fine-tuned. Additionally, they will have a tangible way of measuring the success or failure of the project based on the forecasted benefits specified in the document.

Business case development is not a one-time effort and several iterations of this important document are usually required to achieve a level of accuracy that is acceptable. Project managers can greatly enhance their probabilities of success by incorporating business case development activities into the overall project management plan; these development efforts are certainly part of the critical path. Additionally, project managers should set the expectations that business case accuracy will increase as the project progresses along the early stages of the project. It is not practical, or even feasible, to expect a thorough and accurate business case in the concept phase of a project. There aren't enough resources dedicated, and information is usually sparse at this initial point of the project lifecycle. Phase-end or gate review sessions with project stakeholders must be conducted to evaluate the contents of the business case, assess the necessity for the project idea, and determine action plans for refining it for more accuracy.

Procedures and established checkpoints for measuring business case accuracy should be defined and scheduled for each of the early phases of the project. As stated, completion is not a one-time effort and won't be accurate if it is treated as such. The first iteration of the business case, for instance, will probably lack accuracy, but should be within a +/–30% accuracy range. This means that the *actual* project costs, financial returns, and other business benefits that will result from a project initiative will be within +/–30% of what is *forecasted* in the business case. This first iteration should provide the project approval committee with ample information to determine if the proposed project has enough potential to justify conducting additional planning efforts or if they should simply terminate the project idea at this point. If it's determined that they should proceed with the project and build out the business case further, then the project team should work toward a higher level of accuracy that is acceptable for the next phase-end review.

Organizations define project lifecycles in a variety of ways and deploy myriad project management methodologies. Business case accuracy measures certainly aren't set in stone for the various project phases. Project team members and stakeholders should determine the levels of accuracy that will be acceptable for each of the phase-end sessions. Review sessions other than the phase-end may be conducted as often as deemed appropriate by the project teams. Based upon experience and best practices, I recommend using the following business case accuracy measures as a general rule of thumb for the early, yet critical, phases of a project:

- Concept phase: +/–30% business case accuracy level
- Initiation phase: +/–15% business case accuracy level
- Planning phase: +/–5% business case accuracy level

A graphical depiction of this approach to developing accurate and refined business cases is shown in Figure 4.2.

It is imperative that the business case is at a level of accuracy of +/–5% at the completion of the planning phase because most project expenditures will occur during the next phase—the execution phase. It's best to terminate project efforts prior to the execution phase since this is usually when equipment is purchased, consultants are hired, the project team expands, and efforts gain full momentum. With a business case at a level of +/–5%, project stakeholders can make an informed decision whether to proceed with the project. It is simply good business to evaluate carefully the contents of a business case and terminate project efforts prior to the execution phase if the forecasted benefits will not bring about beneficial change that executive teams are seeking. Even though an organization may have spent time and money in the first three phases of a project that was eventually terminated, that time and money was well spent if it prevented the organization from expending even more resources on a project that would not have delivered acceptable business value. Ideally, it's best to terminate projects as early as possible in the lifecycle once it's determined that the project will not deliver the acceptable results. By canceling a project for justifiable reasons, resources can then be re-directed to investigate options to bring about the desired business outcomes.

Figure 4.3 shows an example where a project was terminated before entering the execution phase based on the results of the business case. Business case results were updated as the project advanced throughout the early planning phases. As the project team drilled deeper into the business case and utilized additional information as it became available, the forecasted benefits were not nearly as lucrative as initially estimated. Quite often a project sounds like a great idea initially but, as the business case is developed and refined, hidden costs are discovered, timelines become extended, and benefits are determined to be fewer than expected.

The business case is a critical component of the decision-making process throughout the entire project lifecycle; from the initial decision to proceed with a project to the decisions made at periodic project reviews to continue, modify, or terminate the project. At the end of each project phase, or whenever the project team deems it appropriate, the business case should be reviewed and re-evaluated by the appropriate stakeholders. Once the stakeholders agree and sign-off on a business case that they feel is +/–5% accurate, the project and operational teams can then execute the project and structure

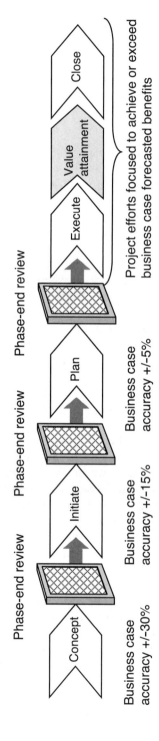

Figure 4.2 Business case development approach

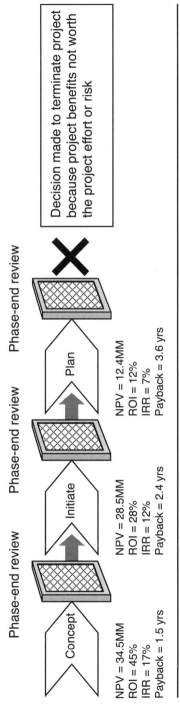

Concept
NPV = 34.5MM
ROI = 45%
IRR = 17%
Payback = 1.5 yrs

Initiate
NPV = 28.5MM
ROI = 28%
IRR = 12%
Payback = 2.4 yrs

Plan
NPV = 12.4MM
ROI = 12%
IRR = 7%
Payback = 3.6 yrs

Phase-end review   Phase-end review   Phase-end review

Decision made to terminate project because project benefits not worth the project effort or risk

Figure 4.3 Terminated project

their work activities to meet or even exceed the forecasted benefits as outlined in the business case.

Approaching the Business Case

Who here would feel a bit queasy if I asked you to present me with a business case for a proposed project by the end of the week? Don't worry—you're not alone! Many people, even experienced project professionals, feel that business cases are burdensome, administrative activities implemented solely to satisfy accounting or other bureaucratic requirements. Others, meanwhile, may realize their importance but rush through them anyway to put the onerous task behind them so they can begin *true* project activities. With such mindsets in existence, it's no wonder so many business cases are sloppily done and are inadequate, incomplete, inaccurate, and forgotten about after sign-off. Here is the shift I am proposing we create here:

Business Case PAINFUL to Business Case REWARDING

If you truly care about your own professional development and personal value to your company, this shift will not seem pointless, boring, unnecessary, daunting. . . . Shall I go on? You will see a *huge* opportunity to separate yourself from the pack, shine brightly among duller stars, and find a new sense of purpose and worth that may make your day-to-day responsibilities a bit more fulfilling. In fact, you will be transitioning from the traditional project professional to a strategic *value enabler, profit creator*, or whatever moniker lights you up. The current toxic mindset toward the most important project document has to change if we're to maximize our strategic investments and protect the senior leaders who are accountable for their outcome.

Back to the nuts and bolts. . . . The project sponsor usually begins the process of developing a business case to justify a project idea. Business case development activities typically will be delegated to a project manager once one is assigned. Project sponsors can't simply dump all responsibilities to a project manager and wash their hands clean of them; they must take an active role in their development. An accurate business case requires insight into many different areas of the business and relies on sensitive business data, including salaries, benefits, workloads, and intra-organizational coordination, to name a few. Project sponsors are usually senior enough to have insight into the applicable areas of the business and maintain relationships with other senior managers who possess resources and information needed for the project. Active involvement of the project sponsor is a necessity for the development of an accurate and thorough business case.

Many individuals contribute to the business case, but a single person should be assigned ownership and be held responsible for its development. In most cases, project sponsors will not be owners of the business case, mainly due to their numerous other job responsibilities, but rather will delegate ownership to a qualified team member. Quite often this person is the project manager, but it may also be another project team member. It can be advantageous to choose project managers because these individuals have holistic views of their projects and are more likely to be able to synthesize the multiple data elements from across their organizations into one document.

The business case owner may be solely responsible, but the completion of it is a team effort. The owner must leverage the project sponsor and other stakeholders to gain commitment and support for the development efforts. The business case owner cannot and must not operate in a vacuum while crafting this vital document. Input from numerous areas of the business is required. Detailed planning sessions must be conducted to identify appropriate resources and, depending on the project, this can include accounting, finance, subject matter experts, and other key personnel. Strategies must then be developed around leveraging these resources to gather the necessary information to build out a solid business case while being respectful of their time.

Business case owners should maintain responsibility for the business case no matter how many pieces are delegated. They hold the vision for their entire team! The business case must convey the big picture and tell a comprehensive story as to why the business should invest in a project and the consequences of pursuing or not pursuing that investment. It's best that it is written solely by the owner, perhaps with the assistance of another person, to ensure a smooth-flowing, comprehensive story and a consistent style throughout the document. This comprehensive story includes elements from various data sources and the business case owner needs to work with individuals from across the organization to gather and synthesize all of the information. In Chapter 7, the value-metrics framework that is used for capturing important data elements and determining key value metrics for projects is introduced. This framework is useful in gathering all of the information required for the business case.

Business case owners do not have to be financial or accounting experts. In fact, it's probably best that they are not to avoid overemphasizing one particular area. These individuals, however, must possess adequate business and leadership skills to be able to gather business information from various sources and articulate a compelling story of how a project investment will bring about beneficial change. In addition to solid business and leadership skills, business case owners will have to employ creative techniques, analytical thinking, organizational skills, political skills, and even detective-type skills in the business case development process. It is of vital importance for the business case owner to communicate regularly with stakeholders to maintain their commitment and support. As business case owners become more skilled, they will be more capable of getting stakeholders excited about their projects by showing them how they will benefit from the successful completion of the project. When stakeholders are excited about projects, they are more willing to share critical information and commit resources.

There are many challenges in creating the business case and then leveraging it in the successful execution and completion of a project. A few of the challenges are:

- Determining and obtaining the required data elements from the various sources within an organization
- Establishing a solid baseline using appropriate metrics
- Formulating project estimates and forecasts
- Calculating financial and other project outcomes
- Producing overall recommendations
- Attaining the expected project outcomes

None of these challenges can be overcome without the support and commitment from influencers and decision makers within the organization. Project teams must produce comprehensive stakeholder management plans to ensure that the appropriate influencers and decision makers are integral components of the core and/or extended teams, and that their responsibilities and time commitments are clearly defined and communicated. The next chapter describes efficient and effective processes and techniques to ensure that the right people are not only involved in projects, but that they committed to the successful execution and completion of them.

Professional Development Game Plan for Success

1. The business case is one of the most important document deliverables for any project. It serves as the basis and financial justification for a project investment. How does your company treat these important documents? Are they viewed as strategic deliverables that must be carefully constructed, evaluated, and maintained, or are they treated as simply one of many mandatory project deliverables that need to be completed in order to receive that all-important checkmark in the box? How many of your projects required a business case for approval? What about across your organization? Who was involved in business case development and approval?

   Action Plan

   a. Investigate and evaluate your company's posture toward the business case. Who drives business case development activities and efforts? What templates and detailed guidelines are provided? What is your perception of the value of your templates and guidelines? Are they clearly documented, easily accessible, and fully understood throughout the organization? How integral is the business case to project approval? Are they scrutinized or just another check-off on the worksheet? What is the business case review process like? Write down three to five of the most glaring issues you see surrounding business case development and approval activities. What is not being executed that should be? What is being executed incorrectly, inadequately, or inaccurately? Now take action! For each of these glaring issues, what can you do, what actions can you take, or what recommendations can you make to address them and to ensure they don't continue? Write your action plans down and schedule that next action!

2. You've heard the expression *garbage in, garbage out*. Business cases are vital inputs into key decisions and project actions. If they are developed poorly and inaccurately, and then presented to management teams (*garbage in*), more than likely poor decisions will be made and ineffective project actions will be executed (*garbage out*). How are your business cases? How much time did you spend developing your last business case? Who did you get involved? How closely aligned was your business case with business goals, and which success criteria did you choose? Did they lead to good business decisions and effective project actions? We didn't have any garbage here, did we?

Action Plan

a. Dig up and evaluate three or four business cases from your past projects. Evaluate their quality, thoroughness, and accuracy. What was the business and financial justification for the project investments? Do they use consistent financial measurements for project evaluation and selection? How useful was the business case for enabling proper project selection, deployment, and benefit attainment? Record three to five of the most glaring issues or shortfalls that are common across all of the business cases. Based on these common issues, what will you do differently or how will you prevent these issues from reoccurring? Write down your action plans.

References

1. Heerkens, Gary R. 2006. *The Business-Savvy Project Manager*. New York, NY: McGraw-Hill.
2. Schmidt, Marty J. 2002. *The Business Case Guide*. Boston, MA: Solution Matrix.

5

Effective Stakeholder Management Drives Value

In the end, all business operations can be reduced to three words: people, product and profits. Unless you've got a good team, you can't do much with the other two.

—Lee Iacocca

Stakeholders: The Right Team Makes a Difference

Project managers are typically skilled at managing their core project teams. They allocate resources efficiently, clearly define responsibilities, motivate their team members, resolve internal conflict, and provide overall project leadership. Where many of them fall short is in managing the resources *outside* of their core project teams. These resources consist of stakeholders from various groups who provide some type of necessary input critical to overall project success. Project managers may *manage down* very well, but if they don't *manage up* or *across* the entire project stakeholder team effectively, they won't receive the necessary support and input that is needed for their projects. Even though most project stakeholders reside outside of the core project team, they play key roles in influencing decisions, generating support, and rallying resources throughout the organization to make projects successful and profitable.

Stakeholders are the specific individuals or groups who have a stake—or a keen interest—in the overall outcome of a project. They are affected by and are capable of influencing project results and are usually experienced at driving change within their organizations. Project managers and core team members, for the most part, do not have the authority to influence senior leaders or make certain decisions to bring about desired change. This is where project teams can leverage stakeholders to wield their authority to make and approve key decisions critical to project success. Stakeholders inherently have a vested interest in a project because the results can affect them either positively or negatively. Their job responsibilities may change, their status in the company can be altered, or their entire organization can be transformed. In any case, a project's chance of success is greatly enhanced when the appropriate individuals are identified and asked to play active roles as project stakeholders. The challenge is managing them in a manner that respects their demanding schedules but also leverages their skills, knowledge, authority, and influence in a way that supports the project in the most optimal manner.

As with the business case, stakeholder involvement must be managed throughout all phases of the project lifecycle to achieve the intended results. Active stakeholder participation creates the positive perception of organizational commitment and confidence in the project, and it greases the skids, or prepares the organization, for acceptance of the project outcomes or deliverables.

Potential project stakeholders include:

- Executives
- Senior managers
- Project sponsors
- Program/Project managers
- Business unit managers
- Subject matter experts (SMEs)
- Process owners
- Legal/Regulatory specialists
- Finance representatives
- Customer representatives
- Suppliers/Partners/Consultants
- End users

As mentioned, many of the project stakeholders will also have demanding day jobs. They have to fulfill their normal roles and responsibilities within their organizations and may be stakeholders on other projects as well. Project teams will not get a ton of time from the stakeholders, so it's critical that they take full advantage of the time that they are given, and that they manage the expectations appropriately. It is the project manager's responsibility to produce sound stakeholder management plans that clearly define stakeholder responsibilities, involvement levels, and other project requirements. These plans must be developed collaboratively with the stakeholders during the early stages of a project to establish the most effective solutions tailored to a project's many requirements.

A project manager's first job is obtaining project support and buy-in from the senior-level stakeholders of the project team. This type of top-down support greatly enhances the probability of getting project support from the various other areas of the business. If an employee is told by his manager to support a project, what is the likelihood of the employee doing it? As close to 100% as you're going to get. But without project buy-in from the top, chances are reduced that other stakeholders will fully support project initiatives. The trickle-down effect occurs in all organizations; leadership still matters. It is in the project manager's best interest to work closely with the project sponsor to obtain project support from senior stakeholders so that commitment to the project is forthcoming.

The best way to obtain support from the top is to clearly show the expected business value and positive organizational impact that the project will deliver. Senior-level stakeholders have a lot at stake within their organizations, mainly their reputations. If they are confident that a project will make money for their company or have some type of positive impact toward increasing the company's overall competitiveness in their industry, they will be more willing to take ownership and fully support, and even lead, project initiatives. *It's amazing how the calendars of senior-level stakeholders will suddenly free up when they are committed to a project that they feel will deliver tremendous value and, therefore, uphold or enhance their reputations within their organizations.* Project professionals can create positive working relations with their stakeholder teams by not only managing them effectively, but by clearly showing them the business value and beneficial change that will be generated as a result of collaborative project efforts.

Establishing this initial stakeholder buy-in and commitment won't occur after one meeting and may even take some time. Here's where our friend, the business case, comes back into play. The business case must be the driving force behind efforts to bring senior leaders on board. If project buy-in proves to be elusive, then the project probably isn't worth it in the first place. If the business case, however, shows a positive return on investment (ROI) and other quantitative and qualitative benefits, senior leaders are more apt to support and commit their time to the project. It is imperative that project professionals present their projects in clear, concise, and unambiguous business terms to respect and take full advantage of the time they get with executive stakeholders. It's hard to refute a project if the business case shows that it will deliver tremendous value, is aligned to the strategic intent, has a positive organizational impact, has a tolerable amount of risk, and increases the firm's overall competitive posture within the marketplace. Senior-level stakeholders think in these terms, conduct their affairs using business vernacular, and will support project professionals who possess this strategic and business mindset as well. See, the business case can indeed be a rewarding experience!

Change doesn't usually occur unless it's driven from the top. For the most part, workers won't alter their established business behaviors and processes unless there is a strong reason to do so, or if that reason is dictated from the higher echelons of the organization. I'm sure many of you have experienced either this resistance to change directly or observed it within your organizations. We all know about that seasoned 20-year veteran who performed a work activity a certain way 20 years ago and has repeated that activity the exact same way for the subsequent 19 years. With strong project buy-in from the top, even these hardened veterans will be willing to modify their work behaviors and support project activities to achieve beneficial change.

Clearly defining and communicating the required stakeholder roles, responsibilities, and levels of involvement is paramount in obtaining stakeholder commitment. If project teams perform these initial tasks effectively, project requirements will be understood and agreed to by all relevant parties. Far too often stakeholders are lumped together into one group and expected to contribute to a project in the same manner with the same time commitment levels. It is unreasonable to expect a senior-level stakeholder to contribute in the same manner and with the same number of hours per week as other stakeholders such as SMEs, process specialists, or business managers. If stakeholders are unsure of their roles, responsibilities, and levels of involvement, they will not be nearly as engaged as they would be if these requirements were clearly established. Project managers must develop and document stakeholder requirements and regularly communicate these requirements throughout the life of a project.

Instituting organizational change to achieve business value from projects can only occur when senior stakeholders assume accountability and responsibility for key areas of the business. Accountability and responsibility for the various project areas must reside with the most appropriate senior stakeholders since they hold the prestige and authority within certain areas of the organization and are capable of influencing behavior to aid in accomplishing important project activities. This is why they make the big bucks! These business leaders aren't getting compensated and rewarded merely to be managerial figureheads, but rather to make difficult decisions, drive change, and make money for their companies. Through sound stakeholder management processes, project professionals can support business leaders in making effective business decisions, driving business value, and delivering lasting beneficial change. If a project delivers the business value and other benefits that were articulated in the business case, project teams will have performed their job duties well and, ultimately, stakeholders will be satisfied with the results of the investment.

Project Sponsor: The Buck Stops Here

There is often ambiguity over who is ultimately accountable for the success or failure of a project. This ambiguity leads to tension within the project team and can spread like a disease. It is crucial to clearly define project account-ability at the onset of a project because money will be invested and someone needs to be accountable for the results of that investment. *The stakeholder pay-ing for the project investment is ultimately accountable to the business and to the shareholders for the results.* Project sponsors, often called executive sponsors, typically *own* projects because payment for the project work comes out of their budgets and they control the flow of project money. Project sponsors also provide the necessary resources for the project on behalf of the organization. *Project sponsors, therefore, are ultimately accountable for project results.* When executives scrutinize the money that was expended on a project investment and are not satisfied with the results, they call on the individual who spent company money. Project sponsors make these investments and the buck stops with them.

Project sponsors can no longer delegate their accountability for project investments by assigning project managers, deploying project teams, or even hiring outside consultants to run their projects. They certainly can delegate re-sponsibility and the operational aspects of project management, but they can't wash their hands clean of the project and expect the transfer of accountability to occur. Project sponsors are always accountable to the business, executives, and shareholders for project results. It makes business sense to bestow ac-countability on project sponsors since they typically initiate or support the initiation of the project, have a particular interest in the outcomes, and are optimistic about the value payoff. Why else would they initiate or support a project idea in the first place if they didn't feel good about the potential value it will bring? Additionally, project sponsors are usually self-appointed because they believe strongly in the need for the project and are willing to pay for it. When not self-appointed, project sponsors are generally assigned by executive teams. This assignment usually goes to those who maintain budgets in particu-lar areas of the business and to those who executives feel can bring about the desired beneficial change.

The project sponsor is the chief advocate for the project at the senior man-agement or executive level and communicates with corporate leaders about the merits of the project. The sponsor provides leadership and oversight to the project to ensure that the project delivers the desired business outcomes. The sponsor strives to obtain priority funding and resources for the project and also provides internal political support, when needed, to keep the project on track. Other key responsibilities of the project sponsor include:

- Championing the project
- Ensuring accuracy and reliability of the business case
- Obtaining budget approval and allocating the project spending
- Assigning project resources
- Supporting and providing guidance to the project

- Selling the project to the organization
- Approving project management plans
- Interacting with senior leaders
- Making key decisions
- Assisting in issue escalation and change management
- Driving the attainment of business value and benefits
- Validating business value and benefits
- Signing off on project deliverables

Project sponsors usually have access to key decision makers throughout their companies and know how to circumvent the numerous obstacles that exist in most organizations. Effective project sponsors promote their projects to other stakeholders and encourage their continued support by conveying the benefits that each stakeholder will receive as a result of the successful completion of the project. Through visible and passionate support for both the project and project manager, and by showing the positive impact the project will have on the organization, the sponsor can receive stakeholder support and commitment that is essential for project success.

The project sponsor is indeed the chief advocate for the project, but does not have to be the only project champion. Project champions are senior-level managers who argue the case for project investments because they believe in their causes and are confident that the investment will bring about positive change for their companies. While there is only one project sponsor, there is no limit to the number of project champions that a project can have. In fact, the more project champions the better. Project sponsors must actively seek out project champions to leverage their power and influence for the benefit of the project.

Project managers, meanwhile, are responsible for executing project activities and delivering the outcomes, but they normally don't possess the authority to make certain decisions or have access to all levels of an organization. In most organizations, individuals mainly communicate and interact within their peer groups making it difficult for project managers to gain access to the senior levels of management. The project sponsor, therefore, must act as the link between the project manager and senior stakeholders and other leaders to expedite decision making and address any obstacles or issues that a project may encounter. The sponsor becomes the focal point for decision making, issue escalation, and other important project priorities whenever the project manager's scope of authority is exceeded. Through active support and involvement, project sponsors can greatly enhance the project manager's ability to obtain valuable input, insight, and support of senior leaders in order to execute a successful project and deliver the expected business value.

Project managers report directly to their respective project sponsors for all project-related matters. Effective project managers regularly communicate with project sponsors and keep them informed about the status, risks, and

issues associated with their projects. Project sponsors are normally too busy to be involved in the day-to-day activities of the project; therefore, the project manager must keep them abreast of all important matters and provide recommendations based on their involvement and insight. *Collaboration between project sponsors and project managers is of the utmost importance and necessary in order to execute effective projects and drive business value.*

Clearly Defining Stakeholder Participation

Stakeholder input and involvement is paramount to any project. The identification of the appropriate stakeholders should be completed as early as possible in the project. Many of the stakeholders will be easy to identify, especially if they have been formally assigned to the project or have volunteered their services. Others, however, may be more challenging to recognize and incorporate into the overall project team. Project teams need to work closely with project sponsors to identify appropriate personnel who can have an impact on the project and who will, in turn, be impacted by the project outcomes. When individuals realize that their jobs may be impacted by a project or feel that they can influence project decisions that could benefit them or their teams, they will be more willing to participate as stakeholders. Identifying and assigning responsibilities to stakeholders is a key element on the critical path of any project. Depending on the magnitude and scope of a project, stakeholder groups may be comprised of a handful of individuals, dozens, or even hundreds of key project participants.

Since stakeholders can have vastly different job duties, it is neither feasible nor practical to expect all stakeholders to have the same responsibilities and involvement in a project. It is the project manager's task to fully understand the impact that stakeholders can have on their projects and assign them the appropriate roles that will bring about the greatest impact. The assignment of responsibilities should be done collaboratively with the stakeholders to achieve consensus and solidify understanding of their roles. Some stakeholders will have more involvement than others, but that does not mean that the stakeholders with less involvement will have less impact on the project. When project responsibilities are clearly established and formalized, stakeholders are much more willing to participate in project affairs and lend their skills, knowledge, and influence to the appropriate areas of the project. When project responsibilities are not clearly documented, stakeholders will more than likely dismiss project activities for other priorities or play a peripheral role in its execution.

Normally, stakeholders have to rearrange their schedules and find the time to commit to certain project activities. It is imperative that the project teams work closely with them to determine the appropriate amount of time that is needed to satisfy project requirements without compromising their other

responsibilities. If project stakeholders understand and agree to their responsibilities and time commitment levels to a project, they will be able to manage their time and provide the necessary input in the project much more effectively. As an example, if it is determined that certain stakeholders should commit 3 to 5 hours per week to a project and the responsibilities for those hours are clearly defined, the stakeholders will be able to focus their efforts and can make a significant impact in a limited time. If project roles and commitment levels are not established, however, stakeholders may not contribute in the most efficient way to a project and may even compromise their other responsibilities to their companies.

When the business case clearly articulates the merits of a project and the beneficial change the project outcomes will deliver, stakeholders typically get energized about the project and want to play an active role in its execution. But, unfortunately, once they realize that this active involvement includes attending meetings, providing timely information, producing deliverables, influencing departments, and many other time-consuming tasks, they may become overwhelmed and eventually lose focus on the project. Sound stakeholder management plans can prevent this from happening. Project managers can begin by establishing stakeholder teams to effectively define and delineate the numerous project responsibilities. Project team structures vary from project to project, but certain stakeholder teams are pervasive throughout most projects. Figure 5.1 shows a typical project team structure.

These stakeholder teams are described as:

- **Executive committee**—a group of senior-level managers representing the overall executive authority of an organization. The executive committee may be the board of directors of a firm, a delegated subcommittee

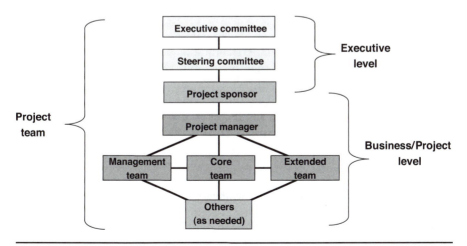

Figure 5.1   Project stakeholder team structure

of the board, or some other representation of senior management. Executive committees aren't normally involved in smaller projects but certainly play a role in projects that affect the overall strategic direction of a company, reshape the organizational structure, or alter the competitive landscape in some way. They may be committed to one hour a week, or even one hour per month, nevertheless, they are still part of the project team. *Remember, projects are strategic plans to achieve strategic objectives. Executive support and input is required.*

- **Steering committee**—a group of senior-level stakeholders responsible for providing leadership and overall guidance on the strategic direction of a project. The steering committee usually is comprised of organizational peers and is charged with senior managerial oversight of the project. It should represent all applicable areas of the business affected by the project and should have authority to make decisions on behalf of those areas of the business. Steering committee members usually attend project kickoff, phase-end review, and project closeout meetings; provide strategic direction for the project; review project progress and findings; and sign-off on project deliverables.

- **Project sponsor**—the stakeholder with genuine executive authority over the project. The project sponsor has full accountability for the project's outcome and has the power to make all project decisions, subject to oversight by the executive and steering committees. Funding and resources for the project usually come out of his/her budget. The project sponsor bridges the gap between the executive levels and the business and project levels of an organization.

- **Project manager**—the individual with day-to-day responsibility for the conduct and outcome of the project. The project manager develops detailed plans and manages resources to bring about the successful completion of specific project goals and objectives.

- **Management team**—a group of stakeholders at the management level who provide managerial insight, information, support, and resources to project efforts. Management team members usually engage in brainstorming sessions and progress reviews and provide input and quality assurance in project deliverables. They typically play pivotal roles in the development of the business case.

- **Core project team**—the project team that comprises the full-time and part-time resources assigned to complete project deliverables and achieve the project objectives. The core project team is responsible for planning project activities, communicating project status and issues, completing the project within budget and established timelines, and satisfying quality expectations.

- **Extended project team**—a group of stakeholders who possess subject matter expertise and provide input and feedback to the core project team. The extended project team may include process specialists, technical architects, design specialists, programmers, training representatives, end users, customers, legal advisors, regulatory specialists, quality experts, or other specialized individuals. This team participates in periodic meetings to provide their insight and knowledge for the benefit of the project and contributes to the development of project deliverables.

- **Others, as needed**—throughout the course of any project, additional resources may be necessary to satisfy unforeseen or unexpected project requirements. Changing requirements may make it necessary to bring on resources with specialized skill sets or to simply reinforce the project team with more resources to meet growing challenges or to expedite project results.

There are several stakeholder teams with differing responsibilities and involvement levels. Responsibilities and time commitments must be clearly established, documented, and communicated to ensure that all stakeholders are fully aware of their responsibilities, can plan their schedules accordingly, and can provide the input that is needed for the project. Stakeholder responsibility charts are effective tools in identifying stakeholder teams and documenting their project responsibilities and involvement. Table 5.1 gives an example of a stakeholder responsibility chart that shows the responsibilities and the required involvement.

As most projects progress through the project lifecycle, stakeholder requirements will change. In some project phases, more stakeholder participation will be required, while in other project phases less involvement will be necessary to satisfy project requirements. A major shortcoming in project management over the years has been treating all project phases equally and assigning the same resources with the same involvement levels to each of the phases. This may work for some projects, but certainly doesn't work for most projects in which requirements differ vastly from project phase to project phase. Today's business climate is dynamic, competitive, and constantly changing, and organizations must be nimble enough to adapt to the fluctuating business environment. This flexibility and adaptability must also make it down to the project level to ensure resources are allocated appropriately to keep pace with the demands and changing requirements as a project progresses throughout its lifecycle.

To illustrate how stakeholder requirements may differ for each of the project phases, Table 5.2 shows examples of three project phases of a technology deployment project. In the initiation phase, the focus is primarily on building the business case, researching potential solutions, developing the project charter, and securing a project budget. When compared to the other project phases, the build-out of the stakeholder team is in its infancy and resource involvement is limited since the viability of the project is yet to be established.

Table 5.1 Stakeholder responsibility chart

	Project Alpha: Stakeholder responsibility chart		
Stakeholder group	**Members**	**Responsibilities**	**Involvement level**
Executive committee	• John S. • Sally F. • Frank R.	• Attend executive committee meetings • Provide strategic direction	2 to 4 hours per month
Project steering committee	• Joan L. • Tom J. • Ashish P. • Kim P.	• Attend steering committee meetings • Review phase-end deliverable results • Make go/no go decisions on project continuation	6 to 8 hours per month
Project sponsor	• Brad B.	• Attend executive and steering committee meetings • Make key project decisions • Provide project funding • Sign-off on project deliverables	8 to 12 hours per week
Project manager	• Kathy S.	• Develop detailed plans • Manage project resources • Coordinate all meetings • Manage the development of deliverables • Provide status updates to executive teams	30 to 40 hours per week
Management team	• Joe B. • James K. • Steve R. • Dave O.	• Provide managerial insight and support • Engage in brainstorming sessions • Provide input for the development of the business case • Provide quality assurance into project deliverables	6 to 8 hours per week

(continues)

Table 5.1 *(Continued)*

		Project Alpha: Stakeholder responsibility chart	
Stakeholder group	**Members**	**Responsibilities**	**Involvement level**
Core project team	• Jan Z. • Jeff L. • David S. • Mary R. • Praveen B. • Jai X.	• Complete project deliverables • Plan all project activities • Maintain project budget • Maintain timelines • Achieve targeted project outcomes • Document results	20 to 25 hours per week
Extended project team	• Jose R. • Gerard L. • Hans T.	• Participate in periodic meetings • Provide insight and knowledge to the project • Contribute to project deliverables	4 to 6 hours per week
Other (as needed)	• Jeanne K. (legal)	• Review contracts	2 to 4 hours per month
Other (as needed)	• Fernando V. (accounting)	• Review budgets	2 to 4 hours per month

Table 5.2 Project involvement summary by phase

Project Beta: Project involvement by phase summary			
Stakeholder group	**Initiation phase involvement level**	**Execution phase involvement level**	**Benefit attainment phase involvement level**
Executive steering committee	4 to 6 hours per month	2 to 4 hours per month	1 to 2 hours per month
Project steering committee	10 to 12 hours per month	6 to 8 hours per month	2 to 4 hours per month
Project sponsor	8 to 12 hours per week	6 to 8 hours per week	2 to 4 hours per week
Project manager	30 to 40 hours per week	30 to 40 hours per week	4 to 6 hours per week
Management team	8 to 10 hours per week	6 to 8 hours per week	2 hours per week
Core project team	10 to 12 hours per week	30 to 35 hours per week	10 to 15 hours per week
Extended project team	4 to 6 hours per week	4 to 6 hours per week	2 to 4 hours per week
Other (legal)	2 to 4 hours per month	N/A	N/A
Other (accounting)	2 to 4 hours per month	2 to 4 hours per month	2 to 4 hours per month

In the execution phase of this technology deployment project, the key activities include executing the project management plan, initiating change control activities, deploying the technology system in the production environment, and addressing any problematic areas that may arise. Note that project involvement levels have been increased significantly in order to complete these labor-intensive work activities.

In the value attainment phase, the operational teams focus on attaining the benefits set forth in the business case. In this phase, the appropriate teams present timely and consistent operational reports that include key project metrics for management review. The operational teams modify or enhance the systems environment to achieve the targeted outcomes and elicit feedback or assistance from the management teams, as needed. Although an important phase, stakeholder involvement is significantly reduced.

In today's competitive business climate, it's imperative to allocate resources efficiently to achieve project results that have a positive impact. Time is money and the stakeholders' time that is devoted to a project can prove to be substantial. Project managers should use these vital project resources wisely and not waste their valuable time in unnecessary or inefficient meetings, or on excessive project activities. Project managers must identify areas where stakeholders will have the greatest impact and focus on those areas to bring about that result. RASCI (responsible, accountable, supportive, consulted, informed) charts can do just that.

Project sponsors may have the ultimate accountability for the outcome of a project, and project managers may be responsible for delivering the project within specifications, but they can't be involved in every single project activity that transpires during the course of a project. The success of a project depends on a combined effort of all of the stakeholders with accountabilities and responsibilities shared across the project team. A RASCI chart is an effective way of identifying and assigning project participation roles for key project activities, decisions, or deliverables. RASCI charts clearly assign responsibilities to the appropriate individuals who can and should own a project activity. RASCI charts are valuable tools for effective stakeholder management. These charts ensure that responsibility, and even accountability, is moved down to the most appropriate level of the project organizational chart to increase the chances of accomplishing the project activity in the most efficient and effective manner. RASCI charts articulate the project involvement for stakeholders and facilitate their active and focused participation.

A RASCI chart clarifies stakeholder participation by the various roles needed to complete project tasks or deliverables. It outlines which stakeholder, or stakeholder group, has what participating role(s) for key project activities:

- **Responsible (R)**—the stakeholder who owns the project activity and does the work to achieve the desired result. This person can be referred to as *the doer* of the project activity. The responsible person should have the appropriate resources to be able to fulfill the project task or complete the project deliverable. They are normally accountable to the person with the accountable (A) role. It's best to assign a single individual to be responsible for a project task, although it may be necessary to assign a group to be responsible to complete the task overall.
- **Accountable (A)**—the stakeholder who is ultimately accountable for the completion of the project activity or deliverable. The accountable person possesses ultimate management accountability, has decision authority, and can allocate resources to achieve the project activity or deliverable. *Each project activity should have one, and only one, accountable stakeholder.* The accountable person signs-off on the work that the responsible (R) person provides. The buck stops here.
- **Supportive (S)**—the stakeholders who provide resources or play supporting roles in the execution and completion of a project activity. There may be several supportive individuals contributing to a project activity. Many of these individuals are assigned or delegated by management teams to assist in the work that is required to complete a project

task or deliverable. These individuals typically have skill sets that lend themselves aptly in supportive roles.
- **Consulted (C)**—the stakeholders who possess the information, knowledge, or capability that is needed to complete a project activity. These individuals possess a particular expertise or knowledge in a business area and must be consulted on a regular or pre-defined basis to obtain information, guidance, recommendations, or other valuable input to guide the execution and completion of a project activity. The opinions of the stakeholders who are consulted are usually well respected and sought out so that the project team can make an informed decision or complete an action. It is imperative to establish two-way communications with these stakeholders and to keep them *in the loop* on all important project activities and decisions.
- **Informed (I)**—the stakeholders who are notified of the results of key project activities and decisions, but are not consulted. Stakeholders who are informed are those affected by a project activity or decision and, therefore, need to be kept abreast of the status but do not need to actively participate in the project effort. These individuals are usually informed after the decision has been made or the activity has been accomplished. One-way communication usually takes place with those who are informed. These stakeholders are kept *in the picture* with regard to project activities, decisions, and deliverables.

RASCI charts convey, at a high level, the approach the project team will be taking in accomplishing key project activities. They complement project schedules and Gantt charts, but do not replace them. Let's face it; most stakeholders won't look through a detailed Gantt chart to determine their roles and responsibilities. A RASCI chart, on the other hand, can be understood quickly, clearly shows where responsibilities lie, and provides visibility into the roles of all stakeholder teams. RASCI charts eliminate ambiguity and help stakeholders focus their efforts on completing key project activities. By carefully and wisely delineating responsibilities across stakeholder teams, project managers can ensure optimal use of resources and provide a targeted approach to meeting stringent project requirements.

General guidelines to assist in the development and implementation of RASCI charts include:

- Each activity should have one, and only one, accountable (A) stakeholder. Remember, the buck stops with this person!
- Efforts should be made to assign just one of the participation types (R, A, S, C, or I) for each stakeholder role that is applicable for a certain project activity.
- Accountable (A) and responsible (R) should be placed at the lowest feasible level of the project organizational chart. By not doing this, the

senior-most members of the project team will be accountable and responsible for *all* project activities, which is not practical.

- A stakeholder can be assigned consulted (C) or informed (I), but not both.
- A single stakeholder may be designated as responsible and accountable (R/A), although efforts should be made to assign just one participation type.
- Two-way communications should be established between the responsible (R) roles and the consulted (C) roles.
- One-way communication should be established from the responsible (R) roles to the accountable (A) roles.
- Efforts should be made to avoid obvious or generic project activities, such as attending meetings, producing status reports, or submitting timesheets. Focus on important, strategic project activities.
- Stakeholder roles may be individuals or groups, but it's best to keep them at the individual level.
- Job titles or functions should be used for the roles as opposed to individual names so that the chart remains valid when people change jobs.

Table 5.3 is an example of a RASCI chart that shows stakeholder roles and their respective participation in the key activities involved in the selection of a network vendor. As can be seen, there is only one accountable (A) stakeholder for each activity. The project manager is accountable for most activities involved in the development and submission of the request for proposal. The network manager is accountable for the overall evaluation of the vendors since this role has the technical expertise in the networking field. The vendor manager is ultimately accountable and responsible for all activities pertaining to vendor negotiations, selection, and contractual matters.

RASCI charts are effective tools in assisting project professionals to identify and assign participation roles for project activities, decisions, or deliverables. These charts can also facilitate project management activities and even stakeholder communication processes. By leveraging the RASCI charts, project professionals can tailor communication messages for the appropriate stakeholders and distribute only the relevant project material to the applicable teams. Stakeholder communications are vital to project success and effective methods that project professionals can use.

Effective Stakeholder Communications to Drive Value

Many of the senior project stakeholders are visionaries within their organizations and plan for the long-term success of their companies. These stakeholders are strategic thinkers and embrace long-term plans focused on significant

Table 5.3 Vendor selection RASCI chart

RASCI chart: Network vendor selection									
Project activity	Steering committee	Project sponsor	Project manager	Vendor manager	Network manager	Application manager	Network architect	Finance manager	Legal manager
Develop request for proposal	I	C	*A*	C	*R*	S	S	C	C
Determine appropriate vendors	C	C	*A*	C	*R*	S	S	I	I
Issue request for proposal	I	I	*A/R*	C	I	I	I	I	I
Respond to vendor questions	I	I	*A*	C	*R*	S	S	S	S
Create vendor short list	I	I	C	C	*A/R*	C	C	I	I
Coordinate vendor presentations	I	I	*A/R*	I	I	I	I	I	I
Evaluate and rank vendor presentations	I	C	C	C	*A/R*	S	S	S	S
Conduct vendor negotiations	I	I	I	*A/R*	C	C	C	C	C
Select vendor	C	C	C	*A/R*	C	S	S	C	C
Finalize vendor contract	C	C	I	*A/R*	C	I	I	C	C

goals. Stakeholder responsibility charts and RASCI diagrams can greatly assist them with their planning and time management efforts. Stakeholders often need to provide resources, in addition to their own time, to support project and other corporate initiatives. The earlier those stakeholder requirements can be established, the more time they will have to adequately plan to allocate time and resources. Stakeholder responsibility and RASCI charts should be developed collaboratively with the respective stakeholders to establish consensus and agreement of the roles. If initial collaboration isn't possible, project teams can develop these tools based on their knowledge of the project requirements and present their recommendations to the stakeholders for approval or modification. Generally, this is the best approach because project teams are more intimate with project details and understand the requirements and input that will be needed from the stakeholders.

Once agreement of the roles and responsibilities has been achieved, it's best to schedule the appropriate meetings as far out as reasonably possible. To conduct stakeholder management in a coordinated and consistent fashion, schedule recurring meetings at the same time on the same day of the week to avoid confusion and to get stakeholders into a project rhythm. Such recurring meetings may include weekly status meetings, stakeholder checkpoint sessions, management working sessions, or project team workshops. Obviously, this will not always be possible, but if you can set a clear path, it will be easier to manage on everyone's part.

Table 5.4 shows an example of a long-term meeting schedule for recurring meetings for the various stakeholder groups. Providing a graphical illustration of the scheduled meetings for the stakeholder teams greatly assists in the long-term planning efforts. Stakeholder meeting schedules should be established for each of the project phases because the requirements may change drastically from one phase to the next.

Effective communication with all of the stakeholder teams is critical. Project communications should be specifically tailored for each stakeholder team and should include the appropriate information at the proper times. It's well known that *under*communication is not a good thing in project management, but *over*communication that includes superfluous information may also prove ineffective, or even detrimental, to project efforts. When busy professionals get inundated with project information that is cumbersome to sort through and difficult to understand, they may simply ignore it. Project professionals should present project information in a clear, concise manner. They need to ensure that it is relevant and clearly highlights the areas that require their attention. Conducting project communications in such a manner facilitates the execution of a project and helps keep the project on-schedule and on-target to meet its objectives.

It's usually advantageous to implement specific communication methods for each of the stakeholder teams. For instance, it may be best for certain projects that all of the communications to the executive and steering committee members come from the project sponsor, while all other communications come from the project manager. Additionally, the type and frequency of the communications should be specifically tailored for each of the stakeholder teams. Executive and steering committee teams, for example, usually don't want to receive meeting agendas and minutes; weekly status reports; and interim or work-in-progress deliverables. What they do want to receive are phase-end and final deliverables; project budget and ROI updates; information concerning key decisions and organizational impact; and other strategic and organization-impacting information. Stakeholder communications should be consistent with the RASCI charts and should include both one- and two-way communication channels with the respective teams. Stakeholders, according to their project participation roles, need communication material to be effective in their project duties:

- **Responsible (R)**—stakeholders who need detailed and thorough project information to support their efforts to complete the project tasks at hand.
- **Accountable (A)**—management representatives who are accountable for key project activities and will need clear, concise summaries of

Table 5.4 Stakeholder meeting schedule

		Project Charlie stakeholder meeting schedule: Planning phase				
Week	**Dates**	**Monday**	**Tuesday**	**Wednesday**	**Thursday**	**Friday**
1	Jan 4–Jan 8	Project kickoff meeting		Management team workshop	Weekly status meeting	
2	Jan 11–Jan 15				Weekly status meeting	Project team workshop
3	Jan 18–Jan 22			Management team workshop	Weekly status meeting	
4	Jan 25–Jan 29				Weekly status meeting	Project team workshop
5	Feb 1-Feb 5		Steering committee checkpoint	Management team workshop	Weekly status meeting	
6	Feb 8–Feb 12				Weekly status meeting	Project team workshop
7	Feb 15–Feb 19				Weekly status meeting	
8	Feb 22–Feb 26		Steering committee checkpoint	Management team workshop	Weekly status meeting	Project team workshop
9	Mar 1–Mar 5				Weekly status meeting	
10	Mar 8–Mar 12			Management team workshop	Weekly status meeting	Phase-end meeting

progress, as well as any risks or issues that may impede that progress. The earlier that risks and issues are identified, the more time the accountable persons will have to react and take appropriate actions.

- **Supportive (S)**—individuals who support project activities and should be provided with specific information that will enable them to perform their supporting responsibilities. These individuals are usually less concerned with the high-level, status-type information, but more concerned with the information that will empower them to fully support their assigned project activities or deliverables.
- **Consulted (C)**—stakeholders who are impacted by the project and are tasked to provide input and to influence the project based on their expertise or knowledge. These individuals may not participate directly, but need to be provided with a level of project detail that allows them to give relevant input for the project and to help guide project decisions and activities in the most useful manner.
- **Informed (I)**—individuals who are usually the end users of the project output, and communications are used to gain their support and commitment to the project. Communication to these stakeholders should be in the form of a management style summary with a strong focus on the project benefits and how they will be impacted positively.

Establishing the communication methods and channels should be completed as early as possible in the project. Quite often this can be accomplished during project kickoff meetings or other meetings that occur early in the project. The priority should always be on establishing communication methods with the senior-ranking stakeholders first. It's best to ask them what type of information and what level of detail they want to see, but project managers should always be prepared to offer their recommendations based on their insight into the project and organization. This is one of the most challenging aspects to project management but can go a long way toward project success when conducted efficiently and effectively. Having informed and engaged stakeholder teams is indispensable to project success and to driving business value.

Effective communication plans identify the applicable stakeholders, the information to be communicated, and how the information will be communicated. Project managers should leave nothing to chance when it comes to stakeholder communications and should clearly document the project communication plans and methods. Project communications don't have to be elaborate or extremely detailed to be effective. In fact, it's best to keep the communications as simple as possible in order to get straight to the point and to ensure all messages are unambiguous and clearly understood by all parties. Effective communications tell stakeholders what they need to know at the time they need to know it and clearly convey what they need to provide so that the project remains on course. Stakeholders appreciate pinpointed communications and will actually read them and take appropriate actions if they know the messages are specifically tailored to them and are easily understood.

There are numerous communication methods available to project professionals in today's business environment. These communication methods include:

- Detailed e-mail
- Brief e-mail with attachments
- E-mail that includes a brief description and a link (URL) to the project central repository Intranet site
- Phone or conference call
- One-on-one meeting
- Group meeting
- Off-site meeting
- Project Intranet site
- Webinar
- Newsletter
- Others, as appropriate

Project communications may take place as often as deemed appropriate by the involved parties, which may include daily, weekly, monthly, quarterly, or even yearly sessions. The project manager should establish the frequency of communications while ensuring they maintain the balance between managing their team members' time and keeping them apprised of all relevant materials. Stakeholders need to be satisfied with the frequency and content of communication messages in order to remain committed to project efforts. Communication plans are eventually dismissed, forgotten about, or not adhered to far too often in projects, especially ones that are longer-term in nature. Project professionals should be relentless in ensuring that the communications go out as planned, but they should also be able to adapt to changing requirements and modify communication methods, if necessary. Finally, it's advisable to be proactive in seeking feedback from stakeholders on the effectiveness of project communications. Some questions you can ask to make sure you are on track include:

- Are you receiving the right amount of project information?
- Are you receiving too much information?
- Are you not receiving enough information?
- Are the communication methods appropriate?
- Is the frequency of communications appropriate?
- What additional information would you like to receive?
- What information can be omitted?
- How can project communications be improved?

It is a mistake to assume that no news is good news. You will eventually hear about the discontent and dissatisfaction of the stakeholders, and it will be far too late to mitigate if you haven't been managing your communications properly. Ill-advised decisions may have been made or inappropriate project actions may have already taken place if you haven't been seeking feedback and ensuring the integrity of your communications.

Project managers should keep a communication log or checklist up-to-date on the project Intranet site. The list outlines all of the communications messages that were distributed along with the associated documents. This is an effective way of managing and keeping track of project communications. Additionally, stakeholders can't use the excuse, "I didn't know that was my action item" or "Nobody informed me that I was responsible" if communication logs or checklists are maintained. Project managers can also revisit the communication history and assess the effectiveness of the communication plans and make adjustments to the approach, if necessary.

Communication methods can vary from one project phase to another. It's necessary to revisit the plan at the end or the start of each project phase to determine if modifications to the plan are necessary. To gain consensus and to set expectations for the communication methods, it's prudent to document the plan. Table 5.5 is a graphical illustration of an example of a stakeholder communication plan.

Stakeholders can make or break a project. They have the power, influence, knowledge, and skill sets that can contribute significantly to the outcome of a project. Project professionals can no longer focus on merely completing projects on-time and within budget, but must focus on achieving the most optimal value from their project efforts and expenditures. This can only be accomplished with the support and involvement of key project stakeholders. Achieving project results that endure is a combined effort of the entire project team. Project managers must coordinate these combined efforts in a focused and efficient manner by implementing sound stakeholder management processes and techniques.

Professional Development Game Plan for Success

1. Stakeholder involvement is essential to project success. These valued resources come from various areas of the business and are capable of influencing organizational behavior, initiating lasting change, deploying improvement plans, and making strategic decisions. Effective stakeholder management is paramount to delivering project results that endure. Do you have a formal stakeholder management process? How did you leverage your last stakeholder team? What did you do to clearly define and document each stakeholder's roles and responsibilities?

   Action Plan

   a. Revisit two or three of your prior projects and evaluate how stakeholder management was conducted. Determine what stakeholder management activities worked well, didn't work, or didn't occur

Table 5.5 Stakeholder communication plan

		Project Delta: Stakeholder communication plan			
Stakeholder group	**Members**	**Communication method**	**Project material**	**Frequency**	**Distributor**
Executive steering committee	• John S. • Sally F. • Frank R.	• E-mail	• Executive update presentation	• Quarterly	• Project sponsor
Project steering committee	• Joan L. • Tom J. • Ashish P. • Kim P.	• E-mail • Group meeting	• Steering committee update presentation • Phase-end presentations	• Monthly • Phase-end	• Project sponsor
Project sponsor	• Ken F.	• E-mail • One-on-one meeting	• Weekly update	• Weekly	• Project manager
Project manager	• Kathy S.	• Intranet site • Weekly status meeting	• Weekly status report	• Weekly	• Project core team members
Management team	• Joe B. • James K. • Steve R. • Dave O.	• E-mail	• Steering committee update presentation	• Monthly	• Project manager
Core project team	• Jan Z. • Jeff L. • David S. • Mary R. • Praveen B. • Jai X.	• Intranet site • Weekly status meeting	• Weekly status meeting	• Weekly	• Project manager
Extended project team	• Jose R. • Gerard L. • Hans T.	• E-mail	• Steering committee update presentation	• Monthly	• Project manager
Other (as needed)	• Jeanne K. (legal)	• E-mail	• Issues and risks log	• Quarterly	• Project manager
Other (as needed)	• Fernando V. (accounting)	• E-mail • One-on-one meeting	• Project budget updates	• Quarterly	• Project manager

at all. Write down five to seven stakeholder management activities that were conducted successfully, were effective, and led to positive results. Now write down five to seven activities that weren't conducted successfully, were dismissed or omitted, were ineffective or led to negative results.

b. Now consider your current or future projects. Based on this analysis, what will you do differently or more effectively in your approach to stakeholder management? How will you treat the executive members of your team? What will you do to obtain commitment from all of the stakeholders? How will you leverage each of their unique skills and influences throughout the organization? Write down five to seven actions you will take, or techniques or processes you will implement, to ensure effective stakeholder management for your project. Be specific.

2. It's no mystery that good project communication is paramount to success. For project communications to be effective, channels must go beyond the core project teams and branch out to all of the stakeholder teams. How are your project communications? Do you communicate enough with the stakeholders? Too much? Too little? Are communications specific for each stakeholder team, or are communications simply distributed to everyone on the project distribution list? Are project communications stored to the online project repository?

Action Plan

a. Revisit two or three of your prior projects and analyze how communications were conducted. How effective were your methods? Did you develop and document a formal communications plan or was it done on the fly? List those methods that worked well and identify areas of improvement.

b. Envision a perfectly executed communications plan for a sizable strategic project. Who were you in the process? How did you lead a smooth effort? Were the stakeholders quickly deleting wasteful e-mails that didn't pertain to them, or were they opening each communication because they knew it was important and relevant to them? Now write down the methodology you used to get this fantastic result! Keep fine-tuning until all of your project stakeholders look forward to being a part of one of your projects.

Reference

1. Berman, Jeff. 2007. *Maximizing Project Value*. New York, NY: AMACOM.

6

Value Metrics: You Can't Manage What You Can't Measure

In God we trust; all others bring data.

—W. Edwards Deming

Applying Value Metrics to Your Projects

Have you ever gotten to the end of a project and had no idea if it was successful? How many times were you unsure if you would receive that elusive stakeholder sign-off? Were you ever surprised that you did receive it? What a stressful way to close out a project! Unless you thrive on distress, approaching uncertain project success is not the most pleasant experience, but it is a current reality. On any given project outcome there will be team members who deem it a complete success and others who feel they may have wasted their time. It may seem rather astonishing that such conflicting views can exist at the conclusion of projects. But to those who have learned to embrace value metrics to guide project execution toward targeted outcomes, these conflicting views come as no surprise.

Project professionals are historically skilled and focused on managing the triple constraints of scope, cost, and schedule, but it's not enough. To bring about the most optimized project results that deliver long-lasting business value, project teams need to incorporate relevant value metrics into their overall project approach to target specific outcomes.

Most project professionals understand the importance of value metrics, but they usually don't know how to approach them. *What should I measure? How do I measure them? Who needs to see them? What do I do about them?* This leaves us with a plethora of projects that completely ignores important metrics or focuses on certain metrics that may not be directly related to a project's success. This is unfortunate because project teams may be executing their projects flawlessly, but at the end of the day they have nothing to show for their efforts because they did not identify, measure, optimize, and present appropriate value metrics.

Metrics are characteristics of a system, organization, project, or process that can be measured and expressed numerically. *Value* metrics are the quantitative objectives, or targeted business benefits, that the project team is commissioned to achieve. Value metrics help to establish the success criteria of a project in quantitative and measurable terms. Clearly defined project success criteria brings objectivity to the evaluation and management of projects and guides decision making toward targeted outcomes. Stakeholders are less likely to second guess the necessity for a project or the status of a project when metrics are established, monitored, and presented. With value metrics clearly defined and understood by the project team, the constant need to make decisions on the fly is greatly reduced—or even eliminated. Decisions that come *from the gut* occur far too often in projects mainly because there are no quantitative metrics in place that can assist with these decisions. The proper use of value metrics empowers the entire project team to make timely, informed decisions that lead to greater overall confidence in ongoing management.

Value metrics should be determined early in a project to provide unambiguous targeted outcomes that team members can focus on achieving. Without properly establishing quantitative metrics, it is extremely difficult to achieve *measurable* business success on any project. The popular adage, "you can't manage what you can't measure," is certainly true and applicable to projects. Establishing, measuring, and acting on the data from sound metrics is a key step in delivering lasting business value.

To illustrate the importance of metrics, let's apply their use to professional development programs and performance appraisals, something that is pervasive in nearly all organizations. Employees are often dissatisfied with their performance reviews and even incredulous that they could receive such poor reviews from their managers. In most cases the employees feel that they performed their job duties well, but their managers did not do an adequate job of communicating clearly defined performance metrics. Similarly, project teams sometimes disagree about the project outcomes. It's tough for anyone to agree on whether or not they hit the bulls-eye if they're looking at different targets. Employees may have worked hard and performed quite well with the tasks on which they were focusing, but if they weren't focusing their efforts on the performance metrics that their managers had in mind, this disconnect will be reflected by poor appraisals.

It is simply good management to clearly define performance metrics for which employees are being rated so that they can focus their work efforts accordingly. Additionally, performance metrics should be documented and revisited periodically to ensure that all involved parties are on the same page and heading in the right direction. The same principle applies to projects. Project professionals need to identify quantitative project goals using the appropriate value metrics and focus project activities toward achieving those goals. Without established value metrics, project performance will be ambiguous and open to interpretation by the entire project team. When this occurs, project management becomes tactical to keep up with the changing project direction that will inevitably occur. Remember, you can't manage a project toward success if you can't measure it. Establishing metrics and incorporating a metrics-based approach is the way to measure project performance and, ultimately, success.

Identifying, tracking, managing, and communicating value metrics can have tremendous benefits for an organization. Value metrics:

- Establish project goals that are tangible and realistic
- Ensure project alignment to the strategic objectives of the firm
- Enhance overall understanding of project status and progress
- Forecast business performance and results with greater predictability
- Enable managers to make informed decisions based on business data—less reliance on gut feelings
- Identify both positive and negative project trends
- Eliminate or reduce inaccurate or embellished reporting—can't pull the wool over their eyes
- Reduce variation in the delivery of products and services to customers
- Provide performance and quality indicators
- Ensure sustainable business results

Project goals that are stated clearly and unambiguously with the use of value metrics provide focus to the project team and establish project success criteria that can't be disputed. We will be getting even more concise as we move forward and dive deeper into this important topic, but for now note these examples of project goals that are stated concisely using specific value metrics:

- Achieve a customer return rate of at least 40%
- Increase employee productivity by 20%
- Achieve a net present value in excess of $8.5MM
- Increase productivity output by 10%
- Reduce vendor costs by 10%
- Reduce the product defect rate from 5% to 2.4%

- Achieve a project payback in less than 2.6 years
- Do not exceed more than 15% outsourced labor
- Achieve a product market share of 25%
- Achieve a customer service rating of 85%
- Achieve an employee satisfaction index of 4.4 out of 5.0
- Maintain network availability above 99.5%
- Resolve all technical issues with the first line of support 90% of the time

With a metrics-based approach, project teams can produce and present performance graphs to depict overall project performance. Executives and senior managers think in business terms and can understand, rather quickly, project performance graphs. With a quick glimpse at these graphs, managers can understand how a project is progressing and can take appropriate actions to address or rectify problematic areas as necessary. Figure 6.1 shows some simple examples of performance graphs that can be effective in tracking and presenting project and business performance. Business leaders still appreciate the *green, yellow, red* indicators for presenting project status, but would much rather see performance graphs that truly represent actual project and business performance.

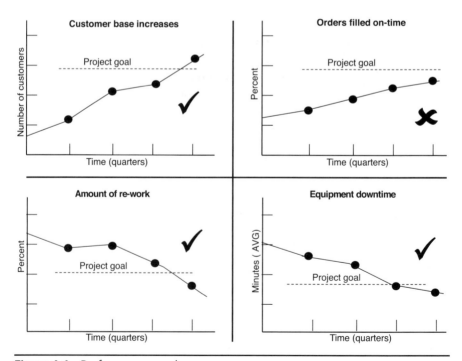

Figure 6.1   Performance graphs

Importance of Labor Metrics in Creating and Sustaining Business Value

People are the most important and one of the most expensive assets for most organizations. For this reason, labor metrics must not be taken lightly in the evaluation and execution of projects. Projects can have significant impacts on the effectiveness of the workforce, especially when managed appropriately using labor metrics and measurements to drive employee behavioral change. Employee costs are extensive and often come close to half of a company's overall expense; therefore, even a slight impact on a portion of the employee pool can produce tremendous results. Project teams need to explore how their projects will impact the workforce, or selected employees of the workforce, and include these important labor metrics in the business case. Projects that can improve workforce productivity and efficiency can contribute greatly to the success and profitability of a company.

Projects can positively impact the workforce in many ways: employee efficiency may be enhanced, productivity may increase, labor costs may be reduced, the knowledge base may be expanded, or morale may increase. Although employees are the primary cost factor within an organization, they also are the primary asset that produces business value, increases business growth, and improves overall competitiveness for their companies. Project outcomes that affect and influence this vital asset base can have a long-lasting impact on an organization.

The knowledge that employees possess can be indispensable for a company. Industrialized nations around the world have been moving toward knowledge-based economies over the past few decades. A significant portion of the overall economic health of these countries relies on the information sector. Plants, machinery, and technology are still important contributors, but information and knowledge contributions have grown rapidly and continue to grow. Companies are still investing in capital assets, but it is knowledgeable people who must utilize those capital assets in smart, effective ways to generate business value. Corporate leaders are recognizing that employee knowledge, productivity, and efficiency are paramount to their companies' success and they are focusing intently on enhancing their most valued assets. With this push toward workforce optimization, an increasing number of projects are being implemented to enhance workforce capabilities. As these projects are initiated, it's up to project teams to identify and manage the most relevant labor metrics to ensure that the workforce is achieving its full potential.

This is another case of, if you can't measure it, you can't manage it—this adage certainly applies to the people factor. If you can't measure your most important assets, you certainly can't manage them. People and the intellectual capital they possess are profit levers for organizations, and management teams must effectively maneuver these profit levers to drive sustained business growth. The knowledge and productivity of the workforce is paramount to the very survival of a company in today's intensely competitive and information-driven world.

You may be thinking, "But most of my projects center around technology deployments, not people." This is not an uncommon assertion. A significant portion of all capital investments is in information technology. What isn't always clear is that the people component of these investments is pivotal to success and cannot be discounted. Where there is technology, there are people leveraging that technology in an attempt to increase their capabilities and perform their jobs better. Companies invest in technology to upgrade systems capabilities, increase computer speed, consolidate disparate systems, replace older equipment, and for numerous other reasons, but technology by itself doesn't add much business value. It is what people do with that technology that brings about business value and beneficial change.

Technology assets require knowledgeable and skilled people to utilize them effectively. A company may implement the latest and greatest technology with all of the bells and whistles, but if the workforce doesn't leverage the features that make the technology great, then what's the point? This happens, unfortunately, far too often in business. Companies feel that if they deploy enough computing power and advanced technologies in their environments, they will fix all of their problems, but a fool with a tool is still a fool, so they say. Computers and technology don't fix problems, people do. Incorporating and managing labor metrics enables project teams to ensure that the workforce is benefiting from their technology initiatives.

It is an unfortunate fact that senior business leaders sometimes dismiss the importance of labor enhancements, efficiency gains, and productivity improvements—especially for office workers—when evaluating possible project investments. When presented with a carefully crafted project proposal that conservatively forecasts workforce efficiency gains of, let's say, 5%, many business leaders respond with, "That just means people will take longer coffee breaks." These same leaders are also fond of saying, "Show me the money." Well, a 5% efficiency gain is money, and it could be a lot of money depending on the size of the organization or the strategic role of the area of the business that is impacted. *It's a management issue if an organization can't produce some kind of business value with extra capacity on their hands.*

To illustrate this point, let's run the numbers (the calculations are shown for reference). If a technology upgrade project is forecasted to produce 5% efficiency gains for a department of 25 office workers, each person will then have extra capacity of 24 minutes per day for a typical 8-hour workday (Calculation 1). In total, that equates to 10 extra hours a day for the department (Calculation 2) and 220 extra hours a month, assuming 22 working days in a month (Calculation 3). As a result of this technology upgrade project, the department will have gained 220 hours of extra capacity. Now that would be a long coffee break if the management team didn't do anything with that extra capacity! This simple example illustrates that labor efficiency gains can indeed enable value for organizations, but only if managers do something with the extra capacity.

1. 60 minutes per hour × 8 hours × .05 = 24 extra minutes per day for each full time employee (FTE)
2. 25 FTEs × 24 extra minutes per day/60 minutes per hour = 10 extra hours per day for the department
3. 10 extra hours for the department × 22 working days per month = 220 extra hours per month

As we have been postulating throughout this book, leadership still matters. A technology deployment project may produce labor efficiency gains, but it's up to management to extract value and produce beneficial change from those efficiency gains. Technology in and of itself generally won't produce any value. Just because bigger, faster, cheaper systems are deployed in production environments, hard dollar cost savings or profit gains aren't necessarily achieved. It's what people do with the bigger, faster, cheaper systems that can bring about value and lasting change.

Herein lies a common mistake that project teams consistently make in their business cases. Too often, project professionals *assume* that hard dollar business value will automatically be generated or saved when employee efficiency gains are expected to be achieved as a result of a project. Let's go back to our previous example. Many of us would want to assign a monetary value to the extra 220 hours a month of additional capacity and include that in the return on investment study. Assuming an average hourly salary of $40.00 per FTE, the monetary value would be $8,800 per month (Calculation 4) and $105,600 per year (Calculation 5). Depending on which way the wind is blowing at the time, a project team may consider this $105,600 additional revenue or cost savings. Can you see where we're heading here?

4. 220 extra hours per month × $40 average hourly salary = $8,800 a month
5. $8,800 per month × 12 months per year = $105,600 per year

Based on this analysis, will this company really generate $105,600 of additional revenue a year by freeing up 5% of office workers' time? Maybe, if they can sell more products. But the assumption that the company will automatically generate $105,600 of additional revenue, as calculated from employees' salaries, is not valid!

Now let's see what happens when project teams treat these hard dollar numbers as cost savings. Will this company really reduce costs by $105,600 per year as a result of these 5% efficiency gains? Maybe, if they eliminate some FTEs and reduce payroll by $105,600 per year. But if no action is taken, costs will not be reduced.

Managers have numerous options at their disposal with extra workforce capacity to enable business value, such as consolidating departments, eliminating functions, reducing headcount, increasing output, increasing responsibility levels, and training employees. I would agree with the *show me the money* folks: if managers plan to do nothing with the extra capacity on their hands, then their projects will not deliver much value to their businesses, if any at all. However, with effective management, tremendous business value can indeed be enabled from projects that increase employee efficiency and productivity.

Still not convinced? Here's another example. A large package delivery company decided to invest heavily in wireless technology to capture package information to provide its customers with near-real-time updates on delivery status. Prior to this technology investment, drivers transmitted package information with the use of pay phones. This required drivers to deviate from their delivery routes several times a day to find these pay phones, dial a pre-defined number, and then transmit all of the package information over the public telephone network. The costly wireless investment would eliminate the need for drivers to go through this process, saving each driver several minutes a day.

Of course there were those who felt that saving the drivers a couple of minutes each day could not possibly justify the cost of building out an extensive wireless network. Those extra minutes probably equates to one more coffee stop for each driver. Well, the project investment certainly was well worth it. With a fleet of thousands of drivers and each driver having extra capacity at their disposal, albeit merely a couple of minutes a day, a substantial number of additional packages were delivered. So instead of taking longer coffee breaks, each driver delivered more packages. More package deliveries mean more revenue for the company. Additionally, customer satisfaction and loyalty increased substantially with the enhanced and near-real-time package tracking system.

In addition to showing the importance of labor efficiency gains, this real-world example illustrates that real-time information about a package could be as important as the package itself. Information is vital in today's business environment. Due to the Internet and other technological innovations, information is instantaneous and in great supply. In fact, all of the information that is literally at our fingertips can be overwhelming and even disruptive if not utilized effectively. The challenge is figuring out what to do with all of this information to remain focused on maintaining or increasing overall competitiveness.

To acquire even more information, employees periodically attend formal training courses. Employee training is often an area of contention for business leaders. Some view training as a waste of valuable time, while others view it as a necessity for a company's vitality and growth. Once again, leadership matters. If employees go to training and do nothing with the knowledge or skill sets they acquired, the training may have been a waste of time; much like a project when the project deliverables immediately go into drawers on project closeout. But when employees apply the newly acquired knowledge and skill sets to their jobs to improve their performance, the training was probably worth it. Training is an integral element to many project management plans. Project managers should include not only training into their plans, but activities to ensure that the training will be beneficial and lasting for the organization. Such activities may include:

- Conducting train-the-trainer sessions
- Delivering internal training
- Producing training documentation
- Creating *quick-tip* guides or *cheat sheets*
- Producing user manuals
- Assigning those who have been through training as Accountable or Responsible (from the RASCI charts) for key project tasks
- Providing periodic refresher classes
- Implementing other creative methods to derive value from training

Knowledgeable and skilled workers are critical—but not enough—to drive optimal performance within an organization. Efficient and effective processes must also be in place. Workforce effectiveness can be enhanced by improving the numerous and varied processes that exist within companies. Organizational and employee processes are vital to a company's success or failure. Nearly everything that happens within an organization is the result of a process. A process consumes resources and is a series of steps designed to produce an effect or desired result. There are processes centered on business areas, including increasing sales, increasing output, reducing outages, improving customer service, submitting expense reports, and optimizing capacity. An organization is only as effective as its processes. Improving and streamlining processes can yield tremendous benefits for an organization. For this reason, more and more projects are being implemented that are focused on improving certain processes within organizations. Through successful process improvement initiatives, employee assets can be optimized and put to work for the benefit of their organizations.

Because labor is a company's most valued asset, employee turnover can be catastrophic. Employee turnover can cost a company significant amounts of money. Many of the costs associated with turnover aren't even obvious, but they are out there and they can come back to haunt companies. The costs of re-hiring alone, for instance, include the costs of hiring, interviewing, advertising, agency fees, referral bonuses, travel, relocation, training, and recruiter costs. These costs can add up quickly.

Businesses with lower employee turnover are more likely to drive profits more effectively than those similar businesses with higher turnover rates. Smart leaders realize the importance of maintaining a steady and productive workforce and have even implemented creative and innovative solutions during rough economic periods. During the recent global recession where lay-offs were pervasive throughout all industries, certain companies were taking measures to keep their employees on the payroll to avoid the massive turn-over and re-hiring costs. Some of these measures included offering sabbaticals to their employees, reducing salaries across the board, requiring mandatory unpaid vacation days that extended holiday weekends, and other creative, in-novative incentives. These companies knew that economic conditions would eventually improve and that an appropriate-sized workforce would be needed once again to maintain or increase their competitiveness. They realized that re-hiring and training new employees would be extremely arduous and ex-pensive, and it would prevent them from maintaining or gaining market share when economic conditions improved.

Project teams need to be cognizant of the importance of the workforce and incorporate the appropriate labor metrics into their project management ap-proach. By incorporating and managing labor metrics throughout the project lifecycle, project teams can ensure workforce optimization specifically tailored for their project deliverables. Labor metrics are numerous and diverse. More common labor metrics that may be incorporated into projects include:

- Absenteeism
- Efficiency
- Productivity
- Resignation rate
- Internal vacancy fulfillment
- Promotions from within
- Profit per FTE
- Staffing levels

Labor metrics alone do not provide value to the organization. They do not in-crease sales, improve productivity, or make key decisions. Project professionals and stakeholders are responsible for making sound business choices based on these metrics that bring about beneficial change. Metrics are only as good as the actions taken to achieve the targeted outcomes of the project.

Common Value Metrics

All projects are undertaken to meet particular goals and objectives in order to bring about beneficial change or added value. These particular goals and objectives, although specific to each project, have common attributes that are universal across all projects, organizations, and industries. The numerous and diverse value metrics that can be applied to projects can be categorized in many ways. Value metrics for the purpose of quantifying and driving business value include:

- Cost savings metrics—to reduce costs
- Business growth metrics—to grow the business
- Time-related metrics—to free-up time and increase capacities
- Performance metrics—to improve performance
- Quality metrics—to improve quality

These categories are applicable to companies of all shapes and sizes across all industries and may be applied to customers, employees, processes, vendors, systems, suppliers, departments, and just about any other area of business. The following sections provide some common value metrics for the five categories listed:

1. **Cost savings metrics:** Many projects are implemented to drive down costs for specific areas of the business. Table 6.1 illustrates some common cost savings metrics that may be applied.
2. **Business growth metrics:** Many metrics are established and managed to drive business growth. Table 6.2 shows common business growth metrics that you can implement.
3. **Time-related metrics:** Time is money. Many projects are implemented to reduce time to complete certain actions or activities for the various areas of the business. Common time-related metrics are shown in Table 6.3.
4. **Performance metrics:** All companies strive for performance optimization. As performance for the various areas of the business increases,

Table 6.1 Common cost savings metrics

Overall costs	Total cost of ownership	Support staff costs
Debts or liabilities	FTE reduction	Facilities
Sales cycles	Elimination of functions	Cabling and racking
Sales reductions	Equipment	Operational expenses
Marketing as % of sales	Hardware	Licensing
Advertising as % of sales	Software	Training
Distribution as % of sales	Telecommunications	Travel
Sales costs as % of sales	System maintenance	Cost avoidance
Net present value	Accident	Capital expenditure
By account	Sales expense	Required headcount
Product delays	Administrative	Penalties/Fees
Service delivery	Cost of solving a problem	Reuse of materials
Consolidation	Taxes	Insurance
Inventory	Overtime	Freight
Overhead	Elimination of departments	Outsourcing

Table 6.2 Business growth metrics

Sales revenues	Name recognition	Geographies served
Profit	Win business from competitors	Employee headcount
Stock price	Merger facilitation	Recognized for community service and charity
Earnings per share	Merger prevention	Recognized as a top producer of quality products or services
Market share	Alliance establishment	Recognized as the performance leader
Repeat business	Alliance enhancement	Recognized as the low price leader
Customer base	Market recognition	Brand recognition

Table 6.3 Time-related metrics

Order response time	Response time for service request	Processing time
Equipment downtime	Time to project completion	Training time
Cycle time	Time to implement	Repair time
Overtime	Supervisory time	Work stoppages
Average delay time	Meeting time	Lost time days
Order fulfillment time	Time to perform internal tasks	Time to perform external tasks
Time saved with process improvement	Mean time to restore service	Inventory turnover time
Time to market	Average time to resolve incidents	Average time to answer customer calls
Average time for system outage	Time to fix a software bug	Number of slipped days
Outage recovery time	Mean time between system incidents	Time to resolve unavailable services
Reconciliation	Time to respond to inquiries	Time to acknowledge receipt of trouble ticket

corporate strength and competitiveness increase. Table 6.4 shows common performance metrics that may be utilized.

5. **Quality metrics:** Quality is paramount to efficient operations and meeting or exceeding customer expectations. Table 6.5 shows common quality metrics that may be applied.

Table 6.4 Performance metrics

Number of units produced per time period	Loans approved	Applications processed
Number of units produced on-time	Percent of equipment downtime	Students graduated
Items assembled	Percent of utilization of equipment	Number of shipments
Items sold	Labor cost per unit of production	New accounts generated
Unit sales	Overtime required per unit of production	Cycle times
Customer closure rate	Number of repeat failures	Reduce activity and unit costs across functions
Size of the average order	Inventory turnover	Time to market
Forms processed	Patients visited	Number of orders filled
Efficiency gains through process improvement	Employee retention	Recruitment of top performers
Unavailable third party services	Professional development enhancement	Employee morale
Employee absenteeism	Number of customers serviced	Percent of incidents resolved by first line of support
Service-level agreement breaches	Percent of calls dropped	Percent of successful software upgrades
Percent of authorized changes to the production environment	Percent of deployments that cause outages	Percent of emergency changes to production environment
Total number of incidents	Percent of accurate sales forecasts	Percent of inaccurate pay statements
Percent of systems over capacity	System downtime	Unavailable service

Table 6.5 Quality metrics

Number of defects per thousand units produced	Defect rate	Number of accidents
Scrap	Re-work	Customer complaints
Warranty cost	Shortages	Number of repeat failures
Programming bugs	Deviation from standard	Product line enhancements
Error rate	Product failures	Customer satisfaction
Number of software defects detected from log files	Number of defects fixed during testing phase	Customer service
Compliance	Regulatory requirements	Greenhouse emissions

Professional Development Game Plan for Success

1. Value metrics help to establish success criteria for projects in quantitative and measurable terms and bring objectivity to the evaluation of projects. Additionally, value metrics guide decision making and project activity toward these targeted outcomes. Do you embrace the use of value metrics? How did you identify and document value metrics for your projects? What were the goals of your last three projects? Were they task-oriented (implement x, y, z) or were they quantitative (achieve x, y, z)?

Action Plan

    a. Revisit two or three of your prior projects and evaluate how effectively value metrics were incorporated into the overall business case and project plan. Where did you miss an opportunity to identify and manage value? Did you consider cost savings, business growth, time, performance, and quality? Were labor metrics taken into account? Write down the value metrics that *should* have been incorporated into each of these projects.

Reference

1. Fitz-enz, Jac. 2000. *The ROI of Human Capital*. New York, NY: AMACOM.

7

Untapping the Full Value Potential of Your Project

Price is what you pay. Value is what you get.

—Warren Buffett

Identifying the Appropriate Value Metrics

I'm certain that many of you can relate to the following true story. A dedicated, management-level professional worked tirelessly on a project initiative that she felt was desperately needed for her organization. She was sure it would solve many of their business problems. She went through all of the standard toll gate processes, developed a high-level business case, and obtained all of the standard *checkmarks in the boxes* to demonstrate that mandated project activities were completed. The project progressed for months and this person became synonymous with this project initiative due to her staunch support of the project and an excellent job of selling it to most areas of the business.

The CFO requested a meeting to review the potential results of this particular project investment because it required a large investment. He simply wanted to hear about the financial benefits that this major investment would bring to the company, but this project supporter panicked and became defensive. *"He's going to destroy my case for this project. We just need this project, it's obvious. Why do I have to show business value? How does he expect me to show positive results?"* You can imagine what happened in that meeting. While she was good at selling the concept of the project and checking boxes, she skipped over the value planning and was held to task for it.

Far too often, time and resources are spent working on a project without proper justification, or even knowing the potential business benefits that the project will deliver. Trust me, eventually you're going to have to pay the piper and show quantitative results. As if on cue, someone will undoubtedly ask the question you're dreading or are unprepared to answer. Build the business case correctly from step one and you will avoid a lot of potential turmoil in the future.

There are typically some obvious benefits to any given project. For example, an investment in the latest plant machinery may increase output production, a software upgrade may improve workforce efficiency, or an enhancement to a claims processing system may process more claims. But project teams need to go further than merely identifying the obvious benefits. They must determine the appropriate value metrics associated with those benefits to truly understand how beneficial the project may be. For instance, it's not enough to simply state that a project investment in the latest plant machinery will increase output production. You must identify, evaluate, and solidify the value metrics associated with that increase. Is it a 5% increase in output production? 7%? 10%? What are the timeframes for achieving these results? These value-metric parameters are crucial to determining if project investments are worthwhile. Management teams may determine that a production increase of 5% may not be worth the effort, whereas a 10% increase is worth the effort, the risks, and all of the associated project costs. Determining the appropriate value metrics for a project helps build an accurate business case that in turn guides effective decision making and project execution.

And that's just the tip of the iceberg! To truly understand all of the possible beneficial outcomes, project teams must not stop with the obvious benefits but should take a structured and analytical approach in capturing all of the potential business benefits that their projects can deliver. Otherwise, they will not discover all of the benefits that reside *below the surface* and, therefore, not attain the most business value from their projects (see Figure 7.1).

As can be seen with this illustrative example, there are so many benefits that are never identified, incorporated into the business case, monitored, reported on and, therefore, never achieved. In the preceding chapter we discussed several different categories of metrics that can be used to drive business value. These metrics focus on costs savings, business growth, time-related savings, performance improvements, and quality enhancements. Project teams need to reference these categories and determine the most applicable metrics for their projects and incorporate them into project activities to drive sustainable value. Otherwise, project teams will leave significant potential and untapped business value on the table.

Achieving the optimal business benefits that will endure is the underlying reason why project investments are pursued in the first place. Before embarking on any project investment, business professionals and project teams should

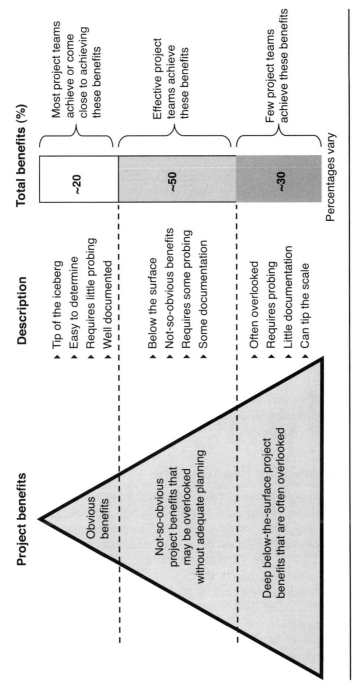

Figure 7.1   Project benefits analysis

ask some high-level questions to determine the initial feasibility of their potential projects:

- Why do we need more business benefits?
- What benefits do we want to achieve?
- What benefits could we get and how valuable are they to the business?
- What are the appropriate value metrics associated with the benefits?
- What problems are the benefits going to resolve?
- How feasible is it to get these benefits?
- What if we do nothing?

When initially identifying and evaluating project benefits, it's not necessary to distinguish between monetary and nonmonetary ones. It is more important to think initially in terms of all the possible project outcomes that can occur. The benefits will be converted to dollars and other quantitative terms at a later stage, if appropriate. Initially, it's an exercise of exploring, brainstorming, and considering all of the possible business benefits that can result from a project investment. After you've uncovered the obvious benefits, dig deeper. Shoot for more no matter how crazy they seem. You never know what you'll find and it could be significant.

Identifying the not-so-obvious project benefits requires probing. Rarely does a project manager, or even the core team, have all of the expertise, knowledge, and skill sets to perform these important analytical functions. Identifying, evaluating, and refining project and business metrics is a collaborative process that requires input from various knowledgeable areas of the business. The next section focuses on the processes and techniques required to accurately identify, synthesize, and incorporate value metrics into the business case and the overall project approach.

The Value-metrics Framework

As we mentioned before, most projects require the input of stakeholders and employees to capture required data elements. These data elements must then be synthesized and presented in a business case to convey the compelling reasons for a project's implementation. The challenge lies in identifying the proper personnel, extracting information from them while being respectful of their schedules, and working with that data to build-out a solid business case. A project team's ability to forecast accurate business outcomes is greatly enhanced when a structured, proven approach is undertaken.

Capturing the numerous data elements necessary for completing a comprehensive business case can be time-consuming, tedious, and even frustrating. Project teams have to reach out to several different departments, analyze numerous reports, conduct detailed analyses, and revisit areas where there may be gaps or missing information. If project teams approach these important project activities indiscriminately, they will most likely fail to obtain the required information needed to craft a thorough and accurate business case.

The process of capturing data and forecasting business value must be one that can be used consistently across departments and at various points along the project lifecycle. Figure 7.2 presents a repeatable, reliable, and proven framework that takes a data-driven approach to accurately identifying and solidifying value metrics. Once these value metrics have been solidified, all project activities focus on achieving these important goals. The success or failure of the project is determined by how closely the organization comes to achieving the identified value metrics.

This framework is iterative in nature and should be repeated as often as necessary as more project team members and subject matter experts are brought on board, and as data elements need to be verified, validated, or refined. It will be necessary for project teams to revisit certain areas or reconvene with specific departments to achieve a greater level of granularity for the data elements. Remember, Rome wasn't built in a day and neither was an accurate business case. This structured process should be used as often as required to get to the appropriate level of detail to craft a fine-tuned and reliable business case.

Before we describe each of these process steps in detail, it's important to re-emphasize that this framework is an iterative one that can be repeated as often as necessary to achieve an acceptable level of detail. This is why the business case will be much more accurate at the conclusion of the planning stage than at the end of the initiation and concept phases (5% as compared to 15% and 30%, respectively, from Chapter 4). As project teams navigate this process, it will become clear which areas need to be revisited, which departments or individuals need to be re-engaged, and which metrics need to be validated or explored further.

So when and where does the process of identifying potential business benefits start? It starts with the project initiator (usually the soon-to-be project sponsor) who has a project idea that may be beneficial to the organization. Unfortunately, the project initiator has no dedicated resources at this point, no management commitment, and limited information at hand. How, then, can the project initiator determine the expected project outcomes and business value of the proposed initiative with a somewhat acceptable level of accuracy? This is why certain folks make the big bucks! The ball has to get rolling at some point and the project initiator has to ensure that it doesn't get rolled down the wrong path or on a path that leads to diminishing returns.

Project initiators have to rely on their experience, insight, vision, and the data at hand to develop hypotheses for their initial project estimates. By taking a hypothesis-driven approach at this early stage, project initiators will be able to formulate initial value-metric forecasts, even with limited resources and information at their disposal. You may remember from your early school

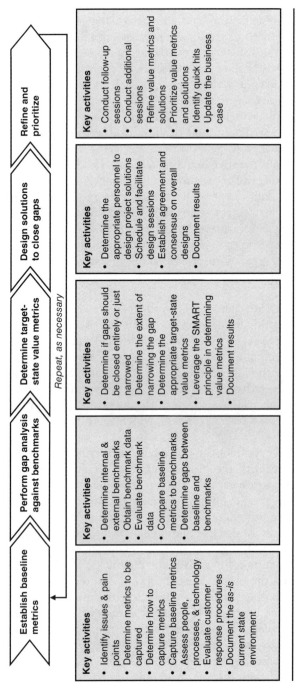

Figure 7.2 Value-metrics framework

years that a hypothesis is an educated guess. In project terms, a hypothesis is a tentative statement, or prediction, that proposes a possible result (business outcome) to some event (project activity) that can eventually be tested. Even though limited resources and data exist at this point, there will be *some* resources and data available for project initiators to formulate initial hypotheses. After all, if no information whatsoever is available, chances are slim that an individual would even propose a project idea in the first place.

If business leaders feel strongly about a proposed project's potential, they should gather all of the available data at hand relating to the problem. They do this by leveraging the resources at their disposal such as product vendors, consultants, and subject matter experts (SMEs) to obtain reference data or to gain better insight into the situation. Chances are these resources have already conducted similar analyses since this may be part of their core business. Upon initial data capture, key observations, and overall insight of the situation, project initiators can then formulate initial hypotheses around their project ideas. Time permitting, project initiators can brainstorm with SMEs to prove or disprove the initial estimates. In formulating initial hypotheses, project initiators can achieve an acceptable level of accuracy for initial project estimates to get the ball rolling down the right path for further analysis.

In following the value-metrics framework, project teams can prove or disprove the initial hypotheses and discover other relevant project data, ideas, and benefits. As the project progresses even further, project teams will be able to affirm, modify, and enhance the project estimates based on new data and more detailed analysis (see Table 7.1).

Establish Baseline Metrics

Identifying value metrics and other business benefits begins with building a comprehensive baseline to identify the as-is environment, or the current state, for the areas of the business likely to be impacted by the project solution. This baseline is built from a combination of documents, organizational charts, interviews, workshops, statistical reports, process maps, performance metrics, and other relevant material. Some of this material will already exist, and some may have to be developed to meet project requirements. Baseline activities involve identifying the pain points, or problems, that the project is attempting to solve, and then capturing metrics around those pain points. For instance, a pain point may be that a system takes too long to respond during peak periods of the day. Baseline metrics that should be captured for this pain point include the duration of the response times, the times during the day in which response times are the slowest, the individuals or departments who are accessing the system, system configuration parameters, and other system or process metrics relating to the pain point. In capturing these baseline metrics, project teams will be better prepared to determine the best approach for improving performance

Table 7.1 SMART value metrics

Value metric	SMART value metric
Reduce turnaround time to generate customer reports	Reduce average turnaround time to generate customer reports from 2.5 days to less than 2 days by the end of 3rd quarter, 2012
Reduce manual processing	Reduce manual processing activities by 30% over the next 60 days by training employees on the new system
Enhance employee productivity with a unified messaging system	Improve employee productivity by 7% by combining e-mail, voicemail, and fax services by the end of fiscal year 2012
Increase sales	Increase sales by 20% six months after the completion of the sales training initiative
Improve output	Improve output from 340 units per standard production shift to 389 once the system has been fully upgraded, targeting June 2012
Decrease unit defects	Decrease the unit defect rate from 6.5% to less than 5% by June 2012
Decrease customer wait times for service calls	Decrease the customer wait times for service calls from an average of 6 minutes to less than 3 minutes by November 2012

results. In some cases it may be a simple tweak to the system or a configuration change to one of the parameters.

A baseline establishes metrics around the current state environment. It is used as a reference for determining project solutions and measuring progress of those solutions. In establishing baseline metrics, project teams can better determine the true current state environment that their projects are trying to improve. It is difficult for business leaders to evaluate what has changed if they don't know where they started. Baseline metrics establish this starting point. An accurate and comprehensive baseline should answer these questions:

- What are the main issues?
- How are resources being utilized? What are the current roles and responsibilities? What are the pain points around resource utilization?
- What are the key process steps? What are the pain points around these processes? Are there unnecessary process steps, or steps that don't add value?
- What technologies are in place? What technologies are obsolete? What is the technology roadmap? What are the pain points around the current technology?
- What performance metrics are being captured and evaluated? Does management leverage these metrics for decision making?

- What are the current costs? What was the budget for the past 1 to 2 years? What is the budget for the next 1 to 2 years?
- How are customer requirements met? What are the customer issues?
- How responsive are we to customer inquiries?
- How timely is our approach? How reliable and accurate is our approach?
- What standard operating procedures (SOPs) and service level agreements (SLAs) are in place? Are SOPs and SLAs adhered to?

Baseline metrics should be relatively easy to collect and understand, and they should be meaningful to the business. Quite often the collection of baseline data will be a new activity for an organization and there may be a bit of a learning curve, but it should not require excessive effort or onerous resource commitments. In most cases, these data elements should be collected anyway as a normal part of conducting business to ensure operational effectiveness. When determining baseline metrics, project teams should avoid those metrics that cannot be collected relatively easily, accurately, or completely; are too complex and not applicable to the project at hand; are disruptive to business operations; or create excessive workloads for employees.

In choosing the appropriate baseline metrics and determining the best way to capture them, project teams should be able to answer these questions:

- What is the purpose of the metric?
- What are the benefits of collecting metric data?
- Who will collect the data?
- Where is the data?
- How should the data be collected?
- Who will verify the data?
- How often should the data be collected?
- Who should analyze the data?
- How should the data be analyzed?
- How will the data be incorporated into the business case?

Project professionals can help their causes by ensuring that the baseline metrics being captured are applicable, appropriate for their respective projects, and beneficial for their companies. If resources are utilized to collect data that is outside of the scope of the project or is not used for useful purposes, project professionals may find out the hard way that these data collection efforts were in vain. Operations personnel, those most likely to collect the data, certainly don't want to take time out of their busy schedules to perform unnecessary tasks for no reason, and they will usually let you know it, sometimes loudly. Baseline metrics vary greatly from project to project. Here are just a few examples of baseline metrics:

- 340 units are produced in a standard 8-hour production shift.
- On average, 22 out of the 340 units (6.5%) are defective.

- On average, finance team members spend 110 minutes a day (23% of their workday) verifying the accuracy of expense reports.
- Accountants spend 14% of their time manually entering data into accounting systems.
- It takes an average of 9 minutes to record an incident into the system and an average of 17 minutes before a technician acknowledges the incident.
- On average, system availability is 98.5%, but only 74.5% during the peak hours of 3:30 p.m. to 4:45 p.m.
- The customer approval process takes, on average, 3.7 days.
- The employee attrition rate has been steady at 10% per month over the past 6 months.
- Overtime costs account for 30% of overall labor costs.
- Sales have been flat, showing no growth for the past 9 months.

Once baseline metrics are captured, then what? It's useful to match them up with other metrics that are similar in nature for comparison purposes, which is the next step of the value-metrics framework.

Perform Gap Analysis against Benchmark Data

With a baseline clearly established, project teams have a better understanding of the current state and know exactly where they *are*. Leveraging benchmark data assists in determining where they *can be*. A benchmark is any standard or reference by which baseline metrics can be measured or judged. Benchmarking is a method for comparing baseline metrics to other established, well known, or industry-standard metrics. Baseline metrics can be compared against a combination of benchmark data elements to determine the most ideal project solutions to close or narrow the performance gaps that may exist between the baseline and the benchmarks.

Benchmark metrics may be internal or external data points, industry best practices, competitor performance, vendor recommendations, performance level charts, or other established performance measurements applicable to a given project. It may be useful in comparing baseline performance metrics with other departments within the organization, which can save time and money by keeping these activities in-house as opposed to going elsewhere. Benchmark data can be obtained in several ways, including competitive intelligence, departmental performance charts, media reports, vendor capability reports, company websites, white papers, technical journals, and discussions with SMEs and specialists. Many companies specialize in gathering and publishing benchmark reports. These reports can be useful but also expensive. Depending on the project, the cost may not be justified.

Benchmarks are a good way to determine where an organization, or segment of an organization, stacks up against the competition, other departments, industry best practices, or expected performance levels. With this information at hand, managers can determine how far off their current baseline performance metrics are from the benchmark metrics. Managers can determine the extent of this gap and will have a better sense of what needs to be done to close the gap. The gap doesn't have to be closed entirely, but managers should strive to narrow the gap enough to be within the ballpark of the benchmarking data measurements.

Determine Target-state Value Metrics

Now that you know where you *are* from the baseline and know where you *can be* based on benchmarking activities, it's time to determine where you *should be* given business requirements, risk tolerance, and project objectives. By leveraging the previous two steps, project teams can better determine the appropriate target-state value metrics for their projects. These value metrics may be benefits that contribute directly to the project return on investment or benefits that enable value in other ways. These *to-be* performance targets serve as the basis for all remaining project activities. The success or failure of the project depends on whether or not these target-state value metrics are attained. It is critical, therefore, to determine the most appropriate value metrics that can be achieved and can deliver the most optimal value to the organization. The target-state value metrics don't have to meet or exceed the benchmark data in which they are being compared, but they must provide beneficial change that is suitable for the business given the numerous requirements and constraints that are involved with any project.

In determining and evaluating the value metrics that should be applied to projects, a good rule of thumb to leverage is the SMART principle. The SMART principle is an effective tool in specifying project metrics in concise, unambiguous terms. The elements of the SMART acronym are:

- **Specific:** The metric must be well defined, explicit, and to the point. It must be clearly understood by all members of the project team.
- **Measurable:** The metric must be expressed in terms where it can be measured, such as monetary-, time-, percentage-based, and so forth.
- **Attainable:** The metric must be attainable given the project and business resources.
- **Realistic:** The metric must be an objective that the project team and the business are both willing and able to work toward, given resource and time constraints.
- **Timely:** The metric should be grounded within a reasonable timeframe.

Table 7.1 showed how the SMART principle can be applied to projects to deliver clear, concise, and focused target-state value metrics.

A question that I hear frequently from project teams is, "How many value metrics should we identify and capture?" This is a good question and there certainly is no set answer. All projects are different and have their own requirements and objectives, but the answer that I would give is to identify and capture a *manageable* amount of value metrics. Manageable means different things to different people depending on the project, but a manageable number that can be applied to most projects is in the range of *4* to *10*. This range is both reasonable and manageable. Project teams may run into trouble trying to quantify and manage more than this amount. Keeping the value metrics at a reasonable number and managing them effectively is highly preferred over identifying a laundry list of metrics and managing them poorly.

Develop Project Solutions around the Target Value Metrics

We now know where we *are*, we know where we *can be*, and we've determined where we *should be*. Now *how* do we get there? Project solutions and associated action plans enable the achievement of the target-state value metrics and business objective. Project solutions should be developed with the targeted end-state vision in mind. With value metrics in place, project teams can better determine how the solution should be designed, what initiatives are required, and what involvement will be necessary from the organization. As project solutions are drafted around the target-state value metrics, project teams can determine with much more accuracy other project parameters as well, such as costs and risks, and can feed this updated information into the business case.

To develop effective project solutions that can achieve the quantitative objectives, project professionals need to build a collaborative environment where all relevant stakeholders can discuss the current problems, targeted outcomes, and long-term solutions to addressing the problems and achieving the project vision. Project solutions are unique for each particular project and require input from those individuals with the relevant experience, appropriate skill sets, and necessary knowledge. For some projects, a proposed solution may be carefully designed and tested in a lab environment, while some solutions for other projects may be constructed in conference rooms using white board sessions. Regardless of the project or method, the project solution must always be developed with the end-state in mind. You need to know where you want to go in order to get there!

Refine and Prioritize

Project solutions are designed according to the target-state value metrics, but as these solutions become fully vetted, project teams will have even more information at their disposal to make better assessments of the project outcomes, costs, and risks. In some cases, the project solution may produce more favorable value outcomes than was previously determined, while in other cases the forecasted performance metrics may have been overestimated or inflated. Project teams need to re-address value metrics when project solutions are deemed incapable of achieving them or prove too costly to do so. Remember, value metrics don't have to be aligned exactly with benchmark performance metrics; they just need to satisfy business and project requirements and demonstrate sufficient returns on the project investment. With the project solution developed or close to being developed, project teams can determine more accurately the project costs and outcomes and can then refine the business case parameters.

An effective business and project management practice is to focus on those project solutions or initiatives that can deliver the greatest business value in the shortest period of time. These solutions should be implemented first and can be referred to as *quick hits*. These quick hits are not only beneficial to the business, but can be advantageous for a project team as well since they demonstrate immediate value that can result in their project efforts being commended by various factions of the organization. Project managers should develop their implementation timelines keeping these quick hits in mind. Figure 7.3 provides an illustrative example of how implementation plans can be structured according to business value and timelines.

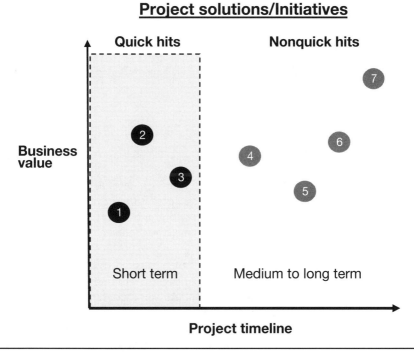

Figure 7.3 Project solutions prioritized by business value

With the use of quick hits, project teams can achieve important business gains quickly and can prove the value, or potential value, of their projects. With a few quick hits under their belts, project teams can gain the necessary momentum, and even psychological advantage, to achieve other breakthrough project goals that may be longer term in nature.

Effective Tools and Techniques for Establishing Value Metrics

We've just discussed an iterative 5-step approach for identifying, evaluating, and solidifying value metrics for our projects. This end-to-end process starts with the initial development of project hypotheses and ends with the eventual completion of an accurate business case. Throughout this entire process, project teams will need to employ effective tools and techniques to gather and synthesize large amounts of project data and to make key decisions based on that data. Far too often project teams don't have an effective game plan in place to capture and analyze the large amounts of project data and end up attempting to use brute force for these crucial project activities, which usually doesn't turn out very well. To be effective in gathering and analyzing data, project teams should use a combination of tools and techniques in a coordinated fashion with the most appropriate areas of the business. The tools and techniques that are most effective in these endeavors are:

- Interviews
- Focus groups
- Data request forms
- Brainstorming sessions
- Process maps
- Other methods, as needed

Interviews

It may seem obvious, but conducting interviews is one of the most effective methods of acquiring project and business information. Interviews can provide real-time information, past performance results, and even future performance forecasts. Through interviews, project teams can determine where the greatest pain points occur, as well as the greatest opportunities for improvement. Interviews may be time consuming, but can be productive in gathering data and gaining insight into the various areas of the business. For many projects, as I'm sure many of you can attest, project team members find themselves conducting dozens of interviews each week during the early stages of the project. These team members hop from meeting room to meeting room or building to building to conduct these interviews. This is usually a good thing (other than the worn out shoes that may result from all of this hopping around), especially when the interviews are conducted in a focused and coordinated manner. Interviews can be counterproductive, however, if not conducted properly and efficiently. The interview process consumes time, and project managers don't need their valuable resources running around in an uncoordinated fashion not satisfying interview objectives. Project managers can prevent this by developing solid interview plans and ensuring that resources are utilized efficiently in order to capture required and specific information from these interviews.

If the project requires a large number of interviews, they can be split between the core project team to handle in parallel as long as they are all following the established guidelines to ensure uniformity and alignment. The interview process must first define clear objectives for each of the interviews. Many of these objectives will be standard across all interviews, but some will have to be specific and tailored toward the audience. For instance, objectives will most likely differ between executive stakeholder interviews and interviews with customers or line-workers.

Project teams need to work with stakeholders to determine an appropriate list of interviewees and schedule the interviews as soon as possible. Finding timeslots on calendars can be difficult unless interviews are scheduled weeks, if not months, in advance. Interviewees differ from project to project, but can include:

- Business leaders who impact or can be impacted by the project
- Project stakeholders
- SMEs and specialists
- Customers and clients
- Users of systems or processes
- Vendors and suppliers
- Consultants
- Any other person or group related to the project

It's best to conduct face-to-face interviews whenever possible to ensure that the interviewees are engaged and not diverted by the normal distractions that occur during a typical business day. Try not to have too many people in the room assisting with the interview. Interviewees may feel they are being interrogated or become defensive with so many outsiders present. The business reality, however, dictates that many of these interviews will have to be conducted over the phone, especially when participants span all corners of the globe as is the case with most multinational corporations in today's global market.

Regardless of where or how the interviews are conducted, there should always be another person acting as a scribe to capture meeting minutes. Capturing meeting minutes is an effective project management technique that is often underestimated and underutilized. How else can you determine what was said in a meeting that transpired several weeks ago? By memory? Doubtful. Additionally, meeting minutes can ensure that all project team members and stakeholders know the outcomes of all of the interviews. All projects should have a central repository where all project materials, from the first draft of the scope to final deliverables, can be stored and referenced. As project teams brainstorm and design project solutions, it's common for questions to arise such as:

- At what times were the systems the slowest for the accounting group?
- From the engineering team, who stated that the supplier takes too long to fulfill orders?
- Exactly what were the pain points for the marketing team?
- Who did the VP of engineering refer us to for further discussion?
- What were the monthly maintenance costs for those obsolete systems?

I'm sure many of you have been in these situations where you're left with a roomful of people with blank stares and scratching their heads. Usually you end up going back to the original source to re-capture the data elements or simply dismiss the data altogether from analysis. These questions, however, can be answered quickly and accurately by simply going back to the meeting minutes, only if they were documented in the first place. I cannot emphasize this enough. If you only knew the number of times that detailed meeting minutes saved my hide during a tough stretch of project. . . . Anyway, are they a pain at times? Sure, but that short-term pain is pale in comparison to the pain you'll experience when trying to figure out what transpired during a meeting that occurred weeks, if not months ago. *Always capture meeting minutes.*

It is important to let the interviewees know why the organization is pursuing the initiative and why they are being interviewed. It is also imperative to explain how they will benefit from the initiative. When the *"What's in it for me?"* question can be answered satisfactorily, interviewees will be much more forthcoming with information. Once they realize they have a stake in the game, they will be more willing to support the project, help out with project efforts, and provide the necessary information and insight. Introductory e-mails that explain the purpose, process, and benefits can sometimes be sent through a senior stakeholder within the organization to increase acceptance.

Efforts should be made to order the interviews strategically in the order of importance, if at all possible. Project teams should strive to start at the higher levels of the organization by speaking with executives and senior managers to gain their high-level, strategic perspectives of the issues and opportunities. Interviews should then be scheduled with those most knowledgeable about the business problem that the project is attempting to solve or the quantitative objectives it is attempting to achieve.

Table 7.2 Interview guidelines

✓	Formally schedule interview as early as possible	✓	Ask for documentation and any other material that may be useful
✓	Send out interview agenda a few days in advance that clearly states the objectives (interviewees can then prepare, if necessary)	✓	Don't rush their answers, but be conscious of the time
✓	Ensure that managers are aware that the employees are going to be interviewed and for what purposes	✓	Don't *bite off more than you can chew* in one session. Ensure that the interview objectives are reasonable for the timeframe
✓	Start by providing context: why they are there, what the project is trying to achieve, and what's in it for them	✓	Determine if a follow-up session is necessary
✓	Understand their roles and responsibilities in the organization	✓	Provide your contact information should the interviewee want to contact you
✓	Ask open-ended questions to allow a stream of consciousness to come through	✓	Ask if they recommend speaking to other individuals or groups
✓	Probe into areas that need further explanation	✓	Summarize key points and action items and agree on timelines for completing the action items
✓	Ask hypothetical, or best case scenario-type questions, such as "What would you like the system to do?"	✓	Finish on time
✓	Confirm or deny information that has already been gathered	✓	Send out meeting minutes and action items as soon as possible
✓	Paraphrase key points or statements so that they are clearly understood	✓	Follow up on the action items, if necessary

Certain guidelines should be followed when preparing for, conducting, and following up on interviews. Table 7.2 lists some key guidelines that should always be followed in the interviewing process. You can use this table as a reference to ensure that you, as well as your team members, are following established best practices for all of your project interviews.

Focus Groups

A focus group session is an interactive method of obtaining real-time information and cross-functional perspectives on specific business areas or issues. Focus groups can be effective in eliciting feedback from specific groups of individuals relating to their perceptions, opinions, and attitudes toward a particular aspect of the business. These sessions are interactive and participants are encouraged to discuss matters with their colleagues in the room. Although the sessions are interactive and conversations are encouraged, project professionals acting as facilitators must keep the group focused on the objectives at hand and guide the sessions toward achieving those objectives. They're called focus groups for a reason. They are not brainstorming or planning sessions; these sessions focus on a few key points to allow participants to engage in concentrated discussions so that project teams can capture key data elements.

These group discussions serve to produce data and insights that would be difficult to obtain without interaction and collaboration. Ideas, opinions, facts, and suggestions can be stimulated when individuals are free to discuss specific areas or issues within the business. In many cases, one person's opinion or insight may produce a chain reaction where others not only agree or disagree with that person, but offer other opinions or insights that provide even more useful material for the focus group. It's important for facilitators to keep these conversations in motion to achieve a consensus or reach key conclusions.

Focus groups can be tremendously valuable when conducted with customers. Customers are not only those individuals external to a company who pay for a product or service, but may be internal to the organization. For instance, customers of the IT department are the users of the various technology systems and customers of the human resources department are the employees of the firm. It is important to understand the voice of the customer by determining their requirements, perspectives, pain points, and recommendations.

The key is to invite the appropriate people to these sessions. Participants are normally those who are greatly impacted by project outcomes and who can provide valuable input in the development of the project solution. All participants should be willing and able to interact and contribute. If they are not, they are the wrong people. It is advisable to have a good cross section of individuals. I recommend keeping the number of participants to a manageable amount, which typically ranges between 4 to 12 individuals. Anything more than this number may be unmanageable, while anything less may not be productive.

As with interviews, attempts should be made to conduct focus group sessions face-to-face, but of course, conference bridges and video conferencing provide options when in-person isn't an option. Certain guidelines should be followed when preparing, conducting, and following up on focus group sessions. Table 7.3 lists some key guidelines that should always be followed for focus group sessions.

Data Request Forms

The interactive techniques of interviews and focus groups are integral to gathering important project information but, due to time constraints that are inherent in nearly all projects, quicker techniques may need to be employed to

Table 7.3 Focus group guidelines

✓	Schedule the focus group session as early as possible	✓	Avoid bringing project bias into the conversation
✓	Define the meeting objectives	✓	Take the matters at hand seriously; if they are talking about it, they are serious about it
✓	Determine the questions or talking points before the session	✓	Accept all points of view
✓	Place the questions or talking points in a logical order	✓	Keep an eye out for the leaders of the group (they may be useful down the road), but don't let them dominate the conversation
✓	Allow time for introductions	✓	Avoid focusing on one person or select persons
✓	Observe nonverbal behavior (e.g., head nodding or short answers)	✓	Debrief with the project team and evaluate the results of the session
✓	Encourage ideas and questions	✓	Capture all of the salient points, including quotes
✓	Determine pain points and wish lists	✓	Capture the names of those who made certain statements; a follow-up may be necessary
✓	Choose a neutral meeting place free from distractions	✓	Send out meeting minutes and action items as soon as possible

capture large amounts of data in short periods of time. Data request forms are a quick way of gathering data. Although noninteractive in nature, the use of surveys, questionnaires, and other data request forms can be useful in obtaining project data and information—such as facts, opinions, performance trends, and recommendations—in a short period of time. Data request forms can be disseminated to a large segment of the population with a single push of a keyboard button. Project teams can tap into the expertise of specific groups and can obtain sizeable amounts of certain data elements utilizing this method.

Whereas interviews and focus groups require a great deal of effort, obtaining information via data request forms requires relatively low effort. Although capturing information with this method is not nearly as labor intensive as interviews and focus groups, development efforts of the actual documents should not be taken lightly. Project teams must give careful attention to developing these documents to ensure that the target audience clearly understands the objectives and instructions; knows why they are completing them; is aware of the timeframes; and knows where and how to submit them once they are finished. Without a quality document and professional process in place, those responsible for their completion won't take them seriously and most likely will ignore them. When done professionally and with the support of the management team, data request forms can prove quite useful in capturing necessary project information.

Project managers may be familiar with and may leverage the Delphi technique when gathering and analyzing data. With the Delphi approach, project teams elicit the opinions of those who possess certain expertise, knowledge, or experience with the goal of attaining an overall consensus for a particular part of the project or business area. The polling of these individuals can even be done on an anonymous basis to ensure participants will be forthcoming in sharing their opinions. Online techniques via companies' Intranet sites are effective ways to ensure anonymity. With online data request methods, participants can maintain their anonymity. All of the responses are eventually combined to form an overall summary that is then provided to the experts for further review and input. Several iterations may be necessary to eventually produce an overall consensus to an approach or solution.

To achieve high response rates for surveys, questionnaires, and other data request methods, it's a good idea to involve senior stakeholders in the process so that they can convey the importance of these data request initiatives. It may behoove a project manager to ask a senior stakeholder to disseminate the information to show that the initiative is being driven from the top. Of course, the project manager will be responsible ultimately for the completion of these forms.

Brainstorming Sessions

Every project is unique and requires specific attention and analysis from qualified areas of the business. In evaluating and determining project metrics and solutions, project teams must perform deep dive analyses and craft solutions that are tailored to business, organizational, regulatory, and project requirements. Quite often this requires creative thinking, brainstorming, whiteboard sessions, and other methods to tap into the vast knowledge pool of project team members and employees. Whereas interviews, focus groups, and data request forms are prescriptive in nature, brainstorming sessions are more free-flowing and are used to generate ideas to solve problems and produce possible project solutions. Brainstorming is a group creativity technique designed to obtain a large number of ideas for the solution of a particular problem or problems. These nonprescriptive methods can be employed at various points along the project lifecycle and can have a tremendous impact on your project.

It's always a good idea for the project manager to be involved in important meetings and discussions, and brainstorming sessions are no exception. *But,* project managers should not treat these sessions as they would other meetings. Brainstorming sessions usually do not follow a set agenda and are conducted to generate creative ideas to solve problems and create beneficial change. I always recommend having an agenda for all formal meetings, even brainstorming sessions, but agenda items for these sessions can be as simple as *brainstorm project solutions* or *discuss project options*. During brainstorming sessions, participants should be free to discuss everything and anything that can lead to optimal ideas. These ideas and solutions result from expert judgment, historical information, industry trends, technology innovations, vendor offerings, and overall experience in the subject at hand.

Participants of these sessions are usually experts in their field, techie-types, certified specialists, and other knowledgeable professionals in a particular subject. In many cases, project managers will have no clue about what is even being discussed during these brainstorming sessions, especially when technical or esoteric topics are being discussed. Sometimes it's best for project managers to just get out of the way and the let the discussions continue and lend assistance only when needed. The assistance that is usually needed is in areas of management intent, project objectives, business requirements, timelines, and other project information in which the participants of the brainstorming session may not be privy. Project managers may also assist in capturing the various ideas that are proposed. Ideas that are documented on paper can be useful in stimulating further discussions or conversations with other groups of people.

Process Maps

As we've pointed out, nearly everything that occurs within an organization is a result of a process. Effective processes can be beneficial for an organization and, conversely, ineffective ones can be detrimental. We need to understand process flows, key decision points, bottlenecks, wasteful steps, and areas for improvement. Process maps are effective tools in capturing end-to-end business processes and discovering key attributes along the process flow. They account for all of the actions from start to finish, including both the efficient and inefficient process steps currently employed to deliver a product or service. They also assist in capturing important process performance metrics, such as process timeframes, delays, amount of re-work, redundant steps, unnecessary steps, and other key metrics. Process maps can help project teams determine the differences between the actual processes being performed and the perceived processes. In most cases, the actual processes are much less efficient and reliable than the perceived processes. Business leaders are usually quite astonished, in fact, when presented with a process map that shows all of the wasteful and nonvalue-adding steps along the process flow.

Process maps help project teams identify the numerous steps that are involved in any process and incorporate them into a single document. This document can then be used to evaluate the end-to-end process and to identify steps that can be eliminated, consolidated, or enhanced to improve overall performance. It's difficult to know and understand an end-to-end process that involves numerous steps and checkpoints without seeing it captured on paper.

Once people see it, they can improve it. Project teams and decision makers should keep an eye out for certain wasteful areas that are common across ineffective process flows. Some of these areas include:

- Long wait times where there is little activity taking place, such as waiting for approval or signatures
- Process steps requiring multiple reviews and approvals
- Steps that add no value to the final outcome, product, or service
- Too many people or departments involved
- Too many hand-offs between different people or departments
- Excessive or redundant manual data entry
- Too many disparate computer systems in use
- Too many first time failures resulting in re-work
- Steps that only serve to add risk to the process flow

Project teams strive to optimize business value from their project investments, and processes are no exception. As project teams develop and analyze process maps, they must distinguish between the value-adding process steps from nonvalue ones. A process flow may be efficient, but if it's not adding business value then what's the point? There will be situations where it will be necessary to include nonvalue process steps in the overall flow, such as for legal or regulatory reasons, but nonvalue-adding process steps should be avoided as much as possible.

By implementing process mapping activities to determine current state baselines and to develop target-state metrics and solutions, project teams can cut out a significant portion of waste and nonvalue-adding activities. It's not uncommon for project teams to discover that nearly half of all current state process activities are wasteful or add no value! Surprised? Take a moment and think about some of the processes in which you are involved? Are all those steps, approvals, waiting periods, data requests, management reviews, and inspections absolutely necessary? Streamlined target-state process maps that eliminate process waste and ensure all steps are absolutely necessary adds tremendous value to the end product or service.

Other Methods, As Needed

The outcome of any project cannot be known with absolute certainty, and it is difficult for core project teams to garner all of the important metrics without consulting knowledgeable areas of the business. By employing the tools and techniques discussed in this chapter, project teams will be better positioned to gather all of the required data elements and use that information to craft project solutions that achieve the targeted value metrics. Project teams should also use other techniques that may be at their disposal to gather business information, data elements, trends, and other required information. The goal of any project is to achieve 100% of the business benefits set forth in the business case. Project teams should use techniques that help them capture data elements, synthesize the data into meaningful business terms, and achieve this lofty goal.

Professional Development Game Plan for Success

1. Numerous data elements for any project must be gathered, synthesized, revisited, and leveraged to determine appropriate target-state value metrics and to develop project solutions that can meet or exceed them. A project team's ability to identify the most ideal business objectives and to design the most optimal solutions around those objectives is greatly enhanced when a structured, data-driven approach is undertaken. What is your process for determining target-state objectives for your projects and designing solutions to meet them? What steps do you take to ensure that you captured all of the required data elements and used them for the development of business objectives and project solutions? Are project solutions always designed with target-state value metrics in mind?

Action Plan

a. Revisit two or three of your prior projects and evaluate how effective you were in capturing the necessary data, synthesizing that data, determining business outcomes from the data, and designing project solutions to meet those outcomes. What baseline and benchmark metrics were captured and leveraged? Evaluate the overall project solution. Was it developed with the end goals in mind? How could the solution have been designed differently or more optimally if more data had been available and specific performance targets had been established? Based on your assessment, write down five to eight activities or processes that were conducted effectively and that led to positive results. Now write down five to eight gaps, flaws, or ineffective activities or processes in capturing data elements, determining target-state value metrics, and designing project solutions around those metrics.

b. Apply these lessons learned to your current or future projects. What can you do to ensure that a data-driven approach is taken to formulate ideal value metrics and to design appropriate solutions to achieve those metrics? What is your approach toward interviews and focus groups? What about surveys and questionnaires? How can you better gather baseline and benchmarking data? Who must you include in brainstorming sessions? Write down five to eight actions you *absolutely must take* on your current or future projects to solidify aggressive, but realistic, target-state business objectives and to design project solutions that can achieve these targeted objectives.

Reference

1. Phillips, Jack J., Timothy W. Bothell, and G. Lynne Snead. 2002. *The Project Management Scorecard*. Burlington, MA: Butterworth-Heinemann.

8

You Need to Know *All* the Costs to Accurately Determine the Benefits

---

Money often costs too much.

—Ralph Waldo Emerson

Everything Has a Cost

Now that we know how to go about capturing required data elements, formulating target-state value objectives, and designing solutions to achieve those objectives, let's focus our attention on those data elements that are absolutely required to provide business justification for our projects and to produce the most optimal and financially attractive solutions. It's time to get down to the essentials, the brass tacks, and this begins with our favorite subject, *costs*. All of the costs associated with a project solution must be identified and included in the business case to accurately reflect the financial merits of the project. These costs include project-related costs as well as other business costs that may occur long after project closure. Too often project teams take shortcuts in cost determination efforts, or simply fail to identify all of the costs associated with their project solutions that result in inflated return on investments (ROIs) and unrealistic expectations. These costs, however, will eventually rear their ugly heads and surface at various points down the road, causing anguish for those managing budgets that were created around these inaccurate business cases. It's best, therefore, to capture *all* of these costs early in the process to avoid inevitable cost overruns down the road. This chapter focuses on the significant, but often misunderstood or omitted, project and business costs.

Net cash flow is at the heart of the financial analysis for a project and shows the money that will be expended over a period of time (costs), as well as the money expected to come into the organization as a result of the project investment (benefits). To conduct an accurate net cash flow analysis, all of the project costs must be identified and incorporated into the financial study. Far too often many project costs are excluded, dismissed, overlooked, or underestimated, which results in a favorable financial justification for a project, albeit an inaccurate one. There are several types of costs that can occur at various points throughout the course of any project. Thoughtful and careful analysis must be given to all of the possible costs that may arise to properly assess the viability of a project and not to overestimate the returns of the project investment. Underestimating the costs and inflating the project returns will eventually come back to haunt a project team, because the team will be expected to achieve the returns that were presented in the business case. All of the hard work in the world can't produce unrealistic project returns.

A cost is the value of money that has been expended to produce, or contribute to the production of, a project outcome. It is the amount of cash that an organization has to pay to acquire products or services that is required to conduct business or execute a project. Having a thorough understanding of all of the project costs is paramount to managing a project successfully. Project costs contribute directly to the returns that are realized for a project investment, as well as to important pricing and project decisions. Project teams often don't delve deep enough into identifying and evaluating costs, which often leads to inaccurate business cases, incorrect project justification, and budget overruns. There are costs to everything and oftentimes these costs are hidden, unforeseen, or unexpected. Equipment or hardware prices, for instance, usually do not include the associated shipping costs that can be 8 to 10% of the overall costs. If a project team plans to order several shipments of equipment but doesn't account for shipping costs, the business case will be inaccurate and the project will run over budget. Taxes, interest, travel, vendor, and other project costs can also be significant and can lead to inaccurate business cases if overlooked or dismissed.

The project team is a sizeable cost and must be a part of the financial analysis. There are cost elements even in the early stages of a project where the focus is primarily defining requirements and evaluating project options. People have to conduct these upfront planning activities and peoples' time is money. Project team costs can be substantial and can include: rates and salaries; travel, lodging, meals; consultants and vendors; relocation of project resources; project materials and shipping; project software; and even office supplies.

Has your cable bill remained flat over the past few years? What about your phone bill? Rent? Utilities? What about your salary? I think we all know the answers to these questions. It's no different in the business world. Costs rise and fall. Project teams need to take into account these cost fluctuations for the various cost elements of their projects. Cost trends and fluctuations need to be examined as project teams embark on each phase of the value-metrics framework in order to tap into the expertise and experience of seasoned professionals.

It is imperative to understand the various types of costs that can occur for any project. Understanding these costs and incorporating them into financial cost models leads to accurate and reliable business cases and project budgets. Let's discuss the most prevalent costs incurred for most projects.

Direct and Indirect Costs

Direct costs are more closely related to project activities than indirect costs. It is important that organizations treat these costs consistently across project teams. Costs incurred for the same purpose in similar circumstances across project teams must be treated consistently as either direct or indirect costs. When an organization treats a particular type of cost as a direct cost for a project, all costs incurred for the same purpose in other projects should be treated as a direct cost as well. The same holds true for indirect costs. Project teams often struggle with the proper allocation of these costs. It may be advantageous to include a finance or accounting representative as a project stakeholder to assist with the allocation of direct and indirect costs. Let's define these costs.

Direct costs—directly related to a work activity, deliverable, or project output. These costs can be directly assigned to project activities relatively easily with a high degree of accuracy. Examples of direct costs include:

- Salaries and rates of project personnel
- Hardware/Equipment
- Hardware/Equipment repair and maintenance
- Software/Special computer programs
- Vendors/Consultants/Partners
- System upgrades
- Travel
- Training
- Equipment rental
- Lease/Rent
- Industry reports and benchmarking information
- Books and periodicals
- Cabling and racking

Indirect costs—indirectly related to a work activity, deliverable, or project output. Indirect costs are usually for activities that benefit more than one project. These costs are incurred for common business activities across an organization and cannot be identified specifically with a particular project or project activity. For example, many project teams within an organization may utilize the services of the security and purchasing departments while executing their projects. Each project team incurs a portion of these costs for using these services. These costs must be allocated appropriately across all project teams utilizing these services. Indirect costs are often referred to as overhead costs. Examples of indirect costs include:

- Security
- Administrative staff
- Purchasing
- Utilities
- Factory overhead
- Office supplies
- Audit and legal
- Accounting
- Research
- Postage
- Telephone
- Library
- Facilities repair and maintenance

It is important to note that when a cost is charged to a project directly, similar costs should not be included in the indirect cost structure for that project. Conversely, if a cost is included in the indirect cost base, then similar costs should not be charged directly. Project teams certainly don't want to incur double costs for the same project activities.

Administrative costs, such as office supplies, postage, telephone, and computer usage, are normally treated as indirect costs. These costs, however, may be charged directly to a project when:

- A project has a need for a service that is beyond the level of service normally provided.
- The goods or services apply directly to and benefit a particular project.
- The costs can be assigned easily to a particular project with a high degree of accuracy.

Direct costs are much more substantial and significant for projects than indirect costs. Concerted efforts, however, should be made to capture all of the costs associated with a project investment and these include the indirect costs. Our business cases need to reflect the true business environment as closely as possible; indirect costs are part of that environment and must be incorporated into these important documents.

Fixed, Variable, and Mixed Costs

To determine accurate financial cash flows, project teams need to gain an understanding of the cost behavior patterns of their projects. It's important to understand not simply the costs but when they occur throughout the life of a project, and even beyond. Knowing the cost behavior patterns is vital to building accurate cash flow models and critical to helping organizations plan for future cash expenditures. The most common cost behavior patterns for projects are fixed, variable, and mixed.

Fixed costs—remain the same over the course of a project and are unaffected by changes or project activity. These costs are not dependent on the level of activity or deliverables produced by the project team but remain fixed within relevant time periods. Fixed costs tend to be time-related, such as salaries, rates, or leases. A retail organization, for instance, must pay rent for store space irrespective of sales. A company, furthermore, must pay salaries and consulting fees for services rendered. Examples of fixed costs include:

- Salaries
- Consulting fees
- Maintenance/Service contracts
- Rent/Leases
- Interest
- Taxes
- Insurance
- Licenses

Variable costs—costs that change over the course of a project with the level of project activity. Whereas fixed costs are usually time-related, such as salaries and fees, variable costs are volume-related and are usually paid per quantity of units produced or services delivered. Examples of variable costs include:

- Sales commission
- Material usage
- Usage-based mobile phone usage
- Travel
- Employee moves/Adds/Changes
- Network bandwidth on demand

Mixed costs—comprise a combination of both fixed and variable costs. These costs, often called semi-variable costs, include both time- and volume-related costs. The fixed cost element must be paid irrespective of the level of project activity and the variable cost component is payable proportionate to that level of activity.

A common example of a mixed cost includes telephone or mobile phone service. Users of these services pay flat, fixed fees usually on a monthly basis but also pay other fees based on their volume of calls. Energy usage is another example of a semi-variable cost. Companies pay standard energy bills for the basic operation of their businesses, but as demand for energy ramps up based on business activity, energy costs rise accordingly.

Figure 8.1 shows two graphical examples of fixed vs. variable costs. In the first example, the x-axis represents the number of units produced. Since variable costs are volume-related, there is typically a linear relationship between the number of units produced and the costs. As the number of units produced increases, the variable costs increase as well. It is not always a linear relationship, however, especially when volume discounts occur when a predetermined amount of units have been reached. In the second example, the x-axis represents time. Fixed costs still remain constant, but variable costs fluctuate depending on project activity or unit production.

Recurring and Nonrecurring Costs

For many projects there are costs that require an initial outlay of cash, such as for the purchase of equipment, as well as other costs that occur as the project progresses throughout its lifecycle. Recurring costs are incurred in a repeating fashion, whereas nonrecurring costs, often called one-time costs, are incurred only once or only at certain intervals of a project. The accuracy of financial analysis is greatly improved when recurring costs are evaluated separately from the nonrecurring costs.

Recurring costs—repetitive costs that occur throughout the course of a project, and even beyond project closeout. Recurring costs can be fixed or vari-

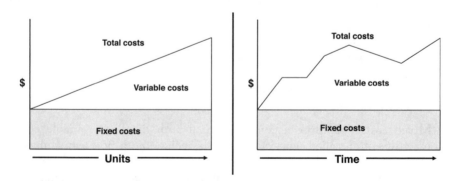

Figure 8.1 Fixed vs. variable costs

able. Many of these costs are often referred to as operating expenses (opex). Examples of recurring costs include:

- Salaries and benefits
- Office space occupancy
- Equipment leases or rentals
- Systems maintenance
- Software leases
- Data/Network usage
- Direct support services
- Travel
- Ongoing training programs
- Supplies and utilities
- Technical support

Nonrecurring costs—occur one time and do not repeat. Nonrecurring costs usually occur once and typically at the beginning of a project. These one-time costs may also occur at various points along the project lifecycle, such as training costs for operations personnel once a project solution has been deployed. Typical nonrecurring costs for a project include the cost of equipment, hardware, or software. Examples of nonrecurring costs include:

- Equipment
- Building/Plant
- Land
- Hardware/Software
- One-time training
- System upgrades
- Cabling and racking

It is important to note that not all physical assets that are purchased for a project will be classified as nonrecurring costs in financial cost models. When companies purchase physical assets, such as land, buildings, or equipment, to create future benefits, these purchases are often considered capital expenditures (capex). Capital expenditures may also include upgrading physical assets or refurbishing property or equipment to add value to them. A fixed asset that is considered to be capital has a useful life that extends beyond the taxable year and, therefore, must be capitalized by spreading the cost over its useful life.

For tax purposes, capital expenditures cannot be deducted in the year in which they are incurred and must be capitalized. The capex costs are amortized or depreciated over the life of the asset and must be reflected this way in the project cash flow model. If the cost is not considered a capital expenditure, the cost is deducted fully in the year it was purchased, thus making it a nonrecurring cost.

As project professionals it's important to know whether certain project costs should be capitalized. Costs that are capitalized are depreciated or amortized over multiple years and must be represented accordingly in the project cost model. Costs that are not considered capital expenditures should be represented simply as nonrecurring costs that were incurred at that particular time period. Again, it is always advisable to include the accounting or finance department when determining which costs are capital expenditures and how they should be depreciated or amortized over their useful lives. We discuss the intricacies of depreciation in detail when we discuss cash flow models in Chapter 10.

Vendor Contracts

Many project deployments require the assistance, subject matter expertise, and industry experience of vendors, consultants, and suppliers. As with everything else, vendor support does not come free and has associated costs. The various cost elements involved with vendor support can be significant and must be carefully considered and incorporated into the business case. These cost elements are not always as straightforward and as easy to determine and forecast as project teams would like. Far too often project cost overruns occur because certain vendor costs were misunderstood or not anticipated. Additionally, it's easy to make a quick phone call to your favorite vendor to bring on additional resources during project implementation in order to lend assistance or expertise. If these additional resources were not planned for, and more than likely they were not, cost overruns will ensue.

To fully comprehend vendor cost elements, project professionals must first understand the various types of contracts that are typical in project work. Different projects require different types of contracts. Companies pursue certain contracts to allow for more or less pricing flexibility and to allocate different levels of risk to the vendor. Let's dive into these types of contracts and see how they relate to our projects.

Fixed-price Contract

A fixed-price contract, often called a lump-sum contract, is fairly straightforward. A company normally outlines a defined scope of work and a vendor specifies the products or services they will offer to complete the work, along with a fixed price. The vendor is then obligated to complete the work set forth in the contract, with possible financial penalties if they do not. This lump-sum cost element is easy to incorporate into the business case. The challenges come when changes to the scope of work are required. These changes usually result in increased vendor costs that may be significant. It is imperative, therefore, to define the scope of work as accurately as possible in the fixed-price contract to prevent change control initiatives and increased costs.

Companies may choose fixed-price contracts, but also offer financial incentives to vendors for achieving or exceeding certain project objectives, such as schedule, cost, and performance. These contracts are referred to as fixed-price incentive fee contracts. Project teams need to be cognizant of such contracts because their projects costs will increase if vendors are able to meet or exceed the incentive requirements.

Cost-reimbursable Contract

A cost-reimbursable contract involves payment, or cost reimbursement, to a vendor for the actual costs incurred for completed project work, plus a fee representing vendor profit. Companies frequently pursue cost-reimbursable contracts on longer-term projects when the quality of the work is more important than the actual costs. As a result, there is often uncertainty as to what the final project costs will be, which poses challenges to project teams building out business cases. To exacerbate these challenges, cost-reimbursable contracts may also include financial incentives to vendors for achieving or exceeding performance objectives.

Time and Materials Contract

A time and materials (T&M) contract contains aspects of both fixed-price and cost-reimbursable contracts. Companies often pursue T&M contracts to augment existing staff by acquiring industry experts to assist with project activities. These contracts are usually used when it's difficult to estimate the extent, duration, or cost of the required work with a reasonable degree of confidence. Vendor rates are usually negotiated and can be on hourly, daily, or even weekly rates. In addition to the labor costs, the price of material used in project delivery will also be billed to the company. Additionally, vendor travel and expenses are usually billed to the company in these contractual arrangements.

Project teams need to do some probing into the T&M contracts to determine actual cost estimates. For instance, if vendors typically charge for a 45-hour work week instead of a 40-hour one, the cost differential can be significant, especially for a large vendor team. Some vendors may even strive to bill upward to 50, 55, or even 60 hours per week per team member. This is certainly not unethical and the type of work may call for the extra hours, but project teams need to take this into account when building their cost models. Travel expenses can add up quickly as well. If the vendor is flying people in each week from various parts of the world to work on the project, these costs can be significant. Project teams need to be aware of these cost elements to accurately reflect the true business scenario in their business cases.

Professional Development Game Plan for Success

1. Even though this is a short chapter, several important concepts relating to project and business costs are discussed. Project professionals must fully comprehend these important concepts to accurately reflect the financial viability of their projects. When all of the cost elements of projects are not captured, or when cost elements are classified incorrectly, or even when costs are placed inappropriately along the project timeline, the project cash flow models will be inaccurate and the forecasted benefits will be inflated and that ultimately leads to bad business decisions. As a project professional you need to prevent this from occurring. With that said, what is your comfort level with these important cost concepts? Are you confident that you can identify all of the cost elements associated with your projects, classify them accurately, and place them at the near-exact points where they will be incurred along the project timeline?

Action Plan

   a. Perform a self-assessment of your knowledge and abilities surrounding project-related and business cost elements. Do you have a basic understanding, a full comprehension, or do you need some development work in this area? Keep in mind that these basic, yet important, concepts are the foundation for more advanced topics we discuss in subsequent chapters, such as cash flow modeling, discounting, depreciation, and calculating ROI measurements. Where do you need to build up your knowledge base? Schedule some time with a member of your accounting group to analyze a project cost model. Read a basic book on financial management. What's one more action you can come up with?

   b. Choose one of your projects for a deep-dive case study. At the end, you should have a crystal clear view of the financial management of this project. Scrutinize the cash flow model of the business case if these cost elements aren't discussed in the document itself. Were all of the costs captured? Were they underestimated, overestimated, or right on the mark? What costs were omitted? Consult with a financial representative to perform this analysis since they will have the *actual* costs that were incurred. How close were the estimated costs to the actuals? Based on this analysis, try to determine what cost elements were off the mark or omitted and why you think they were mistaken or omitted. Were bogus assumptions made? Was it a result of inadequate planning? Or were they simply overlooked? Document all of the areas that could have been improved and learn from them. Don't make the same mistake twice.

Reference

1. Cohen, Dennis, and Robert Graham. 2001. *The Project Manager's MBA*. San Francisco, CA: Jossey-Bass.

9

Project Benefits: ROI Contributors and Value Enablers

Don't be seduced into thinking that that which does not make a profit is without value.

—Arthur Miller

Benefits Must Outweigh the Costs

As important as it is to understand all of a project's costs, it's just as important to understand the different types of business benefits that can occur as a result of a project. These business benefits can be numerous and diverse and, as with costs, are sometimes hidden or misunderstood. Project teams need to explore all of the possible benefits and analyze the most relevant ones to determine the viability of a project investment. The aggregation of all of the business benefits must outweigh all of the project costs for a project investment to be worthwhile. Project costs outweighing business benefits is a sure red flag and a sign that re-evaluation may be required.

A cost-benefit analysis helps to determine how well, or how poorly, a project will deliver value to an organization. In simple terms, this analysis adds up positive factors (business benefits) and then subtracts the negative ones (project costs) to determine if the project is a worthy investment. The challenge is not only identifying all of the costs and benefits, but properly quantifying them in business terms that show an accurate side-by-side comparison that stakeholders can understand. Of course other factors must be considered, such as the time value of money, discount rates, risks, sensitivity analysis, and other factors. But the first step is identifying and evaluating all costs and benefits that are applicable to a given project.

Comparing the business benefits to the project costs helps decision makers determine whether to go forward with a proposed project. Executive stakeholders are responsible to their companies for ensuring that selected projects within their purview represent the best use of company funds, can pay for themselves as quickly as possible, and will improve the companies' overall financial position. The identification of the possible business benefits that a project may or may not deliver is an essential step in determining if the project will produce beneficial, lasting change. To paint an accurate picture for the potential of a project, project teams must carefully weigh the project costs to the business benefits, as shown in Figure 9.1.

We now delve into the various types of business benefits that may result from project investments. Understanding all of the business benefits is often necessary to *tip the scale* in concluding that project benefits outweigh the costs and, therefore, is a good project investment.

Re-defining Project Benefits

The debate over hard vs. soft benefits has been going on for decades and simply won't go away. Business leaders, especially CFOs, are reluctant to approve projects without the benefits expressed in hard, tangible financial numbers. Oftentimes these senior leaders don't even want to hear about the soft

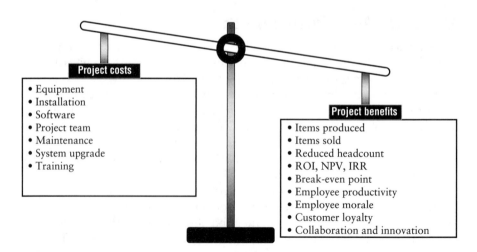

Figure 9.1 Weighing the costs and benefits

(intangible) benefits that a project may deliver. What is my return on investment (ROI)? The *tangibles only* mentality is pervasive across industries and continues to cause heartache for project sponsors and managers around the world who are responsible for crafting business cases to show financial justification for their projects. It's time to set the record straight on hard vs. soft benefits once and for all!

To begin, the terms hard, soft, tangible, and intangible—as they relate to project benefits—are misleading, confusing, and frequently used inappropriately and interchangeably. Most projects produce the misunderstood soft benefits that, unfortunately, many professionals feel don't add any value or contribute to the company's bottom line. These benefits are often dismissed entirely, leaving project professionals at a disadvantage in telling a complete business story about their projects. Most of the soft benefits that projects can deliver are focused primarily on people, behaviors, customer satisfaction, employee morale, or product branding. That is challenging for most project teams to quantify in monetary terms, especially given time and resource constraints. Even though these benefits may be challenging to quantify monetarily, that doesn't mean they don't add value to the business, aren't tangible, or don't contribute to a company's bottom line. Additionally, it doesn't mean that they *can't* be quantified in monetary terms, but given project scope, timelines, and resource limitations, it's usually not practical to do so. Soft benefits are often critical to an organization's competitiveness, but they are usually eschewed for the easier to measure, objectively-based hard benefits and then dismissed from business cases altogether.

Project professionals usually understand the importance of the so-called intangible benefits that their projects will deliver, but leave them out of business cases to avoid the difficult task of quantifying them monetarily. This leads to an incomplete business case. A business case should tell a complete and compelling story. Dismissing important business benefits from this important document does a disservice to the potential project investment, as well as to the stakeholder teams impacted by the potential project. The soft, intangible benefits are more subjective and may appear to be less credible project measurements than the more tangible, hard benefits, but ignoring them altogether is not an option. Soft benefits not only complete the picture that project teams are painting for the stakeholders, but they can sometimes be the items that push a project over the top.

Managers typically focus on hard benefits, also called direct benefits, since they are easily understood and can be converted relatively easily to monetary units. Common examples of hard benefits include the number of units sold or the amount of units produced. It's fairly straightforward to determine project ROIs from benefits such as increased sales and improved production output. Soft benefits—or intangibles—are more challenging to quantify and present in tangible, monetary terms. Improvements to employee morale or enhancements to the corporate image are often cited as examples for soft benefits.

To set the record straight on the proper use and application of hard and soft benefits for our projects, we begin by replacing the terms altogether! These terms have been confusing and frustrating project teams for far too long for myriad reasons. First of all, both hard and soft benefits are indeed tangible and can both be quantified, measured, and managed. Some benefits may be more difficult than others to quantify and express in financial terms, but nevertheless, all of them can be. The notion that certain benefits should be excluded from analysis because they can't be readily converted to financial metrics and, therefore, don't produce or enable business value is preposterous. Business benefits that result from projects are beneficial to organizations or they wouldn't be considered benefits. We need to eliminate the use of the ambiguous terms hard, soft, tangible, and intangible when referring to benefits and replace them with terms that are appropriate for our projects. These terms are *ROI contributors* and *value enablers* and are defined as:

- **ROI contributors**—can be reasonably and appropriately quantified and expressed monetarily and contribute directly to a project's ROI.
- **Value enablers**—enable the achievement of business value, but are determined to be unreasonable and inappropriate to be expressed monetarily for inclusion in a project's ROI analysis, given project requirements. Although these benefits will not contribute directly to a project's ROI forecast, they can be quantified, measured, and managed to bring about significant business value in other ways.

Many project deployments will deliver value-enabling benefits, such as improvement to employee morale, but stakeholders most likely won't want to spend the money and resources necessary to forecast this value metric in monetary terms as part of the ROI study. Project teams should not dismiss certain benefits from their analysis, however, even though assigning monetary measurements to them is neither appropriate nor practical for their projects. All projects will have many benefits associated with them, some more important than others. Efforts should be made to quantify as much as feasibly possible in monetary terms to determine the overall financial returns of the project investments. Quantifying all of the benefits in hard, financial numbers, however, certainly isn't appropriate for most projects since this endeavor could create scope creep, timeline extensions, and cost overruns. Table 9.1 shows some comparisons between the various attributes of ROI contributors and value enablers.

ROI contributors are those benefits that should be included in project ROI studies and usually include value metrics relating to output, time, costs, and

Table 9.1 Benefit comparisons

Project benefits	
ROI contributors	**Value enablers**
Objectively based	Subjectively based (mostly)
Easy to understand, measure, and quantify	More difficult to understand, measure, and quantify
Easy to gain project approval from executive and steering committees with their use	More difficult to gain project approval from executive and steering committees with their use
Can be easily converted to monetary units	Not as easy to convert to monetary units
Common business measurements that are universal	Specific measurements to a company that are usually behaviorally oriented
Easy to incorporate into cost models using common formulas and assumptions	More difficult to incorporate into cost models and require creative formulas and often confusing assumptions
Generally straightforward and feasible	May be confusing and not totally believable
Can be monitored easily	Not as easy to monitor
Do not require excessive estimating in forecasting results	Require estimating techniques in forecasting results

quality. These benefits are objectively based and can be easily quantified in financial terms. Examples of these value-contributing benefits are:

- Loans approved
- Deliveries made
- Equipment downtime
- Time savings
- Work stoppages
- Overhead costs
- Unit costs
- Amount of re-work
- Amount of scrap
- Units produced
- Unit defects
- Service availability

When it's not reasonable and appropriate, given project requirements, to quantify benefits in monetary terms and to include them in the ROI analysis, these benefits should be classified as value enablers. Examples of these benefits are:

- Job satisfaction
- Employee efficiency

- Customer satisfaction
- Employee motivation
- Employee knowledge base
- Employee stress reduction
- Time savings
- Organizational commitment
- Employee complaints
- Work climate
- Innovation
- Community image
- Investor image
- Customer loyalty
- Brand recognition
- Teamwork
- Communication
- Internal conflict

In comparing these project benefit examples, it's clear that the ROI contributors are more straightforward and easier to quantify monetarily than the value enablers, but don't think for a second that value-enabling benefits can't be expressed this way as well. Everything, and I do mean everything, can be forecasted, measured, and converted to quantitative, financial terms. Is it easy? Certainly not. Is it possible? Absolutely. For instance, employee morale is an often-cited benefit that many professionals feel is impossible to quantify. A company that specializes in human resources, employee development, and morale improvement, however, will tell you that it's not only possible to quantify this important workforce metric, but necessary for a company's long-term survival. This is not to say, however, that this is an easy task for everyday project professionals. For this reason, project teams, more often than not, will classify employee morale as a value-enabling benefit and not as an ROI contributor.

Scope, timelines, cost, and management intent are key factors that should be considered when determining whether a benefit is an ROI contributor or a value enabler. Based on the project requirements, project teams can collectively determine which benefits can be reasonably and appropriately converted to monetary units to contribute to the overall ROI study. All other benefits should then be considered as value enablers and expressed in other quantitative and qualitative terms that demonstrate their value to the business.

With this new categorization of benefits, project teams can now determine, based on their distinct project requirements, which benefits should be incorporated into the overall ROI analysis and which ones should not. By incorporating both ROI contributors and value enablers in the business case, project teams can tell the complete business story tailored around their specific project requirements without excluding important business benefits.

Even though certain benefits may not be included in the ROI evaluation, these benefits can still be quantified in other ways and managed to achieve targeted objectives. These benefits can be crucial to the success of a project and to the overall competitiveness of a company.

For certain projects it may not be such a good idea to expend resources on quantifying certain benefits in monetary terms to contribute to the overall project ROI. But for other projects it may make business sense to do so. It's important to note, however, that even though some benefits will be classified as value enablers and won't be included in the overall ROI analysis, it's still advisable to express them in other quantitative terms so that they can be measured and, therefore, managed throughout the course of a project. Quantitative analysis of value-enabling benefits can be extremely valuable to making key decisions that affect the business and in managing projects toward their targeted outcomes.

In using the employee morale example, if baseline measurements indicate that employees are at an average level of 2 out of 5 for morale (5 = highest, 1 = lowest), and at the conclusion of a project the average level increased to 4, important conclusions can be drawn. The management and project teams can say with certainty that the project was a success and should consider other types of initiatives to further improve morale or improve morale for other departments. Conversely, if the average score dropped to 1.5 at the conclusion of the project, key conclusions and lessons learned can also be made about the project; mainly that the project was detrimental to the workforce and, therefore, damaging to the business.

Although simple, this example shows how a value-enabling benefit can be quantified to measure project success. This example can be explored even further with quantitative methods. Other tangible benefits of employee morale could also be easily measured to provide management with important information about their businesses, such as employee turnover and absenteeism. Increases in turnover and absenteeism can certainly be quantified and can indicate negative trends within the business that warrants management attention.

Labeling a benefit as a value enabler doesn't necessarily mean that a hard ROI payoff doesn't exist. It only means that the project team determined it cannot be reasonably or appropriately expressed in financial terms for the project at hand. Oftentimes, only specialized personnel would have to be engaged to determine the tangible benefits and express them in monetary terms. For instance, only a team of human resource experts may be qualified to capture the hard-dollar benefits of improved employee morale. A project team may not find it cost-justifiable to bring such a team on board and will keep the employee morale benefit separate from the project ROI analysis. Value-enabling benefits should never be dismissed from a business case simply because they aren't included in the ROI analysis. They enable other benefits that

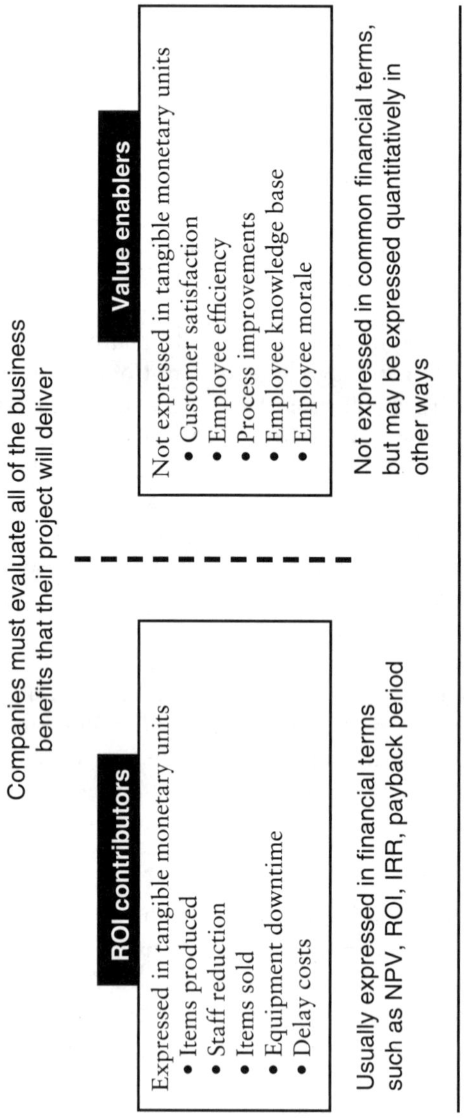

Companies must evaluate all of the business
benefits that their project will deliver

ROI contributors

Expressed in tangible monetary units
• Items produced
• Staff reduction
• Items sold
• Equipment downtime
• Delay costs

Usually expressed in financial terms
such as NPV, ROI, IRR, payback period

Value enablers

Not expressed in tangible monetary units
• Customer satisfaction
• Employee efficiency
• Process improvements
• Employee knowledge base
• Employee morale

Not expressed in common financial terms,
but may be expressed quantitatively in
other ways

Figure 9.2 Evaluating ROI contributors and value enablers

may be even more important than those that contribute directly to the project ROI. Project investments that are difficult to measure certainly don't automatically mean that they are bad investments.

Value-enabling benefits can be converted to monetary terms with the right expertise and analysis but more often than not, they aren't. They are kept separate from the ROI analysis and this is fine for most projects. Attempts should still be made to show the importance of value-enabling benefits and how they can bring about beneficial change for an organization. These benefits must be presented in the business case to tell the complete business story and to accurately weigh all of the benefits the project will deliver. Some of the most important strategic benefits that a project can deliver are often the most difficult to quantify. These benefits can't be omitted from the business case or the overall project approach. Project teams must strike a balance between those benefits that contribute directly to a project's ROI and those benefits that enable business value in other ways. These benefits must be presented collectively to management teams to convey the complete business story. Figure 9.2 shows an illustrative example of how both ROI contributors and value enablers should be evaluated in determining the viability of projects.

For many projects, nonmonetary benefits are just as valuable and have as much influence in the organization as the monetary benefits. But if these benefits aren't included in the business case, it may be difficult to justify a project investment. Figure 9.3 illustrates an example of a business case that includes just those benefits that contribute to the project's ROI. By not including all of the project benefits, the costs and risks outweigh the monetary benefits and is considered to be a bad investment.

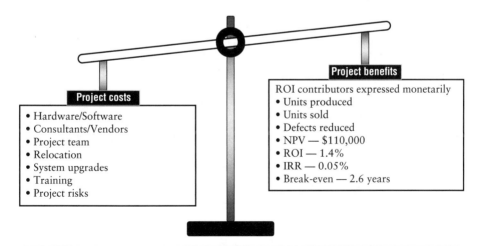

Figure 9.3   Project costs vs. benefits (value-enabling benefits excluded)

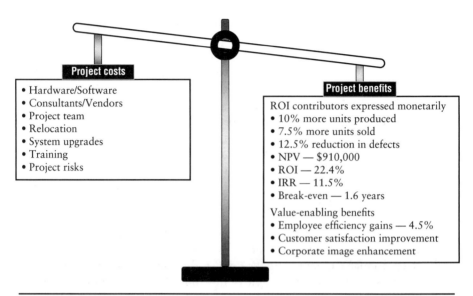

Figure 9.4 Project costs vs. benefits (value-enabling benefits included)

When included in the business case, the value-enabling benefits may tip the scale to provide the necessary justification for a project. These benefits should not be considered less important than the benefits contributing to the ROI. Project teams need to evaluate all relevant benefits carefully to present a compelling story to the management team. Figure 9.4 shows how a project can be considered a good investment when all benefits are evaluated. As can be seen, adding the value enablers to the previous example tips the scale in favor of the project investment being considered a good one.

In a perfect world, all of the right decisions could be made by simply looking at the numbers. There would be clear monetary values for projects and the extent of our analysis would be choosing the projects and solutions with the best numbers. But alas, we're not in a perfect business world and we need to do more analysis than simply making decisions based on the best numbers. But this is a good thing, too, because that would make managers and many project professionals obsolete! So we must still strive to assign monetary value to as many benefits as possible and strategically analyze the potential for the value enablers while having the vision to determine what value can be extracted from them and what actions will be required.

Cost Avoidance and Revenue Protection: ROI Contributors or Value Enablers?

Many projects are implemented to avoid future costs or to protect future revenue streams as a result of unplanned events. As with all project investments, stakeholders want to see detailed business cases and financial justification for these cost avoidance and revenue protection projects. Project teams know the importance of these projects and the possible consequences that may occur if they are not implemented, but they often struggle with demonstrating positive ROIs, because cost avoidance and revenue protection can be rather nebulous when trying to quantify them. Quite often these struggles lead to contentious debates between project teams and stakeholders. Project teams, who possess the most knowledge of the situation at hand, often feel that the potential loss of revenue or increased costs due to an unplanned event is justification enough for these projects. Stakeholders, on the other hand, who are more re-moved from the situation want to see business and financial justification for these project investments.

Companies often implement cost avoidance/revenue protection projects to replace aging, but important, technical systems that are on their last legs. It's common for companies to continue using systems and equipment long af-ter their depreciable lives. Why spend money replacing things that still work? Well, they won't work forever and at some point they do need to be replaced. Operations personnel responsible for maintaining these systems, and the ones constantly applying bandages to keep them running, are usually the ones jumping up and down begging for a replacement. They know the time is near and they know the impact to the business could be significant when the time does come.

Those old, private branch exchanges (PBXs), or phone systems, tucked away in phone closets are classic examples of systems that companies continue us-ing long after their depreciable lives. Those things seem to last for an eternity! When the PBX administrator recognizes that the system is about to make its final phone call and recommends a replacement system, the typical response from stakeholders with budgeting responsibilities is, "Why? My phone works fine. Show me financial justification." The PBX administrator, therefore, would rather keep applying bandages to the aging system than to take on the near-impossible task of showing a positive ROI. But it's only a matter of time before the old PBX does indeed make its final phone call and results in the inability to receive customer orders and inquiries; the inability to correspond with cus-tomers, vendors, suppliers, and other business partners; decreased employee productivity and morale; and a tarnished reputation. You either pay now or you pay later, and most stakeholders don't want to pay now for a project that doesn't demonstrate a positive ROI, and they certainly don't want to pay later with increased costs or decreased revenue. It's no wonder operations personnel keep applying all of those bandages!

Stakeholders are responsible for maintaining budgets and don't like to spend money unless it is absolutely necessary. When they are advised to spend money on a project to protect the business from an event that may or may not occur at some point in the future, they can become rather defensive and appre-hensive. They don't want to unnecessarily spend money on a project to protect themselves from an unforeseen event that may not even occur, and they certainly don't want to be responsible for the consequences of such an event should it occur. Talk about a Catch-22! This is what keeps business leaders up at night. Let's see how we can alleviate some of their anxieties by structuring these types of project proposals in a way that provides enough information so that business leaders are more comfortable in making these tough decisions. But when it comes to uncertainties, risks, negative ROIs, potential revenue losses, or potential cost increases, some anxiety will always remain. That's just business. Nobody said it was going to be easy!

Let's begin by looking at cost avoidance and revenue protection within the context of the business case. See if you can answer these two important questions:

1. Are the costs that are avoided due to a project implementation *direct cost savings* that contribute to a company's bottom line and to an increased project ROI?

2. Are the future revenue streams that are protected, that is, maintained, due to a project implementation *additional revenue streams* for a company that contribute to the bottom line and to an increased project ROI? Think about these questions for a while; close the book if you have to. This may come as a surprise, especially for those who have been treating these situations as direct cost savings and additional revenue streams in business cases, but the answer is a loud and resounding *NO!* Cost avoidance and revenue protection do not contribute to the bottom line nor do they increase project ROIs. I've seen project team members try six ways to Sunday to come up with ways to show positive ROIs for cost avoidance and revenue protection in the context of the business case, but, invariably, they fall terribly short. Let's see why.

When a project team deploys a solution that enables the business to avoid unplanned future costs, they do a tremendous job and the business certainly benefits, but the business doesn't realize direct cost savings as a result of those avoided costs. The costs that were avoided aren't recorded anywhere in the accounting books as direct cost savings. Profit margins, therefore, do not increase. When a project team deploys a solution that enables the business to protect future revenue streams from decreasing, the project team once again did a super job and the business benefits greatly by not losing any revenue, but the business doesn't generate additional revenue. The revenue that was protected isn't recorded anywhere in the accounting books as additional revenue. The business did not make any more money. Project teams must build their financial cost models to reflect the true nature of the business and not simply in hypothetical situations. This is yet another reason why it's imperative to include value-enabling benefits in the business case, such as uninterrupted service, untarnished reputation, and adherence to regulatory mandates, and not merely the ROI contributing benefits.

No matter how one tries to slice it, if a project investment doesn't generate enough money to cover the costs, it won't have a positive ROI in the business case. It doesn't mean the project is a bad one or shouldn't be implemented; it simply means that other factors must be carefully analyzed, such as the risk factors, to make this determination. If it is determined that the project should be implemented because the risks of not implementing it are too great, that project, then, is simply the cost of doing business. A company may not make money on the project, but they won't lose any money or incur additional costs when, and if, an adverse future event does occur. When your mechanic tells you that your car needs new brakes, for instance, do you fork out the cash to buy them? Of course you do. It's the price you have to pay for owning a car. By paying for new brakes now you avoid paying much more in the future when they inevitably fail. Companies often have to pay for projects that don't deliver positive financial returns, but protect them from future events. It's the price of doing business.

With the incessant desire to constantly show positive ROI measurements and with the confusion surrounding cost avoidance and revenue protection initiatives, many project teams do end up producing positive ROIs in their business cases. This is easy to do, albeit inaccurate, when cost avoidance is treated as direct cost savings and when revenue protection is treated as additional revenue. Business cases developed in this manner are laden with bogus assumptions, faulty logic, inaccurate cash flows, exaggerated forecasts, and crafty number crunching. That is not to say that project teams developed these business cases with deceptive motives, simply that they did not fully understand how to treat the cash flows surrounding these projects. This also does not mean that the projects weren't worthwhile investments! It merely means that the business cases were produced incorrectly and inaccurately. Avoided costs are not direct cost savings and protected revenue is not additional revenue. Period.

So how do we approach the business case for cost avoidance and revenue protection projects? Like every other project; carefully, thoroughly, and without cutting corners or sugar-coating the results. All costs and benefits, to include both ROI contributors and value enablers, must be clearly presented. Project teams still calculate ROI measurements, even if they are going to be negative. Stakeholders still need to know how much the project is going to cost them. Plus, there will always be several different options, solutions, and even risk mitigation plans to address business issues and unplanned events, each with its own cost and benefit structure. Businesses need to carefully compare the technical feasibility and financial attractiveness for the various options and solutions. Some solutions may require a total replacement or forklift upgrade, while others may only call for certain maintenance procedures or incremental upgrades. By mandating business cases for all project investments, employees are encouraged and empowered to be creative and to use their business acumen to identify and present the most optimal solutions to address business obstacles and unplanned events.

Not all cost avoidance or revenue protection projects have to be absolute money losers. There will nearly always be some ROI contributing benefits when implementing new projects, deploying new technologies, or enhancing business processes. Investments in newer technologies, for instance, may produce employee efficiency gains, enhance product quality, allow quicker access to vital information, or enable faster delivery times. These benefits must be accounted for in the business case. They may not cover the total costs of the project investment, but they will certainly make the project solution less expensive and more attractive. This is especially useful when comparing competing project solutions.

Unexpected and unplanned events are not predictable and are difficult to plan for in the budgeting process. Money is typically not set aside for such events. Events that occur on a fairly recurring basis, however, are more predictable and can be proactively planned for and included in the budgets. Examples include routine maintenance, inventory overhead, and seasonal-related costs. When businesses discover that unplanned events may occur in the relatively near future, management and project teams must assess the risks of these potential events thoroughly to make the best business decisions and to take the most appropriate actions. Some of the questions that must be addressed include: Is it absolutely necessary that we invest in a project to address these risks? Are the risks low enough where we don't have to take any action? How much time can we deal with the risks before taking action? Project teams can greatly assist with these difficult decisions by gathering the necessary information, performing detailed analyses, and presenting their overall recommendations in the business case.

Project teams and stakeholders need to assess all of the risks involved with unplanned events carefully to make smart business decisions and to avoid overreacting and making poor decisions. Quite often it's not always as doom and gloom as everyone initially thinks. Does Y2K come to mind? Many companies spent a ton of money on Y2K (year 2000) projects to prevent their systems from crashing at the turn of the millennium, as was alleged and even hyped. It's essential for project teams to acquire a full understanding of two key aspects of potential future events, the *probability* and the *impact*. Probability is the possibility that the event will occur, and impact is the overall effect the event will have on the organization. Businesses may be able to avoid costly project investments by finding ways to reduce the probability or impact, or both. By reducing the probability and/or impact of an event, decision makers may be more comfortable with tolerating that new risk posture. Figure 9.5 is a graphical illustration of a probability and impact matrix. Low probability,

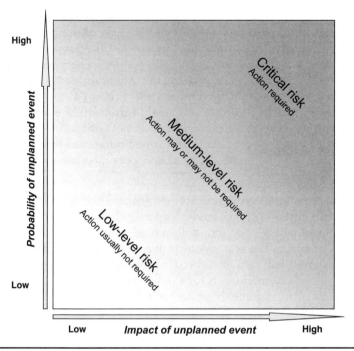

Figure 9.5 Probability and impact matrix

low impact events can usually be tolerated. High probability and high impact events must be addressed. The ones in between pose more challenges for decision makers.

Project managers may be familiar with these terms since they are frequently used in the development of project risk management plans. They often assess the probability and impact of certain project risks as high, medium, or low and monitor these risks throughout the project lifecycle. With cost avoidance and revenue protection analysis, however, project teams must get much more specific than high, medium, or low when assessing the probability and impact of a potential event. Critical and costly business decisions are made based on these assessments, so it's imperative that project teams achieve a level of detail and accuracy in their risk assessments so that business leaders can confidently take the best courses of action. Decision makers need to know the probabilities of certain events, expressed as percentages, with as much accuracy as possible to determine what actions, if any, are necessary. Additionally, if unplanned events are going to impact organizations by increasing costs or reducing revenue streams, management needs to know, with precision, the extent of the additional costs incurred and how much revenue will be lost.

Corporate leaders certainly don't want to pay for projects that have negative ROIs, but if accurate probabilities and impacts of unplanned events are presented that clearly demonstrate the business justification for certain project initiatives, they will reach into the corporate coffers. These leaders, additionally, will not only approve these projects but will embrace them wholeheartedly because they know that the projects will prevent their businesses from suffering major setbacks. Project teams need to articulate the probabilities and impacts of future events in a clear and concise way, with sufficient background information, to gain that confidence from the business leaders. The following example shows how the probability and impact of a certain event can be presented in a business case:

- Based on business growth, customer demand, the age of the system, the warning indicators, and vendor expert judgment, the probability that the customer order system will exceed its data storage and operating capacity within the next six-to-twelve months is 15 to 20%. The impact of this event will be a forced system shutdown resulting in the inability to process customer orders for a minimum of 6 hours. The vendor costs to restore and upgrade the system will be $3.2MM and the revenue lost will be 5.3MM.

There are advanced statistical, scientific, and mathematical methods of determining near-exact probabilities of occurrences and other risk-related elements, which is beyond the scope of this book. More power to those who have these tools at their disposal to assess risks and potential events. But for most project professionals in the trenches such tools aren't readily available and they will have to rely on more conventional methods of estimating risk factors. Determining the probabilities and impacts of future events to an acceptable degree of accuracy requires the input and information from stakeholders, subject matter experts, vendors, consultants, trade journals, industry publications, and past experiences. Project teams need to gather and evaluate all risk elements by conducting interviews, brainstorming sessions, and focus groups; distributing data request forms and surveys; analyzing historical records and past trends; and by employing other methods that may be available to them.

A project team's ability to forecast accurate risk profiles is greatly enhanced when a structured, proven approach is undertaken. In Chapter 7 we described the value-metrics framework that is a repeatable, reliable, and proven method that takes a data-driven approach to accurately identify and solidify value metrics. As project teams leverage this framework, they must also capture all of the risk elements associated with their projects. In using this framework to gather important business information, project teams will be able to determine, fairly accurately, the probabilities and impacts for certain business events since they will be tapping into expert judgment, prior experiences, a vast knowledge pool, historical records, and performance trends.

Evaluating All Possible Outcomes to Determine the Best Project Solution

I'd like to present a case study to drive home a point on choosing and managing a project toward the *big picture* and not merely a specific measure like ROI. Our example is outside of the business realm, but projects are similar to choosing and making life choice changes. When evaluating important life matters such as where to invest your money, where to send the kids to school, or in which neighborhood to buy a house, you have to analyze and evaluate all of the pros and cons of the various options and determine which one best satisfies your needs and requirements. Sound familiar? Let's jump into our example:

Bill decides, with the encouragement of his wife and physician, to improve his overall health and wellness. Although Bill's wife is primarily concerned with his weight loss, his doctor recommends embarking on a well-rounded fitness and nutrition program to attain the following health benefits:

- Weight loss
- Improved cardio fitness
- Increased strength
- Increased energy level
- Improved mood
- Reduced cholesterol level

Bill researches several fitness and nutrition programs that may help him attain these health benefits. He does a thorough analysis of the costs and benefits of each of the programs and presents them to his wife, who happens to be the project sponsor for this initiative since she feels strongly that Bill needs to drop some pounds and, perhaps more importantly, the cost comes out of the family finances that she manages. She interrupts Bill's detailed presentation of the programs and exclaims, "I am concerned about bottom-line results. Show me the program where you will lose the most weight in the shortest amount of time at the lowest cost." In other words, what is the return on my investment!?

Realizing that all of his research efforts were in vain, Bill then presents the least expensive program that promises significant weight loss in the shortest period of time. Without getting into the details of the program, Bill's wife instructs him to embark on this program. She heard the numbers and liked what she heard. The project sponsor is encouraged by this program because she won't have to spend too much money and is confident she can get a good return on her investment quickly in the form of weight loss. What she does not understand, however, is that this program calls for doing nothing but eating a processed lab concoction once a day that has no proven nutritional value whatsoever. The concoction is specifically designed to curb the appetite with one dosage a day. Bill's wife was so engrossed with the bottom-line results that she did not take into account the details, risks, and long-term consequences of the program.

After starving for several weeks and ingesting nothing but this processed lab experiment, Bill did indeed lose weight—a lot of it. The project sponsor was happy because she achieved her project goals. She saved a ton of money by choosing the cheapest program and now feels that she has money at her disposal to spend elsewhere. Or does she? As one might imagine, the health implications from this cheap lab solution start to surface. Bill's energy level dissipates, he has become frail and fragile, his heart barely beats, and his crankiness is driving his wife up the wall. Bill's wife, once the chief advocate for this inexpensive fitness and nutrition program, second guesses her decision and wishes she had never sponsored such a program.

To rectify the situation she sends Bill to see a specialist. I think we all know where this is going. The specialist's treatment ends up costing more, much more, than the most expensive fitness and nutrition program that was initially presented. In fact, the specialist, the therapy sessions, the referrals, and other related costs end up costing more than *all* of the original programs combined! Can you think of any disastrous projects that had similar results? All of the extra money, time, frustration, and adverse health effects could have been avoided if more than simply cheap weight loss was considered and evaluated in the program selection process.

That was a fun and somewhat hyperbolic example of what could happen when only one attribute is assessed for competing initiatives. Similar results can occur and have occurred for projects when they are chosen and implemented based solely on ROI. When projects are selected based only on the numbers and nothing else, companies may end up paying more in the long run, much like Bill's wife. As project professionals, we need to be careful and wary of project solutions that come at the lowest cost but promise the greatest returns. This doesn't mean that inexpensive solutions with high returns are always dangerous, but they can be if all of their attributes aren't evaluated carefully against business requirements and objectives. With low costs, quite often low quality ensues. When quality suffers, customer satisfaction decreases. When customer satisfaction decreases, sales suffer. And when sales suffer, corporations lose money. So much for just ROI!

Financial considerations should always be given top priority in assessing, prioritizing, and choosing projects. Every attempt should be made to convert all project data to monetary value and include them in the ROI study. After all, business is business and money must be made. But basing project decisions solely on ROI doesn't account for the complete picture. All important project attributes should be taken into consideration to choose the best project solution option. The best way to assess competing project proposals is to evaluate how each of them satisfies all of the identified value metrics, or business benefits, that the project is striving to achieve. These value metrics include both

ROI contributing and value-enabling benefits. It's worth reviewing the definitions of these important benefits again:

- **ROI contributors**—benefits that can be reasonably and appropriately quantified and expressed monetarily and that contribute directly to a project's ROI.
- **Value enablers**—benefits that enable the achievement of business value but are determined to be unreasonable and inappropriate to be expressed monetarily for inclusion in a project's ROI analysis, given project requirements. Although these benefits will not contribute directly to a project's ROI forecast, they can be quantified, measured, and managed to bring about significant business value in other ways.

It's certainly not a crime to classify project benefits as value enablers and to keep them separate from the ROI analysis. It would be bad business practice, however, to cram certain benefits into ROI financial models using inaccurate assumptions, bad business logic, and lofty estimates. A project's true ROI will never match the ROI of the business case if these ill-advised procedures are employed.

Stakeholders are accountable to the business for project results. They make the tough, strategic decisions that can either make or break their companies. Project teams can recommend certain projects or project solutions but, at the end of the day, it's the stakeholders, especially the project sponsors, accountable to the business for the results. Project teams need to discern and recommend when it makes business sense to keep some of the benefits separate from the ROI analysis. Project sponsors will eventually have to prove the ROI numbers down the road and will have a lot of explaining to do when the forecasted ROI returns weren't realized for their project investments.

In defense of the *ROI only, show me the money* folks, they were probably never presented with a solid business case that clearly delineated the ROI contributing benefits from the value-enabling ones. They were probably presented with a laundry list of the so called *soft benefits* with no business context or quantifiable value measurements. As project professionals, we need to stop this bad business process and start helping business leaders make those difficult project decisions by clearly conveying ROI numbers and other value-enabling benefits in quantitative, measurable terms. Stakeholders and other business leaders are under pressure and time constraints every single business day. Of course they are going to demand projects that make their companies money, as they should. But let's show them there are other, more effective ways to make project decisions that are better suited for their organizations and better aligned with their business requirements.

Project teams must first begin by prioritizing the business benefits. What does the organization *need* to achieve? What are the *nice to haves*? What benefits *aren't necessary*? In most cases, ROI will be the top priority. With the priorities established, project teams can quickly determine if certain project solutions are even worth pursuing and can then narrow down the options. For instance, if voice recognition technology is a high priority for a company and certain vendors don't offer this feature, project teams may be able to dismiss them from the running, saving valuable time and energy in the vendor selection process.

Once the benefits have been prioritized, project teams can determine how important they are to the organization by assigning a magnitude of importance to them. By assigning each benefit a *weight* of importance, project teams can better determine the most effective project solution to satisfy business priorities and requirements. There will always be several competing project options and solutions from which to choose. The challenge is choosing and implementing the best one for the organization. By prioritizing the project attributes and assigning weights to them, project teams can make informed decisions about which project solutions are best for their organization. The weighted attribute scoring approach, which is discussed in the next section, is an effective way to make an informed business decision on your project solution.

The Weighted Attribute Scoring Approach to Evaluating Project Solutions

Bill and his wife would not have encountered such horrid results if they had chosen a fitness and nutrition program that not only addressed weight loss at a low cost, but satisfied all of the doctor's requirements to some degree. But with inexpensive weight loss being the only attribute in which the project sponsor was concerned, the processed lab concoction diet made some business sense. After all, the ultimate goal of quick, inexpensive weight loss was indeed achieved. But we saw the ultimate results of the program. What would happen if a financial services firm entrusted an untested, unproven, start-up security vendor with all of its security needs because their solution had the best ROI? This solution may be cheap in the short term, but as security breaches arise and the integrity of the company's confidential data is compromised, this cheap solution becomes quite expensive rather quickly when the risk remediation, lawsuits, and damage to their brand kicks in.

If Bill's wife listened to the doctor and determined that weight loss was an important attribute, but not the only attribute, results could have been drastically different. Based on the doctor's recommendations, Bill and his wife could have realistically prioritized and assigned weights of importance to each of the attributes and used these rankings to determine the most appropriate program. Let's say they prioritized these attributes and assigned weights of importance to them in percentages:

1. Weight loss—20%
2. Increased energy level—15%
3. Improved cardio levels—15%

4. Increased strength—10%
5. Improved mood—10%
6. Reduced cholesterol levels—10%
7. Program costs—20%

As with any good attribute weighting exercise, the totals equal 100%. Aligned with their initial plan, Bill's wife still had weight loss and program costs as top priorities, but they also included several other key factors in the decision making process. It's starting to become clear that the processed lab concoction diet could have been eliminated as a viable option early on in the process, but let's dive deeper into the weighted attribute scoring approach to definitively determine the best program for Bill.

The weighted attribute scoring approach is a systematic way of selecting the most appropriate project investments based on business priorities and requirements. The approach involves identifying all of the relevant project attributes and allocating weights to each of them to reflect their relative importance. We then assign scores to them for each project option to reflect how each option performs in relation to each attribute. The result is a single-weighted score for each project option that is then used to compare the overall performance of the various project options. This is an effective method because it shows both the financial and nonfinancial benefits of various project options.

With the weighted attribute scoring approach, project teams and stakeholders can attain a better comprehension of the big picture and can evaluate all of the possible outcomes of various project solutions. We can still prioritize the financial ROI benefits of our projects, but this approach allows for other attributes to be included in the project decision making process as well. The diligence of evaluating numerous and various business attributes reduces the risk associated with a project. If you drop the basket with all of your eggs in it, what are you cooking for breakfast? Evaluate all of the project attributes carefully.

Typically, you'll be faced with numerous solutions initially that can satisfy project and business requirements to some degree. The key is choosing the *best* project solution investment, hence our reliance on the weighted attribute scoring approach to quantify the various project attributes for each project option.

The weighted attribute scoring matrix is easy to develop and understand. As with other important project activities, key stakeholders should be involved in determining the priorities and weightings of the various project attributes. Once the team is assembled, they begin the process by weighting each attribute by its relative contribution and importance to the organization's goals and strategic plan. The team then evaluates each project option or vendor solution by its relative contribution to each of the project attributes. The project team then assigns a range of values for each attribute ranging from low (0) to high (5). These values represent a project solution's ability to satisfy the project attribute. For instance, a 0 ranking for a certain attribute means that a project solution does not satisfy the attribute at all, whereas a 5 ranking indicates that the project solution completely satisfies the attribute. A 3 ranking means the project attribute is somewhat, or moderately, satisfied. Then it's simple multiplication and addition. First, multiply each attribute's weight by the assigned ranking. This gives the overall score for that specific attribute. Then, add up all of the attributes scores to obtain the total score for a project solution. The project proposal with the highest score is the best project.

An added benefit to this approach is that it is collaborative and drives team buy-in for the solution by allowing all key stakeholders to agree on the value of each benefit that will cause the best solutions to rise to the top. Let's apply the weighted attribute scoring approach to the various fitness and nutrition programs that Bill researched. Table 9.2 shows the four programs and the associated rankings and scores that Bill and his wife collectively determined for each of the attributes.

As can be seen, each of the four programs has specific rankings for each of the attributes based on their abilities to satisfy the attribute. For instance, the *heart-healthy* program has a 5 ranking for the *increased cardio-level* attribute because this particular program focuses intently on cardiovascular health and fully satisfies this particular project attribute. The *strength* program has a 5 ranking for increased strength because it completely satisfies this attribute, but only a 1.5 ranking for weight loss, since this program focuses more on bulking up muscles rather than losing weight. The *processed lab concoction* has a 5 ranking for weight loss and program costs, but low rankings for all of the other attributes for obvious reasons. The *general fitness* program has consistently high rankings for all of the attributes and has an overall score of 3.85. Bill and his wife should have chosen this program.

As noted, the weighted attribute scoring approach takes into account the big picture and includes analysis of all of the relevant project attributes. All of the project value metrics that were identified should be used as attributes for the weighted attributes scoring matrix, to include ROI contributing and value-enabling benefits. There may be instances in which stakeholders want to include other attributes in addition to these value metrics, usually to account for additional risk. Common attributes that stakeholders frequently include when evaluating project solutions are:

- Implementation risk
- Employee acceptance
- Impact on existing operations
- Equipment or service downtime
- Impact on safety
- Customer acceptance
- Compliance with government or other regulations
- Alignment with strategic intent and corporate objectives

Table 9.2 Fitness program weighted attribute scoring matrix

Attribute	Weight (%)	Heart-healthy program		Strength program		General fitness program		Processed lab concoction	
		Ranking	Score	Ranking	Score	Ranking	Score	Ranking	Score
Weight loss	20	2	0.4	1.5	0.3	3	0.6	5	1
Increased energy level	15	3	0.45	2	0.3	5	0.75	1	0.15
Improved cardio level	15	5	0.75	3	0.45	4	0.6	0	0
Increased strength	10	2	0.2	5	0.5	4	0.4	0	0
Improved mood	10	3.5	0.35	3	0.3	5	0.5	1	0.1
Lowered cholesterol	10	4	0.4	2	0.2	4	0.4	1.5	0.15
Program costs	20	4.5	0.9	4	0.8	3	0.6	5	1
Total			**3.45**		**2.85**		**3.85**		**2.4**

Table 9.3 Weighted attribute scoring matrix

Attribute	Weight (%)	Project Alpha		Project Beta		Project Charlie		Project Delta	
		Ranking	Score	Ranking	Score	Ranking	Score	Ranking	Score
ROI-contributing benefits									
Financial returns, including NPV, ROI, IRR, and payback period	30	2	0.6	5	1.5	1	0.3	3	0.9
Increased output production	15	2	0.3	5	0.75	1	0.15	3.5	0.525
Reduced defects and re-work	10	2	0.2	5	0.5	2	0.2	2.5	0.25
Total ROI-contributing benefits	**55**		**1.1**		**2.75**		**0.65**		**1.675**
Value-enabling benefits									
Improved customer satisfaction	10	3	0.3	3	0.3	2	0.2	1.5	0.15
Enhanced corporate image	10	3	0.3	3	0.3	3	0.3	1	0.1
Improved worker morale/reduced stress	5	4	0.2	2	0.1	3.5	0.175	2	0.1
Total value-enabling benefits	**25**		**0.8**		**0.7**		**0.675**		**0.35**
Other project attributes									
Low implementation risk	10	2	0.2	4	0.4	2	0.2	3	0.3
Low impact on worker safety	10	3.5	0.35	3	0.3	2.5	0.25	3.5	0.35
Total other decision factors	**20**		**0.55**		**0.7**		**0.45**		**0.65**
Total			**2.45**		**4.15**		**1.775**		**2.675**

These attributes can be classified simply as *other project attributes* in the weighted attribute scoring matrix. Table 9.3 shows an example weighted attribute scoring matrix for four competing project proposals.

As can be seen in the matrix, the project team determined that the ROI contributing benefits were the most important attributes to consider in the evaluation process and, thus, has the highest overall weight of 55%. The value-enabling benefits are important, but not as important as the ROI contributing ones, and have an overall weight of 25%. The other project attributes equal a weighting of 20%. In assigning values for each of the value attributes for each of the project options, we see that Project Beta is the best project solution based on its overall score of 4.15.

There may be cases in which some of the overall scores are the same or too close to determine which project solution has the advantage. In baseball, whenever there is a close play, umpires rely on the unofficial rule of a *tie goes to the runner*. In the weighted attribute scoring matrix, whenever there is a tie, or whenever the numbers are too close to make a definitive decision, priority always goes to the project with the best financial ROI metrics. All things being equal, money trumps all other attributes and the project solutions with the best financial returns should be given top priority. Additionally, whenever the scores are too close and the ROI metrics are similar, projects with less inherent risks should be given priority over those that have more risks. Business leaders strive to minimize their risk exposure as much as possible. With all else being equal, projects that have fewer risks should be chosen over those that have more.

Professional Development Game Plan for Success

1. If you're like most professionals, the terms tangible, intangible, hard and soft, in the context of project and business benefits, have been haunting you for years. How do you deal with these confusing and ambiguous terms? How do you apply them to your business cases? Do you quantify *everything* in monetary terms? How accurate do you think you've been? In other words, did your company receive the money that you forecasted and record it in the books? Do you dismiss those benefits that are difficult to quantify monetarily? Could these dismissed benefits have been quantified and managed in other ways to bring about value to the business?

   Action Plan

   a. Evaluate and analyze your approach to categorizing, quantifying, and presenting project and business benefits in your business cases. Revisit two or three of your prior projects and carefully examine the forecasted benefits and how you presented them. Was there a clear delineation between those benefits that contribute directly to the ROI and those that do not? Do all of the benefits in the ROI analysis truly and directly contribute to the company's bottom-line results? How did you handle the so-called soft benefits? Did you quantify them in other ways to show the value they can deliver? For each of these projects, analyze the forecasted benefits (value metrics) and write down all of the mistakes, faulty logic, erroneous assumptions, omissions, inaccurate categorizations, and improper conversions to monetary units that you can find. Try to find five to eight of these missteps for each of your projects.

b. Now think about your current or future projects. How will you categorize and incorporate project and business benefits into the business case? Consider how we defined benefits in this chapter as ROI contributors and value enablers. Write down three to five strategies you will initiate to properly and accurately incorporate project benefits into your project proposals. Assume that you are accountable to the business for your ROI forecasts and at the end of the project your executives will compare your ROI forecasts to actual business results. With this in mind, how will you approach quantifying and presenting the benefits in your business case?

2. Companies will always have many solutions to any given business problem. The challenge is choosing and implementing the best solution. How do you ensure that the best project solutions are always chosen and implemented? How do you prioritize project attributes and evaluate competing project solutions? Do you even embark on such endeavors?

Action Plan

a. How did you formally evaluate your last two or three project solution options? On review, can you identify any factors that weren't identified that should have been included? How would these additional factors have affected the solution choice? Make sure you review the number of vendors chosen, technologies that were assessed, how far you reached out to gain baseline data and industry best practices. Was there a better solution that wasn't evaluated?

b. What will you do to ensure that all of the business priorities are firmly established and that the best solutions to address those priorities are implemented? Write down three to five strategies you will take to ensure that the best project is chosen to address business issues and satisfy management requirements. Leverage the weighted attribute scoring methodology that was discussed in this chapter. Be creative!

Reference

1. Keen, Jack M., and Bonnie Digrius. 2003. *Making Technology Investments Profitable*. Hoboken, NJ: John Wiley.

10

Building Cash Flow Models to Set Up the ROI Measurements

You don't make spending decisions, investment decisions, hiring deci-
sions, or whether-you're-going-to-look-for-a-job decisions when you
don't know what's going to happen.

—Michael Bloomberg

Concepts That Project Professionals Must Understand

Project professionals certainly don't need to be CPAs or financial experts to be effective in their roles, but they must be proficient and knowledgeable in certain fundamental business concepts that can be applied directly to their projects. Having a solid grasp of these important concepts can greatly assist project teams in achieving optimized and sustained business value for their organizations. Most of us have heard of the terms discounting, return on investment (ROI), net present value, internal rate of return, and payback, but what do they really mean, what do they entail, and how do we apply them to our projects to determine and drive business value? Some of you may be getting a bit apprehensive right now thinking that we will be delving into those esoteric mathematical concepts that caused you heartache in some of your earlier academic courses. Don't worry, these fundamental business concepts aren't overly complex and can be grasped with minimal effort and practice. As project professionals, we must not be intimidated by the numbers, but must understand and embrace them to accurately represent and manage our project investments.

There are key business and financial concepts that are relevant to all projects. In this chapter we discuss these key concepts and focus on their applicability to business and to the overall financial bottom line. Many of these concepts have been used, misused, and even abused over the years, mainly because they weren't fully comprehended. Many of these concepts can indeed be confusing, especially for those without finance or business backgrounds, but rest assured, I'm going to simplify them for you here and you'll be able to leverage them on all of your future projects. Understanding these important concepts is no longer an option. Project investments that have been financially analyzed and evaluated incorrectly or inadequately have proven quite costly for far too many organizations. It's time to get back to the financial basics and to focus on those key concepts that are critical to fully understanding the financial viability of our projects.

My intent is to explain these concepts in a way that they can be understood easily and within the context of project and business management. We will use some fun examples, as well as real-world project examples to further solidify the comprehension of these important concepts. The mathematical theories and formulas inherent in these business concepts are important and I encourage you to spend some time in understanding them. We will address the relevant formulas and show how they are used to calculate key financial metrics, but the reality in today's business world is that we have spreadsheet programs that can do the calculations for us instantaneously. More power to the folks who want to perform the calculations by hand! But for all others, it's important to understand the conceptual background and context in which these subjects apply to our projects and to become familiar with the spreadsheet formulas used to calculate the key financial measurements. Let's dive right in!

Cash Flow Modeling

Cash flow modeling is one of the most important activities in building effective business cases and in determining the actual amounts of cash that will be expended, saved, or generated as a result of project implementations. Cash flow models are constructed by synthesizing all of the information that was gathered during the interviews, focus groups, questionnaires, and various other research efforts and then using that information to create a series of projected cash flows over a period of time, typically the useful life of a project. These models forecast how money will move in and out of organizations as a result of project implementations. Cash flow models help decision makers determine whether projects will generate enough money or achieve levels of cost savings that will cover or exceed the overall costs of their projects.

It's not only important to determine *how* much money will be spent or made, but *when* that money will be expended or generated as well. Cash flow models are effective ways to specifically ascertain when and how much money will come into and go out of organizations. The ultimate goal of cash flow modeling is to determine key financial ROI measurements to draw conclusions about the feasibility and profitability of potential projects. The forecasted outflow and inflow of cash and how far into the future these cash flows occur are key inputs into these important financial calculations.

All project initiatives are undertaken to provide some kind of future benefit. These future benefits, however, have costs associated with them. It's important to identify and separate the various cost elements and place them in the cash flow model where they are most likely to occur. Project costs are represented as *cash outflows* in cash flow models since cash flows out of a company when costs are incurred. *Cash inflows*, on the other hand, refer to money streams that come into a company as a result of a project. For a project to be financially attractive, these cash inflows must be greater than all of the combined cash outflows.

The ultimate goal for any business is to have more money coming in than is going out. Project teams should have the same goal, bearing in mind risk exposure and other key business considerations and requirements. When cash outflows are minimized and cash inflows are maximized, optimal business value can be attained. There are many ways in which projects can increase cash inflows, reduce cash outflows, or achieve an acceptable combination of the two.

Let's start with cash inflows, the money that flows into an organization. There are several ways to generate additional money with the use of projects. Projects that increase production output and sales are the more common ways. If a company produces and sells more widgets as a result of a project, this is an increase to the cash inflows and should be reflected accordingly in the cash flow model. Here are a few other examples of how projects can impact cash inflows:

- Increase repeat business from existing customers
- Acquire new customers
- Win business from competitors
- Merge with another company
- Expand into new markets or geographies
- Increase billable headcount
- Reduce equipment downtime
- Increase order fulfillment time

Now let's focus our attention on cash outflows. Cash outflows are the costs that occur at various points along the project timeline. Some of these costs will increase over time and, conversely, some of the costs will decrease. These fluctuations in costs must be reflected accordingly in the cash outflows portion of the model.

I would like to address the topic of decreased costs because many of our projects are cost savings initiatives and too often these costs savings are incorporated incorrectly into cash flow models. Costs savings are reductions to the cash outflows. *Cost savings are not cash inflows!* Cost savings must be reflected as a reduction to the cash outflows in the cash flow model and not as increases to the cash inflows. Projects that reduce costs *may* produce additional money streams, but cost savings by themselves are not money streams coming into an organization and should *only* be reflected in the cash outflows portion of the cash flow model. For instance, reducing staff is a reduction in costs and not a money generator. Renegotiating vendor contracts is a reduction in costs and does not produce additional revenue streams. Shutting down and consolidating facilities reduces costs but does not generate money.

There *may* be times when cost savings initiatives impact money streams coming into an organization. These impacts can be both positive and negative. If that facility shutdown and consolidation project will result in fewer products being sold, the project may decrease costs, but it will also decrease the money coming into the organization. These changes to both cash inflows and cash outflows must be reflected in the cash flow model. Doing otherwise would result in inaccurate ROI measurements.

Too often project professionals feel the need to show how their projects will generate additional money streams and will reflect cost savings as increases to the cash inflows. This is bad cash flow modeling! Cash inflows and cash outflows must be kept separate. Projects that reduce costs while not impacting cash inflows are still tremendously valuable for companies.

Here are some cost savings project examples:

- Organizational restructuring/Full-time employee (FTE) reduction
- Facilities consolidation and shutdown
- Vendor contract re-negotiation
- Re-work elimination or reduction
- Operating costs reduction
- Material cost savings
- Production costs reduction
- Systems maintenance reduction
- Employee retention improvement

To properly model cash flows, project teams need to collaborate with the various facets of their organizations to fully understand how money will flow in and out of their companies as a result of their projects. Cash outflows and cash inflows are important concepts to grasp and are at the heart and soul of any cash flow model. Table 10.1 is a simple model that illustrates how money

Table 10.1 Simple cash flow model example

		2012		2013		2014	
	Year 0	1st-half	2nd-half	1st-half	2nd-half	1st-half	2nd-half
Cash outflows							
Hardware purchase cost	(75,000)						
Maintenance and operations		(2,000)	(2,000)	(2,500)	(2,500)	(2,800)	(3,000)
Total cash outflow	(75,000)	(2,000)	(2,000)	(2,500)	(2,500)	(2,800)	(3,000)
Cash inflows							
Additional product revenue		20,000	24,000	26,000	30,000	32,000	33,000
New product revenue		5,000	5,500	8,000	17,000	22,000	24,000
Total cash inflows		25,000	29,500	34,000	47,000	54,000	57,000
Total initial cash flow	(75,000)	23,000	27,500	31,500	44,500	51,200	54,000

flows in and out of a business at various points along a three-year time period as a result of a hardware implementation project.

As depicted with this simple example, a large sum of money is initially expended (Year 0) to account for the hardware purchase. Additional costs are incurred for each subsequent half-year for maintenance and operations of the newly purchased asset. The model also shows the cash inflows, or financial benefits, that are expected to be achieved as a result of this new piece of machinery. In this example, the hardware is expected to generate more output of an existing product that will result in increased revenue streams, as shown with the first cash inflow. The second cash inflow depicts cash inflows that are expected as a result of a new product line that the asset is able to produce. Total cash flows, shown in the last row of the model, are the differences between how much money is expected to be spent versus how much money is forecasted to be made over this particular three-year time period.

The key inputs, estimates, forecasts, and assumptions should *always* be clearly defined and documented for all cash flow models. These important parameters greatly impact the cash flow patterns and results. When these parameters are visibly documented, management teams can better understand the logic behind the model, know all of the key assumptions and estimates and can even make adjustments to the parameters to determine how they impact the results. Some of the more common inputs, estimates, forecasts, and assumptions used in cash flow models are:

- Discount rate is 7.5%
- Tax rate is 35%

- 3-year straight-line depreciation is used
- FTE headcount increases 3% per year
- Unit production increases 1.5% per quarter
- Model does not adjust for inflation
- Value-enabling benefits are excluded from ROI calculations, to include improved safety, increased employee morale, and improved customer satisfaction
- Contingency costs are calculated as 10% of project labor costs
- Implementation costs include 10% travel expense
- Hardware maintenance is 10% of yearly hardware costs
- Software maintenance is 15% of yearly software costs
- Sales increase 5% per year
- Fully loaded FTE yearly cost is $105,000
- Cost escalation factor is 2% per year
- Benefit escalation factor is 2% per year

As we continue to discuss the relevant business and financial concepts in this chapter, we build on and incorporate these concepts into this project cash flow model example. For those who have crafted cash flow models before, you know we are only at the tip of the iceberg. At the end of this chapter we will have a fully developed cash flow model that integrates all of these important concepts. Once the cash flow model is fully built, we will then calculate important financial metrics to determine if this project investment example is a worthwhile pursuit. Before we progress, however, there are some words of caution I'd like to offer surrounding cash flow models.

Cash Flow Modeling Words of Caution

With cash flow modeling being at the heart and soul of the financial portion of any business case, some words of caution need to be offered. I've observed some poor business practices and overly broad assumptions made in the development of cash flow models. The most prevalent of these include:

- Dismissing or omitting relevant internal and external factors and influences
- Extending project timelines too far into the future for benefit attainment
- Building models in increments of years instead of smaller, more manageable time periods

As all of us know, nothing is static in today's competitive business world. Business is dynamic and is constantly changing. Too many business professionals, however, develop cash flow models without the consideration of this basic business phenomenon, and they treat their projects as if they were operating in that proverbial vacuum, free from internal and external influences, trends, and pressures. When forecasting cash outflows and inflows, these internal and external business factors are often dismissed or overlooked. These cash flow models, consequently, do not portray reliable or accurate business scenarios and usually overexaggerate the benefits.

Exacerbating these issues, project teams often view their proposed projects as more important and unique than they really are. The *we must implement this project or else* mentality often pervades their thoughts and actions because they view their projects as the panacea, the cure all, for all of the business problems. Well, guess what? Business isn't going to remain stagnant simply because a certain project wasn't implemented. Someone will eventually come up with another way to solve a business problem, address a certain issue, or make money for the company. The business environment will change with or without a certain project. Additionally, the *do nothing* option is always an option, and sometimes it's the best option. Project teams must be objective in building their cash flow models and use realistic data elements and assumptions in their creation.

With this being said, project teams need to be cognizant of all relevant business activities that are currently transpiring, or that will transpire and reflect them accordingly in their cash flow models. Project teams need to explore the business conditions that will exist with or without the implementation of their projects. The current state won't remain the current state forever. All future business initiatives and trends must be considered for inclusion in the cash flow model. Important questions to consider include:

- How are the current revenue streams and cost structures trending?
- What initiatives are underway within the organization that will affect the project?
- How will these initiatives affect the project deliverables?
- Will the project deliverables even be relevant once these initiatives have been implemented?
- What government regulations are being imposed that may affect project outcomes?
- What are the top risks facing the organization?

Project teams must get out of that proverbial vacuum and into the dynamic business world to explore both the internal and external environments to ensure that they are building models that accurately reflect the current and future business landscapes.

As an example, if a major outsourcing contract expires in six months and the leadership team plans to terminate that relationship and partner with another vendor and give the new vendor even more business, project teams should not build cash flow models that extend years into the future reflecting current vendor costs and FTE headcounts. Without knowledge of this upcoming business initiative, cash flow models won't even be close to accurate.

With foreknowledge of this change to the vendor landscape, however, project teams will be better equipped to build models that will reflect the future cost structures, organizational staffing levels, and financial benefits much more accurately. The project team may even determine that it's best to hold off on the project until the outsourcing deal has been finalized. Bottom line, there is a ton of business activity going on out there and it behooves project teams to know what is going on to accurately represent this vibrant business environment in their project cash flow models.

Another disconcerting trend I'd like to warn against is the desire to grossly extend the project time periods for benefit attainment. We know that business benefits derived from projects occur at some point in the future. Far too often, however, project teams develop cash flow models that extend *too* far into the future. When cash flows are unreasonably extended, ROI measurements will be overinflated, inaccurate, and will lead to poor decisions. I've seen cash flow models showing benefits 5+ years into the future when it was well known that the initial equipment purchases for those projects would be obsolete in just 3 years! Project professionals and business leaders need to raise red flags and be wary of cash flow models that seem unreasonably long and show business benefits occurring too far into the future. Business operations, marketing plans, product development efforts, vendor contracts, and competitive forces are constantly being modified and enhanced. On top of that, who knows when the next recession or economic downturn will occur? Time periods for cash flow models should be reasonable and appropriate for a given project at hand, and stakeholders should feel comfortable that the projected returns can indeed be realized, especially since they are accountable to the business for these financial returns.

In certain situations and for certain projects, it may be appropriate to build cash flow models that extend 5 to 10 years into the future. These projects normally deal with long-term, strategic business transformational or merger/acquisition endeavors. But 5- to 10-year cash flow models certainly aren't applicable for most projects. A lot can happen in 5 years, let alone 5+ years. The length of time for cash flow models is obviously dependent on the type of project, and 5-year, and even 10-year, models may be appropriate in certain instances. Uncertainty of the numbers, however, is greatly enhanced as the timeline is extended. How certain are we that a project solution will deliver certain financial benefits in year seven? I would venture to say a lot less certain than our projections for year three. Additionally, with more uncertainty, project teams may be more inclined to massage the numbers or take liberties with their assumptions to achieve desired results. Project teams often have preconceived notions about how their projects should turn out financially and may extend the timeline and finagle the number to achieve those results. Keeping the timeline at a reasonable length can prevent such bad, and borderline unethical, business practices.

So what is the appropriate timeframe for a cash flow model? This is a difficult question to answer without knowing the scope and magnitude of a project, or even the company or industry. Large, conservative companies operating in low-growth industries that have been around for some time may be better able to forecast project results further into the future than smaller, more dynamic start-up companies operating in high-growth industries. Most business professionals have a good feel for the business landscape 2 or 3, and maybe 3 or 4 years down the road, and business metrics for these time periods can be reflected fairly accurately. Quite often project teams automatically assume a 5-year time period for their projects. This invalid assumption is usually made because they've seen other models created in that manner and feel this is the standard. This is not the standard! Projects are unique, companies are unique, and the business environment is constantly changing. In some cases a 5-year time period may be reasonable and true business benefits will indeed be realized that far into the future. For other projects, five years may be entirely too long. Heck, how many employees even stay with the same company for five years these days? Project teams, sponsors, and key stakeholders should, carefully and collectively, determine the appropriate timeline to be used for cash flow models.

The last trend I'd like to warn against is the tendency to automatically assume that cash flow models need to be built in yearly time periods. Project teams often assume that cash flow models need to be built out in increments of years. This is not a valid assumption. Project teams should strive for granularity in building out their cash flow models. I find it's easier, in fact, to more accurately determine cash outflows and inflows when the time periods are in months, quarters, or half-years as opposed to merely years. For instance, instead of making a broad forecast that a profit stream will increase 6% after year two, it's better to reflect profit increases in smaller percentages as they are expected to occur. Profits may increase 2% after year one, an additional 2% after 1.5 years, and finally another 2% at the conclusion of year two, for a total of 6%.

When cash inflows and cash outflows are discounted on a yearly basis, this assumes that all cash flows occur on the last day of the year, which is not indicative of the real business world (more on discounting later in the chapter). Building cash flow models using smaller increments of time, such as half-years, quarters, or even months distributes and balances the cash flows more realistically. Discounting actual occurs, then, when the cash actually flows.

Building cash flow models in smaller increments can enhance a project team's ability in achieving a greater level of detail in the forecast analysis. Additionally, these detailed forecasts improve the accuracy of the ROI results. Table 10.2 shows three examples of how cash flow models can be built using different time periods. The first example shows a cash flow model using increments of quarters, the second in half-years, and the third in years. It's a good idea to build your models in increments of months as well (although more difficult to copy and paste into a document). Be sure to adjust the formulas

Table 10.2 Cash flow model examples

	1.5-year cash flow model						
	Q0	Q1, 2012	Q2, 2012	Q3, 2012	Q4, 2012	Q1, 2013	Q2, 2013
Cash outflows	−15,000	0	0	0	0	0	0
Cash inflows		2,000	5,000	7,000	7,000	8,000	10,000
Total cash flows	−15,000	2,000	5,000	7,000	7,000	8,000	10,000

	3-year cash flow model						
	H0	H1, 2012	H2, 2012	H1, 2013	H2, 2013	H1, 2014	H2, 2014
Cash outflows	−18,000	−3,000	−3,000	−3,000	−3,500	−3,500	−3,500
Cash inflows		5,000	5,000	7,000	7,000	8,000	10,000
Total cash flows	−18,000	2,000	2,000	4,000	3,500	4,500	6,500

	5-year cash flow model					
	Year 0	2012	2013	2014	2015	2016
Cash outflows	−75,000	−12,000	−15,000	−20,000	−25,000	−25,000
Cash inflows		50,000	55,000	60,000	80,000	95,000
Total cash flows	−75,000	38,000	40,000	40,000	55,000	70,000

in your spreadsheet programs to reflect the appropriate time period that you are using.

Time Value of Money

It is imperative that project personnel fully understand the time value of money concept. With a solid understanding of how the value of money changes over time, project professionals can accurately calculate key financial measurements to determine the financial viability of their projects. Additionally, project teams can analyze competing projects that produce different financial results over different time periods with true side-by-side, apples-to-apples comparisons. Project investments achieve financial returns at various points in the future. The financial returns that are realized in two years for one project cannot and should not be compared to the financial returns that another project realizes in three years. Even if the returns of these two projects are exactly the same, they occur at different time periods in the future, and therefore, cannot be considered equal. Confusing? Let's dive deeper.

Except for rare periods of significant deflation, a dollar, euro, pound, or yen is worth more today than it will be tomorrow or at some other point in the future. Conversely, a dollar (or whatever form of currency in use) today is worth less than it was yesterday, or at some other point in the past. The time value of money is the value of money taking into account a given amount of interest that could be earned over a given amount of time. The concept is normally associated with the interest rates that banks offer for deposits, as well as the interest rates that banks charge for loans. As an example, if you invested $100 of today's money for a one-year period that earns 6% interest, that $100 will be worth $106 after one year. The $100 today, therefore, is worth exactly $106 one year from today. So what does that tell us? To start, you would definitely want $100 *now* as opposed to $100 one year from now. The $100 in your drawer is worth more today than it would be one year from now if you simply kept it in your drawer. There is an opportunity cost of keeping the money locked up in your drawer and that is the interest that could have been earned on that money if it were invested.

A project that achieves a return of $50,000 in two years is more financially attractive than a project that achieves the same $50,000 in three years. If an organization implements the first project and makes $50,000 in two years, they can then invest that $50,000 at that point and, assuming the same 6% interest rate as the example, have $53,000 at the end of year three. But if the company chose to implement the second project, they would only have $50,000 at the end of this three-year time period. To reiterate, a dollar is worth more today than it is at some point in the future.

Project teams, sponsors, and stakeholders must utilize the time value of money concept when determining in which projects they should invest. Business leaders always have the option of investing elsewhere if they feel certain projects won't achieve acceptable levels of return. Utilizing the time value of money concept greatly assists with these difficult business decisions. The concepts of future value (FV) and present value (PV) are inherent in the time value of money and rely on the fundamental principles of compounding and discounting.

Compounding

You may remember how to calculate the FV of an investment from one of your early academic courses or even from your personal investment pursuits. The FV of an investment is the calculated value based on a rate of interest paid over a period of time. The basic formula for deriving the FV of an investment is:

$$FV = PV\,(1 + r \times n)$$

where

$$FV = \text{future value}$$
$$PV = \text{present value}$$
$$r = \text{interest rate}$$

$$n = \text{number of time periods}$$

What would the FV be on an investment of $1,000 that earns 5% interest over a 5-year period?

$$FV = \$1,000 \ (1 + .05 \times 5) = \$1,000 \times 1.25 = \$1,250$$

In this example, the investor made $250 in five years. Not bad, or is it? What is the problem with this analysis? Would you be willing to invest $1,000 for 5 years to earn $250? You shouldn't be, and here's why. This basic formula for FV doesn't incorporate the important concept of *compounding*. With the use of compounding, the FV of an investment is calculated on not only the original investment amount, but on the original investment amount *plus* the interest earned on that amount over the entire time period. You may have heard of the phrase *earning interest on interest*. This is where it applies.

Let's see what our original example looks like incorporating the compounding principle. The formula now becomes:

$$FV = PV \ (1 + i)^n$$
$$FV = \$1,000 \ (1 + .05)^5 = \$1,000 \ (1.28) = \$1,278$$

By incorporating the compounding principle and earning interest on the interest that was made over each time period, the FV in our example is worth $28 more.

We've all heard the financial folks on television urging people to start investing at an early age to take advantage of the principle of compounding so that they can retire early as millionaires. The pitch is typically along these lines: "If you're 30 years of age and you start with $20,000 and invest $600 a month earning 8% interest you can retire as a millionaire at age 60." Certainly not a bad deal! Compounding is indeed a powerful investing tool. (By the way, you can check the math with any online FV calculator, this is an accurate example).

Compounding is an important concept for determining the FV of money. The compounding principle, however, isn't used too often in the context of project management, but it sets us up for another important concept that is used extensively, or should be used extensively, in the financial evaluation of projects, and that is the concept of discounting. If you understand how compounding works, then discounting will make much more sense since this is, in a sense, compounding in reverse.

Discounting

In analyzing projects for financial attractiveness, we start by determining the cash flows over a given period of time. For most projects, money is usually spent in the beginning phases, with returns occurring months, or even years, down the road. As we now know, a dollar today is worth more than it is tomorrow or at some other point in the future. If we forecast financial returns for our projects 2, 3, 4, and even 5 years down the road, how can we determine what these returns are worth in today's money? Why do we even want to do that? Knowing the value of a project in today's money helps decision makers in determining if a project is a worthwhile investment. Quite often projects show positive returns in the future, but when these returns are discounted back to PV, they end up being negative financial returns! Additionally, by using the PV of competing project investments that have different returns occurring at various time periods in the future, business leaders can do true side-by-side comparisons of the projects and can make more informed decisions.

So how do we bring forecasted financial returns back to today's value? The answer is with *discounting*. To determine the PV of a future project payoff, the future payoff must be discounted. It is discounted by multiplying it by a predetermined discount rate. The discount rate is similar to the interest rate that is used with compounding, except in reverse. Let's illustrate this point with a fun example.

After four turbulent and challenging years, Johnny and his twin sister Susie finally graduate high school. Their mother is so proud of their achievement and urges them to maintain the momentum by enrolling in college. Knowing the frustrations and distractions that they encountered in high school, the mom decides to incent and motivate them financially to complete a four-year college degree. She shows Suzie $10,000 in hard cash and informs her that once she graduates college, she may have the money. She then shows Johnny $12,000 in cash (Johnny was always her favorite, plus she knew he would need more of an incentive to finish the degree) and offers the same deal to him. The mom then locked the money in two different safes and promised to unlock them when, and only when, they graduated college.

Suzie is a bit disgruntled about the inequitable deal, but nonetheless is excited to receive the $10,000 so she immediately enrolls in a four-year program. Johnny, on the other hand, isn't quite ready to go back into the world of academia and figures since he was offered more money he has the luxury of taking some time off so he decides to travel the world for three years and then go to college. Even though Johnny is offered a more substantial FV payoff, he isn't going to receive it until three years after Suzie gets her lesser payment, assuming all goes as planned. So, then, does he really have the better of the deals? Is the $10,000 that Suzie will receive four years from now a better payoff than the $12,000 that Johnny will receive seven years from now? This is a tough question to answer without understanding discounting and the PV of money concept. As project professionals, we are faced with these tough questions all of the time when analyzing competing project proposals. Rarely do competing proposals have similar returns and similar time periods for those returns.

Let's see if Suzie or Johnny gets the better payoff. The future payoffs must be discounted to PVs in order to do a true side-by-side comparison. The formula for calculating PV is:

$$PV = FV/(1 + r)^n$$

where

$$PV = \text{present value}$$
$$FV = \text{future value}$$
$$r = \text{discount rate}$$
$$n = \text{time periods}$$

Let's start with Suzie, assuming a discount rate of 8%:

$$PV = \$10,000/(1 + .08)^4$$
$$PV = \$10,000/1.36 = \$7,350$$

And now Johnny, using the same discount rate:

$$PV = \$12,000/(1 + .08)^7$$
$$PV = \$12,000/1.71 = \$7,002$$

Suzie has a greater payoff! Even though she was offered less money, by finishing her degree three years before Johnny, the PV of her payoff is more than her brother's payoff. Discounting can be looked at in terms of opportunity costs. By receiving the money three years after Suzie, Johnny eschewed the opportunity to earn interest on that money over this additional three-year time period. Suzie, meanwhile, can put her money into a conservative money market fund, a savings account, or even the stock market if she's willing to take on more risk, and then earn interest for the next three years while Johnny's money sits in the safe. The same concept applies to corporations. As they make money from projects, they can re-invest that money in other projects or in other investment areas to earn interest on that money. If projects don't deliver a profit, then there is no money to re-invest. The longer a company has to wait for a project to deliver financial returns, furthermore, the longer they have to wait before they can re-invest those returns to make even more money.

Since discounting is an important concept in evaluating projects and the basis for most everything else we discuss in this chapter, let's use one more fun example to make sure we are comfortable with the concept.

It's your lucky day. You just won $1.0 million dollars! But, you have the option of receiving:

1. $1.5 million in six years
2. $2.0 million in ten years
3. Take the $1.0 million now

So with Option 1 you can receive $500,000 more than you would receive today, and with Option 2 you would receive $1,000,000 more! (The zeroes were added for emphasis.)

Which one do you choose (sticking with the 8% discount rate)?

Option 1

$$PV = \$1,500,000/(1 + .08)^6$$
$$PV = \$1,500,000/1.59 = \$945,254$$

Option 2

$$PV = \$2,000,000/(1 + .08)^{10}$$
$$PV = \$2,000,000/2.16 = \$926,386$$

Take the money and run! A million today is worth more than $1.5 million in 6 years or $2.0 million in 10 years, assuming an 8% discount rate.

In the examples, we used 8% as the discount rate. Where did we get this rate? What is the significance of this rate? Obviously, the discount rate affects the PV of future payoffs. The higher the discount rate, the lower the PV (the future payoff is discounted to a greater degree). The lower the discount rate, the higher the PV (the future payoff is discounted to a lesser degree). But what is the appropriate rate to use for our projects? How is this rate derived? These are *very* important questions, and the answers lie in a concept in which you may be familiar, and that concept is the weighted average cost of capital (WACC).

Weighted Average Cost of Capital

Many of us have developed cash flow models for our projects and even applied discounting principles to calculate certain financial formulas. Most of us, however, usually simply use the standard corporate discount rate or make a few phone calls to the finance team to ask what discount rate to use. We then normally apply that rate to our models without asking further questions or knowing how this rate was determined in the first place. These procedures certainly aren't wrong or even inappropriate, but in continuing with these procedures, we will never fully understand the significance of the discount rate, how the finance folks determined its value, or even if they determined it correctly. After reading this section, you will still want to ask the finance team about the discount rate to use, but you will be well-equipped to have intelligent conversations with them about your organization's capital structure, cost of debt, cost of equity, WACC and, ultimately, the discount rate.

Many project professionals know that the discount rate is used for discounting purposes and takes into account risk and opportunity costs, but that's pretty much it. The origin of how this rate is determined is quite foreign to a lot of business professionals, even the most astute project practitioners. It's time to set the record straight once and for all on this important concept. Project professionals must no longer perform cash flow analyses without fully understanding how the discount rate was determined and its significance to their projects and organizations.

Let's start from the beginning. When you are assigned to a project, do you ever wonder how all of the project costs are paid? How does the company pay for the labor, hardware, software, vendors, training, travel, and all other project costs? Where does the money come from? Projects, as well as other business initiatives, are funded by using debt, equity, or a combination of the two. More often than not they are paid by using a combination of both debt and equity. Let's discuss debt and equity.

Debt is how much money a company has borrowed from various financial institutions to finance projects, capital purchases, operations, and other areas of the business. Companies pay off their debt over fixed periods of time at certain interest rates. Interest rates may vary across the various financial institutions that are lending the money. Corporations often use a blended rate to account for the rate differences of the various loans and bonds that they acquire. This blended rate is typically referred to as the cost of debt, which is expressed as a percentage. A key advantage to financing projects and other business elements with debt is that companies don't have to forfeit additional control and ownership of their businesses. As long as companies pay off their debts, lenders cannot impose their will or obtain any ownership of the businesses. As soon as debts are paid off, relationships between borrowers and lenders end.

Equity, on the other hand, is money that is raised by corporations by selling stock to individual or institutional investors, in addition to retained earnings from everyday business operations. In return for the money invested in companies, shareholders receive ownership interests in those companies. The amount of ownership depends on how much they invested. The more money they invested, the more ownership they obtain. Corporations do not incur any debt with equity financing, but they do give up ownership and varying degrees of control to the shareholders. Shareholders also expect a certain financial return for their investment. This is the cost of equity, which is expressed as a percentage. If they receive this return, they will normally be satisfied and remain investors. If, however, they are not satisfied with the returns, they may pull their investments and pursue other investment opportunities where their expectations can be met. It is important, therefore, for companies to meet the financial expectations of their shareholders.

Equity comprises three major elements:

1. **Common stock**—basically what it sounds like, common, everyday stock that people buy and sell. It is a piece of paper that represents

some degree of ownership of a corporation. Investors in common stock receive one vote per stock owned to elect board members. If a company goes bankrupt, common stock investors will not get paid what they are owed until creditors, bondholders, and preferred stockholders receive their payments.

2. **Preferred stock**—owned by preferred shareholders, as the name implies. All of a company's earnings and assets go directly to the preferred shareholders before anyone else. Because preferred shareholders are paid before common shareholders, they give up their right to vote in the election of board members.

3. **Retained earnings**—profits that companies make but do not return to the shareholders in the form of dividends. This money is retained by companies usually to be re-invested in its core business functions, to fund projects, to buy new machinery, or to pay off debt.

You may be wondering why companies incur any debt at all when they can finance their projects using retained earnings or other forms of equity. Let me ask you these questions: Did you buy your car with cash or take out a loan? What about your home? Do you buy your daily groceries by taking out a loan? What about your jeans? As you can see, it makes sense to purchase some things by incurring debt and other things by using cash. Businesses operate in the same manner. When a financial institution considers loaning money to a corporation, their representatives will examine the corporation's debt to equity ratio. This ratio shows the amount of debt compared to the amount of equity that the corporation maintains. Investors need this information to know if the corporation has an adequate amount of money available for repayment in the case of default, as well as to ensure that the business is being run in a sensible way without too much dependence on any one source.

Every company maintains some form of capital structure to pay for things to keep their business running and, hopefully, profitable. This capital structure determines what percentage of debt and what percentage of equity will be used to make payments for assets and to fund projects. Capital structures vary greatly from company to company. One company may have a 60% debt to 40% equity structure, while another may have a 40% debt to 60% equity structure, while another may prefer a 50/50 split. Companies who want to retain control of their operations and limit the interference from investors will be heavily focused on debt financing. Companies that are fearful of debt and want to leverage investors will focus more on equity financing.

So what does all of this mean and what does it have to do with the WACC? It is a calculation, expressed as a percentage, of a firm's cost of capital in which each category of capital (debt and equity) is proportionately weighted. The WACC is determined by adding together the weighted cost of debt and the weighted cost of equity. It ascertains how much interest a company has to pay for every dollar it finances. It is often viewed as the *borrowing rate* that is applied to the money that is used to pay for projects and other business purchases. A project's financial return must be greater than the money being borrowed to fund the project.

The WACC is the most appropriate rate to use when discounting cash flows for projects. Since projects are being financed at the WACC, it makes good business sense to discount future payoffs at this rate to determine the profitability of projects. It uses weighted percentages of both debt and equity that takes into account the company's tolerance for risk. The WACC is obtained by adding the weighted cost of debt and the weighted cost of equity. The basic formula is:

$$\text{WACC} = (\%\text{ debt} \times \text{cost of debt}) + (\%\text{ equity} \times \text{cost of equity})$$

One important aspect concerning the WACC calculation that should not be overlooked is that interest costs on debt are tax deductible (much like home mortgages). The cost of debt, then, is typically expressed as an after-tax value. The formula for after-tax WACC is:

$$\text{WACC} = (\%\text{ debt} \times \text{cost of debt})\,(1 - \text{income tax rate}) + (\%\text{ equity} \times \text{cost of equity})$$

where

  % debt = the amount of debt, as a percentage, of the capital structure
  Cost of debt = the blended interest rate owed on all debts
  % equity = the amount of equity, as a percentage, of the capital structure
  Cost of equity = the minimum rate of return that shareholders expect to receive for investing in a company and taking on risk

Table 10.3 presents a common corporate capital structure and shows typical costs for debt and equity. We will use the numbers in this table to perform a WACC calculation.

In applying the values in the table to determine the WACC, we obtain:

$$((40\% \times 13.3\%) \times (1 - 35\%)) + (60\% \times 9.2\%) = 8.98\%$$

In this example, 8.98% is the WACC, or borrowing rate, that project professionals should use in discounting cash flows to assess the financial attractive-

Table 10.3 WACC calculation example

	Capitalization (%)	Cost (%)	Income tax rate	Weight (%)
Debt	40	13.3	35	3.46
Equity	60	9.2	N/A	5.52
WACC	100			8.98

ness of their projects. Projects must have a financial return greater than 8.98% for them to be profitable.

The WACC is an interesting and important business concept. Now when you make those calls to the finance folks, you can have fruitful conversations around the intricacies of this fascinating topic.

Depreciation

Depreciation is a noncash expense that reduces the value of an asset over a period of time as a result of wear and tear, age, or obsolescence, and before we can calculate the key financial measurements to evaluate our projects, we must first account for depreciation. Many assets that are purchased for projects lose their value over time, or depreciate, and must be replaced at the end of their useful lives. With depreciation, corporations can expense these assets over a period of time instead of all at once.

What does all of this mean and how does it relate to our projects? Spreading out expenses in such a manner reduces the total tax liability for companies. Depreciation expenses are subtracted from overall cash flows, thus reducing the amount of cash flows coming into an organization. Since corporations have to pay taxes on the income that they make, any reduction in this money is a reduction in the income taxes that need to be paid, which is a real financial benefit for a company. Since it is a noncash expense, depreciation lowers the company's reported earnings while increasing free cash flow. If depreciation isn't accounted for, companies would show greater income streams and would, consequently, have to pay more in taxes. Project teams need to identify all project assets and determine if, and how, they should be depreciated.

Depreciation expenses typically begin when assets are placed into service or into production environments. There are several accounting methods that are used to compute depreciation expenses. Some of the more popular methods include straight-line, fixed percentage, and declining balance. Methods of computing depreciation may vary according to the assets that are purchased. Additionally, the accounting methods and the length of the depreciable lives of assets may be subject to the tax laws of a particular country. Project teams should consult with their accounting and finance departments to determine the appropriate method.

In most cases, straight-line depreciation is used because it is the most common method and easiest to use. With this method, the original cost of the asset, less its salvage value at the end of its useful life, is expensed in equal increments over the time of its useful life. The salvage value is an estimate of the value of the asset at the time it can be sold. Quite often there is no salvage value at the end of an asset's useful life. As an example, an asset that costs $10,000 may be expensed at $2,000 per year using straight-line depreciation for a useful life of 5 years with no salvage value ($2,000 × 5 = $10,000). Now

Table 10.4 Cash flow model incorporating depreciation

	Year 0	2012		2013		2014	
		1st-half	2nd-half	1st-half	2nd-half	1st-half	2nd-half
Cash outflows							
Hardware purchase cost	(75,000)						
Maintenance and operations		(2,000)	(2,000)	(2,500)	(2,500)	(2,800)	(3,000)
Total cash outflow	(75,000)	(2,000)	(2,000)	(2,500)	(2,500)	(2,800)	(3,000)
Cash inflows							
Additional product revenue		20,000	24,000	26,000	30,000	32,000	33,000
New product revenue		5,000	5,500	8,000	17,000	22,000	24,000
Total cash inflows		25,000	29,500	34,000	47,000	54,000	57,000
Total initial cash flow	(75,000)	23,000	27,500	31,500	44,500	51,200	54,000
Depreciation expense	(75,000)	(12,500)	(12,500)	(12,500)	(12,500)	(12,500)	(12,500)
Total pre-tax cash flows	(75,000)	10,500	15,000	19,000	32,000	38,700	41,500

let's revisit our previous example and see how depreciation affects the total cash flow. Table 10.4 illustrates how depreciation expenses lower the overall cash flows for our project example.

As can be seen, the total initial cash flow has been reduced after taking depreciation into account. The $75,000 purchase price for the asset was spread out and expensed in equal payments over the three-year time period. With cash flows reduced, the company will pay less in taxes. This is not too different from what you do when you prepare your tax returns. When you write-off certain expenses, your total taxable yearly income is reduced, thereby lowering the amount of taxes you owe to the government. Let's explore the topic of taxes and see how cash flows are further impacted.

Income Tax

They say there are only two things certain in life: death and taxes. Corporations may be able to avoid the former, but they certainly can't avoid the latter. Taxes lower the overall financial benefits that companies achieve. The higher the taxes, the lower the financial gains; the lower the taxes, the higher the gains. For instance, if the income tax rate is 30%, a $10,000 operating gain generated by a project becomes $7,000 once taxes are taken out. But if that income tax rate was 35%, the $10,000 financial gain then becomes only $6,500. As can be seen with this simple example, taxes can have significant impacts on project results and should, therefore, be included in cash flow models.

But it's not all bad. As we know, there will be times when we will have to implement projects that simply won't deliver positive returns. We still have to perform the necessary analyses, as well as the financial calculations to determine the extent of the losses. Projects that lose money for a company, or lose money in certain time periods, lower the company's overall operating gains. By lowering the operating gains, the tax liabilities of the company are lowered, meaning they will have to pay less in taxes. To reflect this benefit in the project cash flow model, we simply apply the income tax rate to the operating loss. Using a 30% income tax rate for a $2,000 project loss would be reflected as a $1,400 loss in the cash flow model $(-\$2,000) \times (1 - .30) = -\$1,400$.

Project professionals should build their cash flow on an after-tax basis. Taxes are a real expense and can significantly affect the cash flows of projects. Let's go back to our original example and see how taxes affect the overall operating gains. Table 10.5 illustrates how a 30% income tax rate affects overall cash flows.

Now that we have the after-tax cash flows firmly established, we can proceed to discounting these future payoffs to PVs to calculate the necessary ROI financial measurements.

Table 10.5 Cash flow model incorporating taxes

	Year 0	2012		2013		2014	
		1st-half	2nd-half	1st-half	2nd-half	1st-half	2nd-half
Cash outflows							
Hardware purchase cost	(75,000)						
Maintenance and operations		(2,000)	(2,000)	(2,500)	(2,500)	(2,800)	(3,000)
Total cash outflow	(75,000)	(2,000)	(2,000)	(2,500)	(2,500)	(2,800)	(3,000)
Cash inflows							
Additional product revenue		20,000	24,000	26,000	30,000	32,000	33,000
New product revenue		5,000	5,500	8,000	17,000	22,000	24,000
Total cash inflows		25,000	29,500	34,000	47,000	54,000	57,000
Total initial cash flow	(75,000)	23,000	27,500	31,500	44,500	51,200	54,000
Depreciation expense		(12,500)	(12,500)	(12,500)	(12,500)	(12,500)	(12,500)
Total pre-tax cash flows	(75,000)	10,500	15,000	19,000	32,000	38,700	41,500
Income taxes on cash flow		(150)	(600)	(1,800)	(5,400)	(7,410)	(8,550)
After-tax cash flow	(75,000)	10,350	14,400	17,200	26,600	31,290	32,950

Discounted Cash Flow

We've discussed cash flow modeling, time value of money, discounting, depreciation, and taxes, and now it's time to combine all of these and move on to the topic of discounted cash flow (DCF) modeling. A DCF model is a project cash flow summary that has been adjusted to reflect the time value of money. DCF analysis takes future cash flow projections and discounts them to arrive at PVs that are used to calculate ROI financial measurements. If the PV of financial benefits is higher than that of all of the costs of attaining those benefits, the project opportunity may be a good one. Project investments with the greatest DCF are usually the best project investments.

We now know from the preceding section that the most appropriate rate used to discount FVs to PVs is the WACC. Although not usually the case, separate projects within a corporation may require different discount rates. These differences are usually a result of the risk factors inherent within each of the projects. The baseline discount rate, however, is almost certainly the WACC that can then be adjusted depending on the levels of risks of the various projects. With projects that have higher risks and more uncertain future cash flows, companies may choose to use higher discount rates. With a higher rate, FVs are discounted more, which lowers the PV of earnings. The lower the PV of earnings, the less financially attractive projects become.

Let's go back to our previous example and see how the after-tax cash flows are affected when discounting them to PVs. Table 10.6 shows the cash flows that have been discounted to PVs using an 8% discount rate. For each half-year period, we used the PV formula to obtain these values: $PV = FV/(1 + r)^n$. Keep in mind that since we are dealing with half-year time periods, the discount rate, r, had to be divided by 2.

As noted, the after-tax cash flows are lowered since they were converted to PVs by applying the 8% discount rate to them. The $75,000 cost of the asset is not impacted because Year 0 *is* the PV.

We now have the cash flow model to the point where we can start calculating key financial measurements to determine the financial attractiveness and feasibility of our projects.

Table 10.6 Cash flow model incorporating discounting

	Year 0	2012		2013		2014	
		1st-half	2nd-half	1st-half	2nd-half	1st-half	2nd-half
Cash outflows							
Hardware purchase cost	(75,000)						
Maintenance and operations		(2,000)	(2,000)	(2,500)	(2,500)	(2,800)	(3,000)
Total cash outflow	(75,000)	(2,000)	(2,000)	(2,500)	(2,500)	(2,800)	(3,000)
Cash inflows							
Additional product revenue		20,000	24,000	26,000	30,000	32,000	33,000
New product revenue		5,000	5,500	8,000	17,000	22,000	24,000
Total cash inflows		25,000	29,500	34,000	47,000	54,000	57,000
Total initial cash flow	(75,000)	23,000	27,500	31,500	44,500	51,200	54,000
Depreciation expense		(12,500)	(12,500)	(12,500)	(12,500)	(12,500)	(12,500)
Total pre-tax cash flow	(75,000)	10,500	15,000	19,000	32,000	38,700	41,500
Income taxes on cash flow		(150)	(600)	(1,800)	(5,400)	(7,410)	(8,550)
After-tax cash flow	(75,000)	10,350	14,400	17,200	26,600	31,290	32,950
Discounted cash flow	(75,000)	9,952	13,314	15,291	22,738	25,718	26,041

Professional Development Game Plan for Success

1. Cash flow modeling is necessary to build effective business cases and to determine the actual amounts of cash that will be expended, saved, or generated as a result of a project. The more accurate the cash flow models, the more accurate the forecasted ROI measurements. There are several important concepts inherent in cash flow modeling in which project professionals must be knowledgeable, capable, and skilled. These concepts include cash outflows, cash inflows, estimating, forecasting, time value of money, discounting, depreciation, and taxes. How comfortable are you with these concepts? Would you be able to build out a cash flow model on your own? Are you competent with spreadsheets and formulas?

   Action Plan

   a. Carefully analyze two or three cash flow models from within your organization. These models don't need to come from a project in which you were involved. In fact, it's best to try to get your hands on models from other projects so that you will have no preconceived notions while conducting this exercise. Based on what you learned in this chapter, evaluate these cash flow models. Did they incorporate all of the key elements? Were the assumptions and forecasts clearly listed and reasonable? Were appropriate discounting principles applied? Were the timeframes for benefit realization reasonable? Were the models easy to follow and understand? As a result of your analysis, write down three to five strengths for each of the models. What was effective in the models? Now write down three to five weaknesses, flaws, inaccuracies, or ambiguities that you've identified for each of the models. What was not so effective?

   b. As a result of this analysis, what activities or techniques will you incorporate when building out your next project cash flow model to ensure it is as accurate as possible? Write down five to eight key actions you will take or techniques you will implement. If you are not normally involved in cash flow models, think of ways in which you can be. These skill sets can go a long way for your professional development and career. Start writing!

2. As we discussed in detail in this chapter, the WACC is the most appropriate rate to use when discounting cash flows for your projects. Do you know your company's WACC? Do you know how your company determined this important percentage? Knowing how the WACC was determined can tell you a lot about your company.

Action Plan

   a. Let's see if you can find out a bit more about your firm. You already know your company's mission statement and strategic objectives by heart, right? Now let's see if you can determine how your company finances projects and other business initiatives. Do the necessary research, make the appropriate phone calls, or set up the appropriate meetings to determine your company's percent of debt, cost of debt, percent of equity, and cost of equity. Once you have this information, you can determine the WACC. Is this the discount rate you use on projects? Why or why not? Have you identified any issues or inconsistencies? Write down the formula, calculations, and key observations. This exercise should generate a lot of interesting discussions with folks within your company as well as provide you with a good understanding of how your company spends money on your projects.

   b. If all of this is gibberish to you, find a basic financial management class and take it. It's an important foundation to have in this field.

References

1. Heerkens, Gary R. 2006. *The Business-Savvy Project Manager*. New York, NY: McGraw-Hill.
2. Kodukula, Prasad, and Chandra Papudesu. 2006. *Project Valuation Using Real Options*. Fort Lauderdale, FL: J. Ross Publishing.
3. Schmidt, Marty J. 2002. *The Business Case Guide*. Boston, MA: Solution Matrix.

11

ROI Financial Measurements

A nickel ain't worth a dime anymore.

—Yogi Berra

ROI Is Merely One Component in the ROI Evaluation

When financial investors analyze companies to determine which stocks to purchase, they look at more than merely revenue or income. They evaluate a variety of metrics to achieve better insight into the overall financial and business health and the stability of companies. Such metrics include price-to-earnings ratio, debt-to-equity, return on assets, return on equity, net profit margin, and dividend yield. With detailed analyses of *all* of these key measurements, investors can make better and more informed decisions about their investments.

The evaluation of project investments is no different. As project professionals, we must embrace and use four key measurements when analyzing and evaluating our projects. These key measurements include:

1. Net present value (NPV)
2. Return on investment (ROI)
3. Internal rate of return (IRR)
4. Payback period

All of these measurements are returns on project investments. For this reason, we are using the general term ROI to refer to all four of these project measurements. In determining and evaluating *all* of these ROI measurements, we can gain a better understanding, acquire deeper insight, and determine the financial strength and viability of project investments with confidence. Let's jump into these important ROI measurements.

Net Present Value

NPV is one of the most important, if not *the* most important, financial measurement used when evaluating projects. NPV calculates the amount of money, in today's dollars, that a project is expected to make for a company. This calculation does not deal in percentages, abstract numbers, or ambiguous terms; it states, in hard cash, how much money a business will make or lose as a result of a project. If the NPV is positive, the company will make money; if it is negative the company will lose money; and if it is 0, the company will neither make nor lose money, but will cover the total costs of the project and break even. NPV is paramount in determining the attractiveness and viability of projects and has become a standard measurement tool for many organizations in the project selection process.

Technically speaking, NPV is the net present worth of a time series of cash flows, both incoming and outgoing. It accounts for the uneven cash flow streams that are typical in project investments. It is the sum of the present values of each of these individual cash flows. It can be viewed as the difference between the discounted present value of benefits and the discounted present value of costs. The formula for NPV is:

$$NPV = CF \text{ (year 0)}/(1 + r)^0 + CF \text{ (year 1)}/(1 + r)^1 + CF \text{ (year } T)/(1 + r)^T$$

where

CF = cash flow
r = discount rate
T = total time periods (useful life of the project)

By calculating the NPV, companies will know the amount of money that is expected to be generated and returned to the company's cash reserves that can then be used to pay shareholders, reduce debt, or re-invest in other projects or business initiatives. For these reasons, NPV is an important number and a valuable measurement in planning for future business initiatives.

Let's go back to our project example and determine its NPV. Since we've already calculated the present values for each of the time periods, as shown in the last row of Table 11.1, all we have to do now is add them up to determine the NPV. In doing the addition, we come up with:

(75,000) + 9,952 + 13,314 + 15,291 + 22,738 + 25,718 + 26,041 = \$38,053

The NPV for our project investment example is \$38,053. It's a positive number, so that's a good thing. It's definitely a nice chunk of change, considering it came in only three years, so that's also a good thing. It's not an extraordinarily

Table 11.1 Cash flow model example

	Year 0	2012		2013		2014	
		1st-half	2nd-half	1st-half	2nd-half	1st-half	2nd-half
Cash outflows							
Hardware purchase cost	(75,000)						
Maintenance and operations		(2,000)	(2,000)	(2,500)	(2,500)	(2,800)	(3,000)
Total cash outflow	(75,000)	(2,000)	(2,000)	(2,500)	(2,500)	(2,800)	(3,000)
Cash inflows							
Additional product revenue		20,000	24,000	26,000	30,000	32,000	33,000
New product revenue		5,000	5,500	8,000	17,000	22,000	24,000
Total cash inflows		25,000	29,500	34,000	47,000	54,000	57,000
Total initial cash flow	(75,000)	23,000	27,500	31,500	44,500	51,200	54,000
Depreciation expense		(12,500)	(12,500)	(12,500)	(12,500)	(12,500)	(12,500)
Total pre-tax cash flows	(75,000)	10,500	15,000	19,000	32,000	38,700	41,500
Income taxes on cash flow		(150)	(600)	(1,800)	(5,400)	(7,410)	(8,550)
After-tax cash flow	(75,000)	10,350	14,400	17,200	26,600	31,290	32,950
Discounted cash flow	(75,000)	9,952	13,314	15,291	22,738	25,718	26,041

amount of money, considering that the initial investment was $75,000, so we shouldn't sign off on the project just yet. But so far things are looking good for this project investment. Let's explore the other financial measurements to ensure the results trend favorably and that there are no hidden surprises.

Return on Investment

We've all heard this term used loosely a thousand times, if not more. ROI has become *the* buzzword over the past few years and people like to throw it out there at every given opportunity. ROI is appealing to most business professionals because it seems fairly straightforward. Well it is, but unfortunately, too straightforward to be the sole indicator of a project's financial viability or attractiveness. In fact, we need to be careful with lending too much credence to this financial measurement, because there are inherent flaws in it when dealing with long-term projects, multiple cash flows, depreciable assets, and taxes. But it does offer a comparison of the overall project financial benefits to the overall costs, which is beneficial. For this reason, ROI should be included in the evaluation of projects.

ROI is expressed as a percentage and is based on financial returns over a pre-determined time period. ROI analysis compares the magnitude of investment gains directly with the summation of all of the investment costs. A high ROI indicates that project financial benefits compare favorably to the total costs incurred by the project. ROI can be increased by minimizing project costs, maximizing the returns, or accelerating the project returns.

The basic formula for ROI, not taking into account the time value of money, is simply the return, or incremental gain, achieved from a project solution divided by the cost of that project solution:

$$\text{Basic ROI} = (\text{total benefits} - \text{total costs})/\text{total costs}$$

If a project investment costs $100 and quickly produces financial benefits of $150, it has a 50% ROI: ($150 − $100)/$100 = 50%.

This basic ROI equation may be used for projects with immediate paybacks, typically less than a year. But for those projects that produce benefits after one year, which is the majority of our projects, the ROI formula must incorporate the time value of money:

$$\text{ROI} = (\text{NPV total benefits} - \text{NPV total costs})/\text{NPV total costs}$$

Since ROI only deals with the total costs and the total benefits of a project, and doesn't deal with the cash flows resulting from these costs and benefits, it's best to keep depreciation and taxes out of the equation, since they deal primarily with cash flows (one of the reasons why ROI should not be the exclusive measuring tool for project evaluation).

Let's go back to our project cash flow model example and determine if the return on investment is a favorable one. We need to incorporate only two numbers into the ROI formula, the NPV of the benefits and the NPV of the costs. The total benefits for the project are listed in the Total Cash Inflows row, and the total costs are listed in the Total Cash Outflows row. We need to apply discounting to these values to determine the present values. We then simply add up the present values for each of the time periods to get the NPV of the total benefits and the NPV of the total costs. Table 11.2 shows these calculations.

Now all we have to do is plug the NPV values into the ROI formula and we obtain:

$$ROI = (211,147 - 87,804)/87,804 = 140\%$$

The NPV for this project example is 140%. This is a high number that indicates that the financial benefits of the project far outweigh the costs. This is good, but somewhat expected in simply looking over the numbers in the cash flow model. I would like to point out that ROI results are *extremely* dependent on the length of the analysis. ROI results can become quite high when the analysis covers many years, especially when financial benefits keep occurring far into the future. To illustrate this point, let's compare the ROI results for our cash flow model for various time periods. At the exact mid-point of our project (1st-half of 2013), the ROI is only 1%. At the end of 2013 the ROI is 46% and in mid-2014 the ROI is 94%. (Go ahead, run the numbers, it will be good practice for you!) Increases in ROI values come as no surprise as benefits keep occurring and rising; I want to point out the magnitude of these increases. For this reason, I can't emphasize enough the importance of keeping the cash flow analysis to a reasonable time period. As project professionals, we must show accurate ROI results, not inflated ones.

There are additional flaws inherent in the ROI formula when it is applied to corporate projects. When two projects have the same ROI, let's say 25%, they are both financially attractive and equally beneficial to an organization, right? Let's run some numbers to see if you are right or wrong. Table 11.3 shows three projects and their associated benefits, costs, and ROIs. As can be seen, all three have the same returns on their investments, but all three generate differing NPV benefits. In most cases, Project November would be the best project to implement because it makes the most money for the company. This is yet another reason why we look at more than ROI when evaluating projects.

We now know that our project has a favorable ROI and that it will make us money due to the positive NPV. Let's now focus on the yearly return rate we can expect from this project. We can determine this rate by calculating the IRR.

Table 11.2 Benefit and cost NPVs

	Year 0	2012		2013		2014		NPV
		1st-half	2nd-half	1st-half	2nd-half	1st-half	2nd-half	
Total cash inflows		25,000	29,500	34,000	47,000	54,000	57,000	
Discounted cash inflow		24,038	27,274	30,226	40,176	44,384	45,048	211,147
Total cash outflows	(75,000)	(2,000)	(2,000)	(2,500)	(2,500)	(2,800)	(3,000)	
Discounted cash outflows	(75,000)	(1,923)	(1,849)	(2,222)	(2,137)	(2,301)	(2,371)	(87,804)

Table 11.3 Project ROI comparisons

Project	NPV incremental benefits	NPV costs	ROI (%)
Project Lima	$5000	$4000	25
Project Mike	$2000	$1600	25
Project November	$8000	$6400	25

Internal Rate of Return

IRR has been confusing business professionals for a very, very long time. IRR is typically calculated in business cases, mainly because it's simple to do with spreadsheet programs once the cash flow model has been developed. Most professionals know that a high IRR is a good thing and a low one is a bad thing, and they take this into account when evaluating projects. The interpretation of the IRR results, however, is a different story. Is the IRR really the ROI? If not, what's the difference between ROI and IRR? What is the significance of IRR? Why do we even need it? These are not only common questions, but good ones. Let's get to the bottom of this important, yet confusing topic once and for all.

The IRR, expressed as a percentage, is the *yearly* rate at which an organization expects to recover its investment in a project. It is the annual compound interest rate that can be gained from the money that was invested in the project. The IRR determines whether a project's yearly rate of return exceeds the interest rate that a company is paying on the money that was borrowed to fund the project. This is the borrower's rate that we've discussed, or the weighted average cost of capital (WACC). (See, this WACC thing really is an important concept after all.) If the IRR is greater than the rate of financing the project, then a surplus will remain after all of the finance costs are paid. When the project exceeds the WACC, the project is a good investment, financially speaking. The IRR provides decision makers with a better feel for how good the project investment really is.

Technically, the IRR for a project investment is the rate for which the NPV of cash inflows equals the NPV of cash outflows. It's the rate where the NPV of all cash flows equals 0. If we take our NPV formula, then, and assign an NPV value of 0, we can determine the IRR by solving for r:

$$0 = CF \text{ (year 0)}/(1 + r)^0 + CF \text{ (year 1)}/(1 + r)^1 + CF \text{ (year } T)/(1 + r)^T$$

IRR tells us how high interest rates would have to go to wipe out the value of a project investment. So if debt and equity finance charges (key components of the WACC) increase to the point where they are equal to the IRR, the project won't make money for the company, won't lose money, but will break even. In a sense, a company would be funding a project with a loan, let's say at 12%, and using that loan money to invest in a project that earns the same 12%. The project investment value is wiped out; the financial value is $0. Financially speaking, what's the point? Projects with higher IRRs, therefore, are safer from the dangers of rising interest rates than ones with lower IRRs.

IRR is expressed as a compound yearly percentage rate, whereas ROI spans the entire length of a project investment. For this reason, IRR will be a lower number since it only looks at an annual rate instead of the rate spanning multiple years. We've already seen how ROI numbers can be grossly exaggerated when project cash flows are extended too far into the future. Since IRR is a yearly rate, the numbers usually aren't overly exaggerated. When they are unusually high, the cash flow model may be flawed or it may mean that a calculation was done incorrectly.

IRR gives no indication about the magnitude of the overall project return; it doesn't account for the amount of wealth generated. It is more of an indicator of the overall efficiency, quality, or yield of a project investment. A small investment may lead to a tremendous IRR. In many cases, a smaller IRR is preferred if it brings in a larger net cash flow, or NPV. Some companies use IRR as hurdle rates for new project investments. For example, a company might decide that a new computer system requires an IRR of 15% or more for the project to be approved.

Let's see what the IRR is for our project cash flow example. Again, more power to the folks who want to perform this calculation by hand, but for expediency purposes we will rely on the spreadsheet to do the work for us. In calculating the IRR, we must apply the formula to the after-tax cash flow, not the discounted cash flow (DCF)! The IRR applies the appropriate discounting to make the NPV equal to 0. In performing this calculation, the IRR for our after-tax cash flow is 15.49%. This seems like a reasonable number since we know we will receive an adequate NPV for the project and the ROI was positive. It is quite a few percentage points higher than the WACC, which is a good thing. So our project is expected to achieve 15.49% yearly returns on the money that was used to finance it. So far, so good. Now let's see how long we have to wait before we start seeing some of this money. We do this by determining the payback period.

Payback Period

Business leaders are concerned with knowing when their project investments will turn a profit. They want to know exactly when they are going to go from being in the red to being in the black. Positive cash flows can put business leaders at ease, or at least more at ease than negative cash flows. The payback period is the period of time required for a project's financial benefits to repay the sum of the project investment costs. The payback period shows how rapidly, or how slowly, a project returns the initial investment back to the company. For this reason it is often called the *time-to-money* period.

In most cases, shorter payback periods are preferable to longer payback periods. Shorter paybacks are ideal because businesses can begin to make money earlier and will have money at their disposal to invest elsewhere. A project with a shorter payback period, however, does not necessarily indicate it's the best project option. Projects with longer paybacks may be more profitable and have greater IRRs. The payback period is more aligned with liquidity than anything else. With liquidity, businesses have money at their disposal that they can re-invest.

The payback period is a popular tool because of its relative ease of use and because business leaders can understand the results quickly. Project teams can reply to those business leaders who like to say *show me the money* with, "You will see the money in 2.5 years when the payback period is reached."

Can you guess when a payback period can never be determined? Paybacks can never be calculated when cash inflows do not eventually outweigh cash outflows. These are projects that don't make any money for a firm. It doesn't mean that they are necessarily bad projects; it simply means that the ROI contributing benefits do not produce positive results. NPV, ROI, and IRR may still be analyzed for such projects, although the analysis will be negative numbers and percentages.

The payback period is often used as a measure of risk; the longer the payback, the riskier the project. For this reason, companies often establish certain parameters around payback periods based on their risk tolerances. For example, a risk-averse company may want to implement only those projects that have a payback of less than 2 years. This is also referred to as the cutoff period. So for this risk-averse company, any project that has a payback of more than 2 years is cut off from further analysis!

Here's a quick payback example: If a $10,000 project investment was made and it returned $2,500 per year, the payback period would occur at the end of the 4th year. This investment has a 4-year payback period. But I think we know by now the problem with this simple analysis. Yup, it doesn't incorporate the time value of money principle. Project teams need to determine the discounted payback period. Let's go back to our original example and see how the payback period can be determined. The quickest and easiest way to determine the payback period is to create a row of cumulative cash flow totals, which is simply a running total of the current DCF value plus the previous value or values. Table 11.4 shows the cumulative cash flow values increasing by time period. The time period where the values go from being negative to being positive is where the payback occurs. In this case, the payback occurs somewhere in the first half of year 2014.

A graphical illustration of the cumulative cash flows can be a powerful tool. Figure 11.1 shows exactly where the project breaks even and pays back

Table 11.4 Cash flow model incorporating cumulative cash flows

	Year 0	2012		2013		2014	
		1st-half	2nd-half	1st-half	2nd-half	1st-half	2nd-half
Cash outflows							
Hardware purchase cost	(75,000)						
Maintenance and operations		(2,000)	(2,000)	(2,500)	(2,500)	(2,800)	(3,000)
Total cash outflow	(75,000)	(2,000)	(2,000)	(2,500)	(2,500)	(2,800)	(3,000)
Cash inflows							
Additional product revenue		20,000	24,000	26,000	30,000	32,000	33,000
New product revenue		5,000	5,500	8,000	17,000	22,000	24,000
Total cash inflows		25,000	29,500	34,000	47,000	54,000	57,000
Total initial cash flow	(75,000)	23,000	27,500	31,500	44,500	51,200	54,000
Depreciation expense		(12,500)	(12,500)	(12,500)	(12,500)	(12,500)	(12,500)
Total pre-tax cash flows	(75,000)	10,500	15,000	19,000	32,000	38,700	41,500
Income taxes on cash flow		(150)	(600)	(1,800)	(5,400)	(7,410)	(8,550)
After-tax cash flow	(75,000)	10,350	14,400	17,200	26,600	31,290	32,950
Discounted cash flow	(75,000)	9,952	13,314	15,291	22,738	25,718	26,041
Cumulative cash flow	(75,000)	(65,048)	(51,734)	(36,444)	(13,706)	12,012	38,053

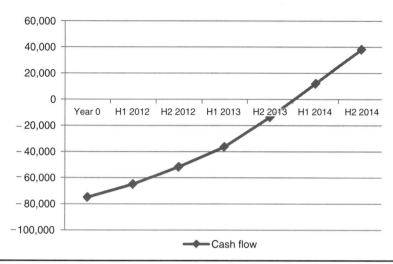

Figure 11.1 Cash flow break-even point

its initial investment. In this example, the payback is in the beginning of year 2014.

We now know that our project investment will pay for itself in just over 2 years. We also know it has a high ROI of 140% over a 3-year period. We also know the project produces a good IRR of 15.49% and will make the company $38,053 over a 3-year period. All and all, this seems like a good project investment.

Sensitivity Analysis to Evaluate Changing Business Variables

The ROI measurements are calculated based on input variables of the cash flow models, such as cost, schedule, production, quality, and time. The values for many of these input variables are not known with absolute certainty, but rely on estimates, forecasts, and assumptions. As these input variables change in the real world, the actual ROI measurements will change as well. It is imperative, therefore, to structure cash flow models to account for the changing business environment and fluctuating input variables to evaluate several possible options based on these changes. Project teams should analyze and determine how changes in the input variables impact the overall project ROI measurements. For instance, if material costs rise by 5% instead of remaining flat as expected, what impact does this have on the NPV? Or, if productivity gains increase only 2.5% instead of the expected 4%, how many months does this push back the payback period? Sensitivity analysis is a powerful tool to determine how *sensitive* the financial ROI results of a cash flow model are to changes in the values of the input variables.

Sensitivity analysis is a method of determining how variations in the business environment impact the results of the cash flow model. By systematically changing the input variables to reflect possible business scenarios, project teams can determine the effects of these changes on the overall ROI measurements. Nothing is static in the business world, risks and uncertainty are prevalent in all areas of business, and business leaders need to know which input variables have the greatest impact on overall results. In performing sensitivity analysis, businesses can evaluate different scenarios based on risks, uncertainties, trends, and other important business factors, and then make strategic decisions based on this evaluation.

Sensitivity analysis can be used on the fly during presentations or strategic meetings to demonstrate how results vary with changes to the input variables. Business leaders like to ask *what if* questions to account for risk and uncertainty and then evaluate how changes to certain business variables impact overall ROI results. With a laptop hooked up to a projector, project teams can instantaneously present the answers to these questions simply by changing the values of the input variables of the cash flow model. Common questions that are asked in evaluating the results of cash flow models include:

- What if sales increase only 2% as opposed to 5%?
- What if the benefits occur in year 4 as opposed to year 3?
- What if we reduce only 5% of staff instead of 7%?
- What if time savings are only 12 minutes as opposed to 15 minutes?
- What if the price of materials increases more than what is accounted for in the model?
- What if it takes longer for our staff to understand and know how to operate the equipment?
- What if we produce only 2% more units as opposed to 5%?
- What if we use a discount rate of 7% instead of 8.5%?
- What if the tax rate increases to 35% instead of 30%?
- What if we factor in a 7.5% contingency cost?
- What if travel costs increase to 15%?
- What if maintenance costs were only 10% as opposed to 15%?
- What if the cost escalation factor is only 2% per year as opposed to 3%?
- What if the benefit escalation factor is 4% per year as opposed to 3%?

Stakeholders will be quite impressed when you answer these questions in real time! Sensitivity analysis adds credibility to cash flow models since ranges for input variables can be analyzed as opposed to merely single numbers. Evaluating ranges of values more accurately reflects the dynamic business world. Additionally, investigating a wide range of input values can offer tremendous

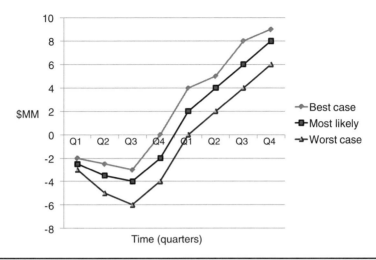

Figure 11.2   Various project NPV scenarios

insights into not only the most likely scenario, but the worst case scenario as well as the best case. Leaders want to know these scenarios to know exactly what they may be getting into. When the best case varies greatly from the worst case, the uncertainties, risks, and variability involved in the project may be too much for leaders to stomach and they may want to pursue other options. Project teams should be prepared to present the best case, most likely, and the worst case scenarios. A graphical depiction of these scenarios can be quite useful for stakeholders to quickly understand the complete project story. Figure 11.2 shows such a graphical depiction.

Project teams should definitely know which input variables have the greatest impact on the overall ROI results. These input variables, then, can be further scrutinized for accuracy. If the business decides to implement the project, managers can ensure that the right amount of focus and attention is paid to these high-impacting business elements. If it's determined, for instance, that a mere 1% difference in output production results in a 10% difference in NPV, management can then focus intently and take appropriate actions in optimizing output production and ensuring that it doesn't slip even the slightest amount.

Project teams can go beyond presenting the best case, most likely, and the worst case scenarios for the overall project by getting even more granular with the analysis of the various input variables. It's always best to present several possible scenarios to account for the dynamic business environment and to clearly identify which elements have the most impact on the business.

Table 11.5 Sensitivity analysis table

	Project Zulu			
	NPV ($MM)	IRR (%)	ROI (%)	Payback year
Most likely scenario (base case)	$2.6	13.3	45	20 months
Project costs				
10% below base case	$2.9	13.8	48	18 months
5% below base case	$2.75	13.5	46.5	19 months
5% above base case	$2.5	13.1	43	21 months
10% above base case	$2.35	12.9	41	22 months
Unit production				
10% above base case	$3.8	14.	65	15 months
5% above base case	$3.2	13.8	55	17 months
5% below base case	$2.4	12.6	36	24 months
10% below base case	$1.8	12.0	30	27 months
Time saving				
10% above base case	$2.8	13.8	49	18 months
5% above base case	$2.65	13.4	47	19 months
5% below base case	$2.4	13.2	42.5	22 months
10% below base case	$2.3	12.95	40	23 months
Project completed				
10% earlier than base case	$3.0	14.2	50	17 months
5% earlier than base case	$2.8	13.8	48	18 months
5% later than base case	$2.6	13.3	44.5	22 months
10% later than base case	$2.4	13.1	41.9	23 months

Table 11.5 shows an effective way to present variation for the significant input variables of a project. In the table, variations of the input variables are compared against the most likely scenario, or base case, to show how this variation affects the overall project ROI measurements. In this particular case, variation in production has the greatest impact on project results and should, therefore, receive the most management support and commitment.

Professional Development Game Plan for Success

1. Organizations rely on key measurements to evaluate their project investments to achieve their strategic goals. These measurements include NPV, ROI, IRR, and payback period. Regardless of your title, role or job function within your organization or project team, you need to

possess a solid understanding of these important business and project measurements. How deep is your knowledge of these important concepts? Can you have intelligent conversations of these concepts with executives? Are you able to calculate these measurements in spreadsheets and understand their implications to the business? Do you need some training?

Action Plan

   a. Assess your level of knowledge and understanding of these critical ROI measurements. To help guide your assessment, conduct discussions with competent project professionals, reference applicable documentation, practice these calculations in spreadsheets, and analyze some of the past business cases and cash flow models. How do you stack up? Based on your assessment, determine the appropriate actions that you can take to improve your knowledge and abilities in these key areas. You may consider attending formal training, taking an academic course, joining a study group, reading some books, perusing relevant websites, or even volunteering to be a part of cash flow modeling endeavors. Write down three to five actions that you *will* take within the next year to increase your business acumen and improve your ROI measurement knowledge and abilities. Now put the next action on your calendar and stick to it.

2. Too many project teams don't calculate all of the necessary ROI measurements to effectively and decisively evaluate their project investments. When is the last time your project teams calculated NPV, ROI, IRR, and payback period in their business cases? If ROI is the only one you can remember, you have the chance to make change in your organization that has a great impact!

Action Plan

   a. Examine three to five random business cases. What ROI measurements were calculated? Were they consistently and uniformly calculated across all of the business cases? What conclusions can you make in evaluating the ROI measurements of these business cases? Record three to five of your conclusions and write down any actions that you can pursue to ensure consistency and uniformity across the board when calculating ROI measurements. Be specific. This is important for your company. Start writing!

References

1. Heerkens, Gary R. 2006. *The Business-Savvy Project Manager.* New York, NY: McGraw-Hill.
2. Schmidt, Marty J. 2002. *The Business Case Guide.* Boston, MA: Solution Matrix.

12

Achieving Optimal Results in the Value Attainment Phase

Management by objective works—if you know the objectives. Ninety percent of the time you don't.

—Peter Drucker

Measuring, Achieving, and Optimizing Business Value Is a Formal Process

Your project was expertly *project-managed* and the solution has been successfully deployed. You go back to your clearly defined and thorough business case and (shocker!) many of your business benefits haven't been attained. Even with highly effective project management and successful deployments of project solutions, this happens far too often. Even when project return on investment (ROI) metrics are carefully calculated and targeted business benefits are agreed on and documented, many projects still fail to deliver on business and financial objectives. It's time to start realizing *all* of their intended business benefits your project investment was built to attain. Results-oriented value attainment plans can help your business achieve this lofty goal.

Value attainment focuses on achieving all of the ROI-contributing and value-enabling benefits that were identified and documented in the business case. Value attainment processes are conducted in a structured and organized manner to maximize the chances of achieving the targeted business and financial outcomes. A value attainment plan is a document that focuses on attaining, optimizing, and sustaining business value. This plan can be viewed as an extension of the business case because it establishes clear guidelines on how to capture, measure, manage, and achieve the targeted value metrics outlined in that important document. The value attainment plan also establishes formal accountability for managing, achieving, and sustaining each of the targeted business benefits. This documented accountability that is available to the project stakeholders greatly increases the motivation of the responsible parties to achieve their documented benefits.

Value attainment plans keep project teams focused on achieving the forecasted financial returns and other business benefits from their project investments, even after project solutions have been deployed. With these plans fully documented and agreed to, stakeholders and business leaders can be confident that project efforts are focused in the right direction and concentrated on achieving the targeted quantitative business objectives, after all, isn't that what we're trying to do here? When a detailed plan is put in place, project teams are also better equipped to measure progress, make adjustments, or take other actions to increase the chances of attaining these targeted benefits.

Since value attainment plans establish procedures for measuring and reporting the status of benefit attainment, business leaders are kept abreast of the progress on a regular basis with quantitative metrics. These metrics are typically presented utilizing dashboard reporting techniques to ensure the results can be quickly and easily understood by busy professionals. Stakeholders, then, will have the knowledge to more efficiently allocate resources, make strategic decisions, and perform operational adjustments to increase the probability that the goals can be achieved. Management may even be inclined to re-prioritize or revise the project scope based on the progress, or lack of progress, that is being made toward the attainment of the desired business value. Additionally, with a strong emphasis and focus placed on attaining the forecasted business objectives, project benefits may be achieved earlier than anticipated, which can result in the ability to close out the project ahead of schedule, a true rarity!

Project teams may also capitalize on the positive, *unexpected* benefits that may surface as a result of tracking, measuring, and presenting value metrics. These unforeseen, positive benefits will come as a welcome relief to project teams since typically when unforeseen results occur, they are usually negative in nature and detrimental to the business. But as value metrics are tracked and unexpected, positive trends begin to appear, business professionals can act on these positive trends and deliver even more value to the business. This is what some might call *gravy*. If plans aren't in place to capture data, analyze the results, and identify trends, however, these unexpected, positive benefits will never be discovered and can never lead to increased value to the business.

Value attainment plans can greatly assist any organization in any industry achieve their desired project outcomes. Effective execution of these plans ensures that companies remain focused and aligned with the original intent of their projects. The ultimate goal for any project team is to achieve, and even exceed, the forecasted returns for their project investments. Value attainment plans are vital components to achieving this ultimate end goal. Let's now discuss how to put this important plan together.

Developing the Value Attainment Plan

The value attainment plan is a vital document that should be created to ensure that a project manager's hard work actually produces the desired business results. This plan must be tightly woven into the overall project management plan and become one of the key project deliverables. Since the project management plan is a living document, the value attainment plan is normally completed once the value metrics have been identified and agreed to and the business case finalized. Both the ROI-contributing and value-enabling benefits are direct inputs to the value attainment plan.

Who is responsible for the development of this plan? As with most project documents, project managers are ultimately responsible for producing and maintaining the overarching value attainment plan. Project managers, however, may have limited involvement or control over how project outputs and deliverables are executed once handed over to the business (a major reason these plans never get developed in the first place!). For this reason, it's imperative that project managers include the appropriate business representatives, operations personnel, and other key business members in the development of these plans. Project managers may be responsible for developing the overarching plan, but it's the business personnel who are usually responsible for achieving the results set forth in the plan. These business representatives, therefore, must assume accountability for the benefits within their purview and be intimately involved in the creation of the plan to ensure that the most appropriate actions are planned for and executed. Since these valued resources are accountable for achieving their respective benefits, they will be assigned the role of *benefit owner* and will maintain ownership of their respective benefits until they are achieved.

Business case documents clearly articulate all of the business benefits that are expected to be achieved as a result of project implementations. Projects are successful when these forecasted benefits are achieved and, conversely, failures when they are not. It is imperative, therefore, to assign ownership and accountability to each and every one of these benefits to the persons most closely associated with them and most likely to take the best courses of action to achieve them.

The value attainment plan must explicitly state what benefits will occur; when they will occur; how they will be measured, reported, and optimized; and who is responsible for their manifestation. The project manager develops the overarching plan and the various benefit owners construct the detailed plans for each of the targeted benefits. The project manager, then, consolidates the various plans from each of the benefit owners and incorporates them into the overall value attainment plan.

A sound value management plan possesses key attributes, including:

- Formalizes the process of capturing business value
- Is an extension of the business case and is aligned to corporate strategic objectives
- Defines accountability and responsibility for achieving project benefits
- Establishes timeframes for achieving the benefits
- Specifies measurement techniques and frequencies
- Specifies performance reporting processes and frequencies
- Has strong stakeholder support and commitment
- Is tightly linked to change and risk management processes
- Ensures objectivity in the measurement results
- Identifies key dependencies for each benefit

There can be no ambiguity in accountability when it comes to achieving the business benefits for costly project investments. Project managers can eliminate any such ambiguity by creating executive summaries of value attainment plans that clearly list each of the targeted business benefits and their respective owners. Table 12.1 shows an example of a value management plan executive summary. With this executive summary, business leaders, or anyone else for that matter, can quickly determine the project quantitative objectives, the persons accountable for their attainment, and other important information.

Depending on the project, it may be advantageous to assign multiple owners to a single business benefit. This usually occurs when a single benefit is applicable to and spans multiple geographies or departments. Project managers need to be careful, however, to keep the number of benefit owners to a manageable amount. Table 12.2 illustrates how multiple owners can be assigned to a single business benefit.

The details of the value attainment plan come from each of the benefit owners. These benefit owners are intimately familiar with those areas of the business in which the benefits apply. They will know the minute details of how to measure, achieve, and optimize the benefits better than anyone else. I don't recommend assigning overall project ROI measurements, to include net present value, internal rate of return (IRR), ROI, and payback period, to benefit owners; the project sponsor, along with the project manager, should maintain accountability for the overall ROI metrics of the project. Project ROI results are dependent on certain benefits to be achieved. These ROI-contributing

Table 12.1 Value management plan executive summary

Project Sierra					
Business quantitative benefit	**Description**	**Benefit owner**	**Baseline**	**Target date**	**Dependencies**
ROI-contributing benefits					
Increase package deliveries by 5%	New package sorter will enable faster and more reliable placement on vehicles	Steve R.	25,000 deliveries per month	Q3, 2013	Training department must develop and deliver hands-on training of the new sorter
Reduce vehicle maintenance costs by 10%	Vendor negotiations resulted in improved pricing and more vendor involvement	Ashish J.	$2.3MM per month	Year end 2013	Vendor management team needs to finalize the contracts
Reduce maintenance FTE headcount by 5%	Due to more vendor involvement in maintenance activities, a reduction in staffing levels is required to eliminate duplicate work efforts and decrease costs	William S.	125 maintenance FTEs	Q2, 2014	Receive executive and HR authorization
Value-enabling benefits					
Increase customer satisfaction index rating to 3.5 out of 5	Customers will receive packages quicker as a result of faster sorting	Alfonso R.	Current customer satisfaction index is 2.8 out of 5	Year end 2014	Marketing team must develop new and improved online customer satisfaction surveys
Improved driver morale to a level of 4 out of 5	Vehicles will operate more smoothly and with fewer malfunctions due to vendor maintenance expertise	Ashish J.	Current employee morale at a level of 3.5 out of 5	Year end 2014	Union leaders must approve and authorize the survey forms

Table 12.2 Benefits spanning multiple geographies and departments

	Project Tango: Value management plan executive summary				
Business quantitative benefit	**Area**	**Benefit owner**	**Baseline**	**Target date**	**Dependencies**
ROI-contributing benefits					
Reduce FTE headcount by 10% across the company	North America	James K.	1,250 FTEs	Q4, 2014	Finalize early retirement incentives
	Asia Pacific	Lucy L.	650 FTEs	Q3, 2014	Hire career development services consultants
	Europe/Middle East	Hans F.	900 FTEs	Q2, 2015	Receive legal approval for each country
	South America	Alfonso R.	700 FTEs	Q4, 2014	Develop transition packages and training
Value-enabling benefits					
Reduce employee absenteeism by 10%	Marketing	Ken F.	15%	Q4, 2014	All employees are trained on the new policies and sign-off on them
	Operations	Tom C.	17%	Q3, 2014	Union reps approve of the new plans in writing
	Finance	Cesare P.	22.5%	Q2, 2015	Implement floating holiday policies
	Engineering	Steve S.	14%	Q4, 2014	Finalize plan of offering rewards of days off for performance

benefits and not the overall project ROI metrics, therefore, should be assigned to benefit owners. Benefit owners, however, should track the financial impact that their benefits generate in their specific areas of the business.

Project managers should guide and assist the benefit owners in the creation of these detailed plans. Project managers should also produce standard templates for each of the benefit owners to complete to ensure uniformity and consistency across the board. These templates should include key areas to facilitate the monitoring, measuring, reporting, and optimizing of the targeted benefits. The key areas for value attainment plans include the following:

- **Benefit title**—The benefit title must be clearly stated in quantitative terms. This should come directly from the business case. Benefits include both ROI contributors and value enablers. The SMART principle should have already been applied, so the benefit should be specific, measurable, attainable, realistic, and time-based. Examples of benefit titles include:
  - Increase unit production 20% by the third quarter of 2012
  - Reduce maintenance costs 10% by mid-year 2013 by outsourcing all maintenance operations to a single vendor
- **Current baseline**—The benefit title explicitly states what the business is trying to achieve and the baseline states how the business is currently performing, in quantitative terms. Business leaders need to know current baselines to determine the extent of the gap that needs to be closed to achieve the targeted benefit.
- **Detailed benefit description**—Although the benefit is stated in unambiguous terms incorporating the SMART principle, there still may be additional information that can be useful for stakeholders. This additional information should be included in this section of the plan.
- **Benefit owner**—The benefit owner is accountable for measuring the benefit, reporting its progress, taking appropriate action to ensure its attainment, and ultimately achieving or exceeding it. The benefit owner maintains ownership of the benefit until it has been achieved and/or the stakeholders are satisfied with the level of attainment. The benefit owner is usually responsible for that area of the business being impacted and will usually maintain operational accountability for that area of the business even after benefit attainment and project closure.
- **Benefit owner contact information**—All contact information for the benefit owner, such as mobile phone number, e-mail, department, and office location should be included so that he or she can be easily contacted by the various project team members.
- **Beneficiaries**—All of the applicable groups, departments, or individuals benefiting from the targeted benefit should be identified and documented. For some projects, the entire organization may be positively

impacted, but for others, only certain departments or certain segments of the business may be impacted. Specific office locations or even certain geographies may be sole beneficiaries. Benefit owners should get as specific as possible in determining the beneficiaries so that the most appropriate measurement and management activities are employed. Beneficiaries will usually have to modify existing work behaviors or experience some other type of change to realize the project benefit. For this reason, they must not only be clearly identified and documented, but should be involved in the various activities of benefit attainment. It may behoove the business to offer incentives to the beneficiaries to ensure their support and lessen their resistance to change. Examples of beneficiaries include:

- Marketing department
- Network engineering team within the operations department
- Production personnel at the White Plains, New York, manufacturing facility
- All Asia Pacific office workers

- **Start date**—The start date is when the benefit owner starts, in earnest, to measure, optimize, and achieve the targeted business benefit. This usually occurs immediately after the project solution has been implemented and the value attainment plan has been completed, but it can occur at any point along the project lifecycle. Remember, there are usually *quick hits* that can be achieved early in projects that can be instrumental in garnering project support and commitment.

- **Milestone date(s)**—The benefit owner should include key milestone dates and associated objectives to more effectively track the progress of benefit attainment. These milestone dates may come directly from the cash flow model in the business case, since these models specifically convey when financial benefits begin to surface and resurface. Examples of milestone dates and objectives include:

  - Achieve 15% of the targeted 20% cost savings by Q2, 2013
  - Have two of the four departments consolidated by year end and achieve 25% of the forecasted cost savings at the end of Q2, 2013
  - Increase unit production by 50 widgets per day in Q3, 2013 and by 75 widgets per day in Q1, 2014

- **Benefit attainment date**—This important date is when the benefit is expected to be fully achieved. The business case and cash flow model should clearly identify this important end date. Not all of the project benefits listed in the business case will occur at the same time.

- **Benefit dependencies**—The benefit owner should identify all of the dependencies that exist and the associated actions that need to occur for the benefit to be achieved. They should focus their attention in the areas of people, processes, and technologies to help them identify these dependencies. Dependencies include any initiatives, changes, or modifications that need to occur within specific areas of the business before the targeted benefit can be achieved or before certain actions can be taken to achieve the benefit. Benefit owners should determine where in the organization these actions are required, who will be impacted, and when they need to happen. Examples of benefit dependencies include:

- Formal and hands-on training need to be delivered to the users of the system before the end of the year.
- Educational material, reference guides, and quick-tip cheat sheets need to be developed and distributed before the system goes live.
- All essential staff members must be relocated to the new office building before the end of the year.
- New processes need to be developed, documented, and rehearsed before going live in the production environment.

- **Risks to achieving the benefit**—The risks to achieving the targeted benefit should be identified and documented, as well as their likelihood (high/medium/low) and impact (high/medium/low). Quite often risks can be easily and quickly addressed if stakeholders simply know of their existence. But if risks are not identified and communicated, they won't be addressed and may pose serious threats to achieving the benefit. When risks are identified, they can be tracked and managed to ensure they don't jeopardize benefit attainment. Examples of risks to achieving certain benefits include:
  - Lack of leadership involvement from the engineering team
  - Equipment shipment dates are not met
  - Lack of internal experience and expertise to deploy the technical solution

- **Risk mitigation strategies**—Mitigating risk is reducing the extent of exposure to an identified risk and/or decreasing the likelihood of its occurrence. Approaches to mitigating risks should be clearly articulated as well as any actions that should be taken to minimize any negative effects that may result from the risk. Risk mitigation strategies for the risks identified include:
  - The project manager will invite the vice president of engineering to executive steering committee meetings to ensure active leadership involvement from the engineering team.
  - The project team will submit all equipment purchase orders to the purchasing department two weeks ahead of schedule and will request that all orders pertaining to the project be expedited to ensure equipment shipment dates are met.
  - The project sponsor will hire external consultants to provide leadership and expertise for all technology deployment efforts.

- **Measurement processes and frequency**—Benefit owners need to determine how and when to measure key metrics and data elements surrounding their assigned benefit. They should determine the most appropriate performance measurements methods and techniques, in both monetary and nonmonetary terms, if applicable. If baseline metrics were already established, benefit owners may be able to use the same, or similar, measurement processes and techniques. The measurement systems should provide real-time, or near real-time, information so that problems or trends can be identified and addressed as quickly as possible. Examples of measurement processes and techniques include:
  - Producing quarterly production reports
  - Analyzing monthly sales reports
  - Generating 24-hour network availability statistics
  - Distributing satisfaction surveys two months after deployment
  - Tracking and analyzing monthly help desk calls
- **Performance reporting processes and frequency**—Benefit owners need to determine how and when to present the progress benefit attainment. They should work closely with project managers in determining these important activities and incorporate them into the overall stakeholder communication plan. Quite often there will be numerous reports, statistics, graphs, trend lines, and other performance-related information. Benefit owners must determine the most appropriate ways to package all of this information into reports that are easily understood by the various stakeholders. It's best to visually represent performance metrics by displaying them in charts, graphs, and diagrams. We've discussed the importance of building cash flow models in increments of months, quarters, and half-years, as opposed to just years. The performance reports and frequency of the reports should be aligned with the cash flow trends within the project cash flow models. For instance, if the cash flow model forecasts a 10% productivity improvement at the end of Q2, a performance report should be produced at the end of Q2 showing productivity levels.
- **Benefit optimization processes and techniques**—The purpose of tracking and measuring the progress being made toward the attainment of business benefits is to increase the likelihood that these benefits will actually be achieved. Based on the performance measurements and the progress, or lack of progress, being made, benefit owners may have to take additional actions. They may have to make adjustments to a system, expedite certain initiatives, allocate resources more effectively, or perform other actions to get the project back on track to attain the targeted benefit. Benefit owners should proactively plan for these actions and document them in this section of the value attainment plan. Examples of optimization processes and techniques are:

- Work with the systems vendor to fine-tune configuration parameters to improve performance levels
- Further streamline processes to achieve time savings
- Allocate additional resources to the project to expedite results
- Automate approval processes to prevent delays

Tables 12.3a and 12.3b show an example of a value attainment plan for a process improvement initiative that includes all of the elements described.

Executing the Value Attainment Plan to Achieve Results

With the value attainment plan fully vetted, it's time to achieve the forecasted business value and targeted benefits. The benefit owner and project team members should carefully follow the value attainment plan and carry out all of the specific actions prescribed within it. Central to these actions is monitoring and measuring the current performance against the targeted outcomes to ensure the business benefits are on track. These measurements should be repeated at intervals outlined in the value attainment plan to determine overall performance improvement, or even degradation, trends, and performance patterns. Based on each of the measurement results, benefit owners should resolve any issues in a timely manner and take appropriate actions to adjust and optimize business performance. Business analysis and decision making certainly doesn't stop once the project solution has been implemented. In fact, performance analysis efforts should be elevated since the deployed project solution finally starts producing business value for the organization.

We've incorporated the value attainment phase into the traditional project lifecycle approach to prevent organizations from continuing down the road that leads to nowhere. In this case, the road to nowhere is unrealized or partial business value. By incorporating the value attainment phase, organizations can apply strategic focus to ensure they are going down the road that leads to successful project completion and optimized business value. As we discussed in Chapter 3, projects should not be terminated until operational teams and business units have had the opportunity to achieve the project objectives articulated in the business case. Figure 12.1 re-introduces the value-centric project lifecycle methodology, highlighting the critical value attainment phase. As a result of this phase, optimized business value *can and will be achieved* and operational teams will assume control of an *enhanced* steady-state of operations on project closure. It's no longer business as usual!

With value attainment efforts, organizations can terminate the reckless and costly practices of closing out projects, disbanding entire project teams, and losing focus on project objectives right at the point where project teams have the greatest opportunities to affect and drive business value and benefit

Table 12.3a Value attainment plan

	Help desk process improvement		
Benefit title	Increase the percentage of incidents resolved by the first line of support of the help desk by 20%. This increase will result in the first line of support resolving 90% of all recorded incidents.	Current baseline	• Help desk receives an average of 5000 incidents per month • First line of support resolves 70% of these incidents • Second line of support resolves 20% of the incidents • Third line of support resolves 10% of the incidents
Detailed benefit description	The first line of support of the help desk is escalating far too many incidents to second and third lines of support, which is taking too much time away from strategic roles. As a result of this process improvement initiative, the first line of support should be able to resolve at least 90% of all incidents.		
Benefit owner	Charles D. Vice President of Operations	Contact information	• Operations team • Office: 212-123-1212 • Mobile: 917-111-1122 • CD@mail.com • 1200 Broadway, New York, NY 10001
Beneficiaries	• All U.S.-based employees • All Mexico-based employees • All Toronto-based employees		
Start date	Q2, 2012	Milestone date(s)	• By Q4, 2012, first line of support resolves 78% of all incidents • By Q2, 2013, first line of support resolves 85% of all incidents	Benefit attainment date	December 31, 2013

Table 12.3b Value attainment plan

	Help desk process improvement		
Benefit dependencies (people and process technology)	• An outside consulting firm needs to assess the current situation, perform a gap analysis against target-state objectives, and deliver a plan by Q1, 2012. • All members of the first line of support of the help desk need to attend process training by Q3, 2012. • A software upgrade to the ticketing system needs to occur by Q3, 2012. • Second and third lines of support need to provide detailed documentation to the first line by Q4, 2012.		
Risks to achieving the benefit	First line of support may not possess adequate skill sets to resolve the more complex incidents.	Risk mitigation strategies	In addition to formal training, second and third lines of support will informally train the first line on the more complex incidents that are encountered.
Measurement process and frequency	• Help desk reports will be generated by the ticketing system on a weekly basis. • These reports will include the total amount of incidents for the week and the percentages resolved by first, second, and third lines of support. • Any anomalies will be highlighted and the operations manager will provide comments to address them.		
Performance reporting process and frequency	• All operations managers and supervisors will receive these weekly reports. • Project stakeholders will receive monthly reports. • Executive steering committee members will receive quarterly reports.		
Benefit optimization processes and techniques	• If performance improvements aren't forthcoming or less than anticipated, the benefit owner shall investigate the scripts that the first line of support is presenting to the customers. Perhaps the scripts aren't detailed enough or not focused in the appropriate areas. • Benefit owner shall make periodic assessments of the overall quality of the investigative procedures and will make adjustments as necessary. • Will investigate advanced training and other vendors if performance improvements are dismal.		

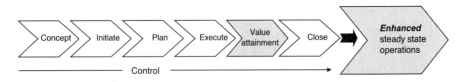

Figure 12.1   Value-centric project lifecycle

attainment. Projects cost money. Without concerted efforts to achieve or exceed forecasted business value, much of that money is wasted. Too many important business activities and changes take place once a project solution is deployed to simply forego focused and rigorous value attainment efforts. A few of these strategic activities and changes are:

- Redeploying, consolidating, and even terminating employees
- Changing well-established business processes and norms
- Operating with new technological systems
- Conducting business with new partners, suppliers, and vendors
- Working in new geographic locations
- Conducting business with new customers
- Competing with new competitors

The value attainment phase is where the rubber meets the road. This is where businesses excel or fall short. Project teams and stakeholders must be thoroughly engaged in the value attainment phase to actively manage these critical business activities and strategic changes and to motivate employees in the acceptance of these changes. They must ensure that these strategic and value-impacting endeavors are conducted in the most efficient manner possible to achieve the targeted business objectives, as well as to ensure minimal disruptions to their organizations. Doing otherwise increases the chances that their companies will revert back to their old ways and resume business as usual, which is usually suboptimal, since projects were initiated to change these established ways.

Establishing project continuity is imperative to maintaining momentum and focus on value attainment. When this continuity isn't enforced, project team members go on to their next assignments and operational teams are the ones left holding the proverbial bag in the form of project deliverables. We've seen what happens when this occurs. Some degree of project management must remain intact during the critical value attainment phase. It doesn't have to be 100%, or even 75%, but a sufficient level of project management commitment must remain to drive the project toward the ultimate goal of benefit attainment.

In today's business environment, multitasking is simply part of doing business. Project managers have become quite adept at this skill and are capable of working on several projects simultaneously. If it's determined that only a fraction of project management is required for this phase, then I'm sure project managers will be able to achieve exceptional positive results with that level of commitment. This phase is simply too important to dismiss project management entirely. The project manager was responsible for the development of the value attainment plan. It makes good business sense to keep this person on board, in some capacity, to achieve the results. As with other project phases, detailed RASCI charts should be developed to determine the appropriate levels of involvement for all key project personnel, including the project manager.

Measuring the performance of benefits using quantitative metrics is a key business activity of the value attainment phase. These measurements aren't taken to merely present the results to the stakeholders, but to identify trends, analyze performance patterns, perform root-cause analysis, and to identify additional business opportunities that may surface. Too often business decisions are made and actions are taken without adequate, quantifiable justification, which leads to unfavorable results. By tracking metrics and producing performance reports, business leaders can make better decisions and implement actions most suitable to their businesses.

Some of you may have heard the expression, *measure twice, cut once,* when used in the context of carpentry or construction. Good carpenters ensure that measurements are taken more than once to achieve high degrees of accuracy before they start cutting. If measurements are made inaccurately, their projects will not be built to specifications and they will spend additional time and money replacing wood and other materials. It's no different in the corporate world. Business professionals must measure and measure often. Based on these measurements, leaders can then take appropriate actions to meet the specifications detailed in the business case. Measurement and performance reports come in many flavors and should be presented in a manner where all stakeholders can clearly understand them. Figure 12.2 shows an example of a project performance report. As can be seen, a lot of important information can be gleaned from such a report, such as trends, variances, progress, and timelines.

Benefit owners and project managers should conduct periodic performance reviews with key stakeholders to discuss the measurement results and any implications that may arise from the results. Project managers should encourage feedback and seek input into appropriate courses of action to expedite or enhance the progress being made. Stakeholders should collectively determine ways to maximize the benefits and to identify opportunity areas to create even more value for the business. Business leaders are often quite surprised with the value-enabling opportunities that surface when business performance metrics are monitored, evaluated, and presented. The details of the value attainment plans may even need to be updated based on the progress that was made or the new opportunities that may have surfaced.

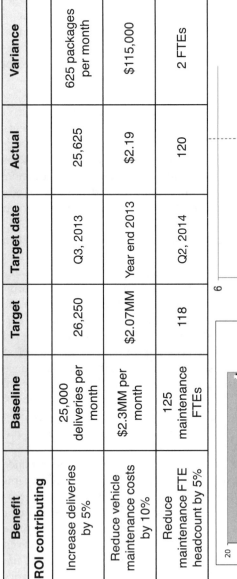

Benefit	Baseline	Target	Target date	Actual	Variance
ROI contributing					
Increase deliveries by 5%	25,000 deliveries per month	26,250	Q3, 2013	25,625	625 packages per month
Reduce vehicle maintenance costs by 10%	$2.3MM per month	$2.07MM	Year end 2013	$2.19	$115,000
Reduce maintenance FTE headcount by 5%	125 maintenance FTEs	118	Q2, 2014	120	2 FTEs

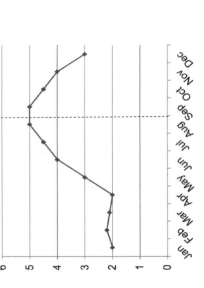

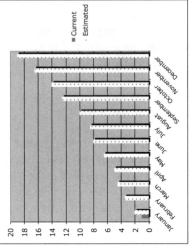

Figure 12.2   Performance report examples

As we all know, it's not always possible, or even practical, to get key stakeholders in a room all at once. For this reason project managers must maintain good communication channels in the value attainment phase to facilitate the presentation of project results and to elicit feedback and input into improvement areas. To ensure that feedback and input are provided, project managers may find it useful to assign *homework* to specific persons so that they can research certain business areas or investigate possible solutions. These homework assignments are usually assigned during key meetings and are due by the time of the next key meeting so that the results can be discussed. Project managers may want to maintain an action item register to keep track of all of the outstanding action items and homework assignments.

Education and training are also key elements of the value attainment phase. Project teams typically conduct training sessions during or immediately after the project solution has been deployed. This is good, but they usually don't follow up to ensure that the training was successful or they don't train employees on how to achieve *peak* business performance. Training should be delivered and educational material should be disseminated to the appropriate groups impacted by the project solution. The training and educational material, furthermore, may have to be updated based on key project findings. For instance, a benefit owner may conclude that certain process steps can be eliminated to increase product delivery time to the customer. Enhancements to training material are good indicators that project teams are focusing on value and finding new or improved ways to optimize that value. As with performance reports, there are many different flavors to educational and training methods and material. Project teams should determine the most appropriate method for each of the specific groups involved. Such training can be formal, informal, hands-on, computer-based, internally driven, externally driven, and even self-paced.

Risk and change management processes need to be carefully implemented during the value attainment phase. There are risks associated with any type of business initiative or action. These risks will be greatly minimized when business initiatives are based on quantifiable performance metrics as opposed to abstract targets, but nonetheless, they will still exist and should be carefully evaluated and mitigated. Before implementing any change to the production environment, change control procedures should be carefully followed and the upcoming changes should be clearly communicated. The impacted teams and business units need to be informed well in advance of these upcoming change initiatives so they can take appropriate precautionary measures and develop back-out plans should the changes not go according to plan.

At the conclusion of the value attainment phase, business leaders will be able to determine the true business value of their projects. They will be able to compare the forecasted results articulated in the business case against the actual results that they achieved. They will also be able to better determine why the targeted outcomes were or were not achieved. Once stakeholders are satisfied with the results or collectively determine that the project is at a point where it can be terminated, the project manager can then advance the project to the closeout phase.

Business and project professionals must learn from their project efforts and determine what they did well, what they did poorly, and what they can improve on. They must also make a commitment to continuous improvement to ensure that the business stays focused on achieving increased value in order to remain competitive. These important concepts are discussed in Chapter 13.

Professional Development Game Plan for Success

1. Value attainment plans are valuable tools for ensuring that specific and measurable business benefits can be achieved and even exceeded. How does your company manage value attainment? Is there a formal value attainment plan? Maybe it's called a benefit realization plan or benefit management plan? How effective are they in facilitating value and benefit attainment?

   Action Plan

   a. Assess your company's posture on value attainment plans. What plan templates are available and readily accessible? How much value do they add? What is the process for assigning benefit owners? Does your company enforce and support the execution of the plans? How is accountability maintained? Based on your assessment, determine appropriate action plans that you can take to improve your company's posture toward value attainment plans. Consider the template of the plan itself as well as the execution of the plan. Write down three to five strategic but detailed actions that you can take or recommendations that you can make to improve your company's position toward value attainment plans.

   b. If your company does not embrace the use of value attainment plans, build your own business case (now that you know how to build an effective one!) to educate the appropriate management personnel on their importance and necessity for achieving maximum results from your projects. You may want to consider developing a template or putting together a slide presentation that discusses the merits of these plans. Who can you review your ideas with? Who should you be presenting them to? Go to your calendar and schedule the next step.

2. Organizations achieve consistently better business results from their projects when value metrics are monitored, evaluated, adjusted, and

presented. Based on your project experience, how well are value metrics identified, monitored, and presented to management teams for review and input? Look for examples of how your measurements lead to actions that lead to improved business performance and record these. Did you use the most appropriate tools for tracking and presenting value metrics? Is this even a priority for your company or department? How effectively do you use the tools at your disposal in your job?

Action Plan

a. Revisit two or three of your prior projects and assess how well value metrics were identified, monitored, adjusted, and presented. Evaluate the effectiveness of *how* performance reports were generated. Did the process lead to strong performance metrics that make business decisions easier? If not, where did they fall short? Were there more effective ways to generate them? What could have enhanced this part of the process? Evaluate the effectiveness of the *contents* of these reports. Was the information timely, relevant, and useful for decision making? Did the appropriate teams review the reports? Were they generated and disseminated at appropriate times? Create your own standard operating procedures for developing your value metrics and reports. Make it good enough to share with your team.

b. Now write down what you will do or actions you will take on your current or future projects to ensure that the appropriate value metrics are properly tracked, measured, analyzed, tweaked, and reported. There are no wrong answers here. Your focus should be on those things you will do to ensure the targeted business benefits will be absolutely attained. This may require investigating various measurement tools, obtaining password permissions to use such tools, researching how measurements can be formatted or incorporated into management reports, or leveraging resources skilled in certain tasks for knowledge transfer sessions.

13

From Project Closure to Continuous Value Improvement

Without continual growth and progress, such words as improvement, achievement, and success have no meaning.

—Benjamin Franklin

Beyond the Typical Lessons Learned

The primary purpose of lessons learned has typically been to review project management performance and execution to gather insights, both positive and negative, that can be usefully applied to future projects. Project teams usually identify which facets of the project were conducted successfully and which ones posed challenges and obstacles. The intent, then, is for project team members to learn from their past experiences to capitalize on the successes and to avoid the failures for future projects. Additionally, the output of lessons learned sessions should be made available for the rest of the organization so that other project teams can leverage the positive attributes and avoid repeating the same mistakes. Unfortunately, most organizations don't devote enough time and energy to this beneficial project activity and end up repeating the same mistakes over and over again. Since there is no transfer of knowledge or best practices from one project team to the next, the more appropriate moniker for this important project activity is lessons *not* learned. It behooves project managers, sponsors, and stakeholders to embrace this project activity and devote the necessary time and effort to ensure that the entire organization benefits from its outputs.

Lessons learned sessions are also sometimes known as postmortems, project audits, and post-project reviews. I don't like these names because they have negative connotations and imply that they can only be useful on project closure. Besides, who really wants to be an active part of something called a postmortem? I recommend sticking consistently to the term lessons learned as this clearly states the positive intent to learn from project lessons. Project teams can learn valuable lessons from their projects by taking these sessions seriously. Some of the questions project teams should attempt to answer in their lessons learned sessions include:

- What did we learn from the project?
- What strengths can we build on?
- What can we do better?
- How can we apply these lessons to our future projects?
- How can other project teams leverage these lessons learned for their projects?

The answers to these basic questions can go a long way for future project teams, as well as for the professional development of project professionals.

The concept of lessons learned is certainly not new. Sports coaches constantly apply lessons learned in the strategic management of their teams, game plans, schedules, and coaching staff. Lessons learned are applied at the end of the game to determine which strategies worked and which ones didn't so they can make adjustments before they face their next opponent. The good coaches, furthermore, not only apply lessons learned at the end of games, but utilize them at periodic points *during* the game, such as during time-outs, halftime sessions, between innings, between sets, and at various other points throughout the game. A bell should be going off in your heads right now: *apply lessons learned throughout all phases of the project lifecycle and not just during project closeout!* The lessons learned that are applied during project closeout, however, do serve as the grand finale and should be conducted and documented with precision and care to ensure their lasting effect throughout the organization.

Lessons learned are not only reserved for athletic competitions and project endeavors; people apply lessons learned on a daily basis. When you go out to a new restaurant, for instance, and find the service to be dreadful and the food awful, will you go there again? Probably not. That's a lesson learned, albeit the hard way!

Some of the areas for improvement in a typical lessons learned session are that they are predictable, lack depth, and don't add much value for professional development or for other project teams. Common takeaways from most lessons learned sessions include rather shallow, insubstantial lessons, such as:

- Not enough time
- Not enough people
- Not enough management support
- Too many hidden costs
- Too many other commitments for project team members
- Not enough planning
- Too many unrealistic expectations

For the most part, there will *never* be enough time, resources, or management support and there will *always* be hidden costs and other commitments. We need to stop rushing through this important project activity and avoid producing a laundry list of so-called lessons learned.

The process involves much more than a quick brain dump of what comes to mind, but rather requires detailed and thorough analysis that requires analytical thinking and even investigative work to uncover some of the not-so-obvious project lessons. For lessons learned to be useful, all project teams throughout organizations must be able to leverage them and apply them to their projects. So instead of saying there wasn't enough time, find out *why* there wasn't enough time, *how* planning could have been conducted more efficiently to account for the necessary time requirements, *how* to better optimize resources' time, and *what* meetings or activities distracted from project commitments. Now this information would be useful for other project teams trying to navigate the complexities and obstacles of their projects.

The focus of lessons learned is nearly always on the qualitative side of project management and execution and not on the quantitative side of business results and value. Of course it's important to capture the qualitative side of lessons learned, because project teams can benefit greatly with this information. But it's absolutely essential to discuss and evaluate, in detail, whether or not the business benefits and project financial returns were achieved. These are the reasons for the project in the first place and can't be glanced over during lessons learned. This is what business leaders really need to know so they can continue implementing those strategies that increase value and avoid those that do not produce desirable results.

By executing the value attainment plan, project teams compare the financial and quantitative forecasts from the business case against the actual results. Quantitative lessons should be learned during the value attainment phase and at project closure. A few of the results-oriented, quantitative questions that should be asked during lessons learned sessions include:

- Why wasn't the projected net present value achieved?
- Why did the investment break even long after the forecasted payback period?
- How did we fall 11% lower than our forecasted IRR?

- How did employee productivity increase even more than the expected percentage?
- Why didn't customer satisfaction increase to the targeted level?

By asking and discussing these types of quantitative questions, project teams aren't merely providing lip service during lessons learned sessions but are getting to the heart and soul of why the project contributed, or didn't contribute, to the overall success of the company.

It is absolutely necessary to revisit the business case during lessons learned sessions, because this document served as the basis for the project investment and specified the expected outcomes. In addition to comparing actual results against forecasted results, you will also gain extremely valuable insight into the effectiveness of the initial business case so that you can leverage these for your own professional development.

Inaccuracies in the business case may cost businesses money and may even lead to the implementation of undesirable project investments. It's imperative, therefore, to revisit and scrutinize the assumptions, the costs, the benefits, the cash flows, the estimates, and financial calculations to uncover any and all lessons that could be learned and usefully applied elsewhere. Keep in mind that other project team members are developing business cases for their projects and are struggling with similar assumptions, estimates, cost determinations, and cash flow projections. They can benefit greatly by leveraging a detailed and comprehensive results-oriented repository of lessons learned surrounding the business case.

There will always be those stakeholders who like to ask, "Why did you make this assumption?" or "Why didn't you include these cost elements?" Monday morning quarterbacks always find their way into lessons learned sessions! These questions, however, are good ones, and project professionals should be prepared to answer them. Many of these Monday morning quarterbacks may find out, much to their chagrin, that business cases were prepared inaccurately because they did not engage in the development process to the level expected of them. Additionally, they may have hurriedly signed off on these important business documents without proper analysis. The successful execution of projects requires the commitment and input from *all* stakeholders. This is why they are stakeholders in the first place. The evaluation and analysis of stakeholder involvement is not off limits during lessons learned sessions. Stakeholders play strategic roles for many projects, and businesses can't afford to have them making the same mistakes from project to project. (For those not familiar with American football, a Monday morning quarterback is someone who criticizes the performances of the various football teams and players who played on that Sunday—yes, like many of our stakeholder friends on project completion.)

If the project team concludes that the business case was solid and the contents were reasonably accurate, but the project failed to deliver the expected outcomes, the lessons to be learned will usually apply to the execution of value attainment efforts. These lessons learned can be anything from the lack of follow-on training to incomplete documentation to inadequately skilled resources. The only way to get to the root-causes of why the quantitative results weren't achieved is to do a detailed and comprehensive review of all of the activities that contributed, or did not contribute, to the attainment of the expected benefits. Each and every one of the targeted benefits should be carefully analyzed to uncover the lessons to be learned as to why these results fell short or possibly even exceeded the forecasts. Table 13.1 shows an example of how lessons learned can be applied to the business objectives set forth in the business case.

To capture the relevant results-oriented lessons learned, project managers must include business owners, key stakeholders, and other representatives, as appropriate, in these thought-provoking discussions. Quantitative lessons learned go beyond the core project team and way beyond typical project management checklists. These strategic sessions focus on the business and operational issues of value attainment and growth. Benefit owners, operational teams, and key stakeholders are the ones who are capable of influencing their organizations and should, therefore, be included in lessons learned sessions. These strategic players will serve as stakeholders and decision makers for other projects and can apply these results-oriented lessons learned to those projects as well.

It's imperative to not only identify lessons learned, but to document them, store them to an easily accessible online repository and ensure that all project teams are leveraging them. Lessons learned must be an integral component to all phases of the project management lifecycle, so include the beginning stages. In Chapter 2 we talked about the importance of planning and how too many project teams rush into the execution phases of their projects. An important component to the planning process is the evaluation of lessons learned from other projects. Lessons learned is not only a post-project activity or an activity that occurs at periodic points along the project lifecycle, but must be a front-end activity as well. Project professionals can glean tremendous insight from reviewing other lessons learned, such as where they need to beef up resources, where they should allow more time for certain activities, which change agents to include, and which cost elements may produce overruns. Transferring knowledge from one project to another offers tremendous benefits, improves project performance, and ultimately leads to project success and value attainment.

Value Attainment Doesn't Stop!

Now that the project is over and all of the benefits have been achieved, the organization can take a breather and go back to doing business as usual. Right?

Table 13.1 Quantitative lessons learned

Project Sierra			
Business quantitative benefit	**Actual result**	**Variance**	**Lessons learned**
ROI-contributing benefits			
Increase package deliveries by 5%, from 50,000 to 52,500 per week	Package deliveries increased by only 2.4%, from 50,000 to 51,200	−2.6% (1,300 packages short of goal)	Project team did not provide enough advanced notification to the warehouses of the new package sorter. As a result, the warehouse teams could not free up their resources to attend training on the new package sorter. They were, therefore, unable to leverage the advanced features of the new equipment. For future initiatives that involve warehouse employees, a minimum of four months notification is required to allow for planning and schedule adjustments.
Reduce vehicle maintenance costs by 10%	Vehicle maintenance costs decreased by only 6.5%	−3.5%	All of the vendor costs were not accounted for in the business case. These costs included shipping, taxes, and vendor travel. The project team did not delve deep enough into the vendor cost structures and made poor assumptions. For future projects, supplier management and finance representation will be included in vendor pricing discussions and business case development activities.
Reduce maintenance FTE headcount by 2.5%	Headcount was reduced 2.5%	0%	The project team did an excellent job of involving senior executives and human resource representatives in the early planning phases of the project. This allowed for proper and thorough planning that resulted in the achievement of this goal.
Value-enabling benefits			
Increase customer satisfaction index rating from 3.2 to 3.5 (out of 5.0)	Customer satisfaction index rating decreased to 3.0 out of 5.0	−0.5 from the objective	We overpromised and underdelivered. We should not have been so aggressive in our marketing campaign, promising so many benefits for a solution that hasn't been thoroughly proven or tested. We will not employ such tactics in the future unless we have concrete evidence that the solution produced expected results in a small scale or prototype environment.
Improved driver morale to a level from 3.5 to 4.0 (out of 5.0)	Driver morale increased to 4.2.	+0.2 from the objective	The maintenance program improved the reliability of the vehicles, and drivers did not encounter nearly the amount of vehicle malfunctions as before the program. Additionally, drivers appreciated the quick tips guide that the project team developed to assist them in troubleshooting basic problems. For future projects, we will ensure such guides are developed.

Wrong! Too many business professionals, unfortunately, take this view and feel that the completion of a project indicates the end of the game; the whistle has blown, it's time to put this one behind us and move on. When the whistle blows in sports, it may indicate the end of a game, but do the coaches and players stop planning, hitting the weight room, running wind sprints, and improving their overall performance? Of course not. They know they have to contend with other opponents on other days. These opponents certainly haven't stopped upgrading their game plans and improving their performance. In the business world, the competition hasn't stopped striving for that elusive competitive edge, nor should you. Just because a project has been completed, it doesn't mean that all of the heavy lifting is done. In fact, there's more lifting to do and the weights aren't getting any lighter. Projects may have been executed flawlessly and achieved their targeted objectives, but perfection can never be achieved; there's always room for improvement and the competition isn't standing still. Continuous value improvement of project results is not only possible but necessary to remain competitive in the challenging business environment.

Maintaining and, more importantly, increasing the business value that was achieved from project deployments requires a culture of continuous improvement. Without such a culture, organizations often find themselves backsliding and losing the momentum that they achieved with all of their project efforts. When projects come to a close and resources are deployed elsewhere, too often the focus on maintaining and increasing those project value returns comes to an end. When this occurs, organizations often go back to their old ways of doing business, which leads to deteriorating performance and results. Figure 13.1 gives an example of how business results may suffer when companies lose focus on business value and continuous improvement during project closure. As can be seen, all of the business gains that were achieved during the value attainment phase quickly dissipated on project closeout.

The purpose of the value attainment phase is to achieve, and even exceed, peak performance and results. Once these performance results have been attained, the bar has been set, proverbially speaking. The performance bar has been raised and set to a higher level due to the tireless work of the project team. It's now up to the management and operational teams to ensure that performance results never slip below this new level. Business leaders must make concerted efforts to ensure that their teams don't backslide and go back to doing business as usual, resulting in poorer performance. Managers should keep their measurement systems in place and continue monitoring, evaluating, and adjusting results for peak performance. This value focus must become a normal part of doing business. It is an essential component to a culture of continuous improvement.

Nobody says that business leaders and stakeholders can't continue to receive performance reports on project closure. It is good business practice for

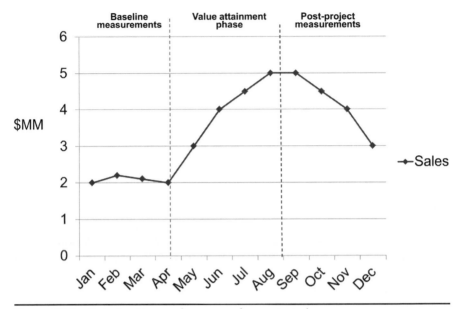

Figure 13.1   Deteriorating performance after project closure

leaders to stay abreast of performance metrics. Managers rely on quantitative reports to assess the business and to make strategic decisions based on business measurements. Business performance reports that can be quite useful for managers include budgets, sales reports, production trends, time and cost savings reports, network statistics, staffing levels, productivity parameters, and marketing forecasts. Quantitative data prevents leaders from always making key decisions from the gut. Since measurement systems are already in place due to value attainment efforts, operational teams can continue to generate, analyze, and present performance reports. The project may be over but decision makers still need to evaluate business results to ensure they are not backsliding to pre-project performance levels and are trending in the right direction.

As we've stressed throughout, the business environment is dynamic and constantly changing. If business leaders don't take concentrated measures to ensure their businesses are keeping pace with this dynamic environment, the changes will overwhelm them and they are more apt to lose control of the business or respective areas of the business. Even though a project may have delivered quality products or services, these project outputs have to be continually adjusted and readjusted to the changing business environment. The moment organizations cease improvement or optimization efforts is the moment they open themselves up to performance degradation and diminishing profits.

When performance objectives have been achieved from project efforts, business leaders must update and formalize both internal and external business contracts, such as operating- and service-level agreements (OLAs/SLAs), with the new performance standards. These elevated performance metrics become the new baseline which continued performance is measured. If the help desk, for instance, can now accommodate 250 service requests per day instead of the pre-project number of 200, this becomes the new standard and the help desk's new obligation to the business. If it takes financial analysts 15 seconds to access critical reports during peak periods of the day instead of the pre-project time of 45 seconds, this is the new standard and IT's new obligation to the business. I think you get the point, but to reemphasize: *Performance should never fall back to pre-project performance levels*. Maintaining a quantitative focus on results after project closure and constantly striving to improve those results can prevent backsliding and lead to maintained or increased performance levels. Figure 13.2 shows how performance charts *should* look several time periods beyond project closure.

With business distractions occurring every single day, it's tempting to eschew strategic continuous improvement initiatives to focus on tactical firefighting issues. This is especially true when businesses are achieving acceptable levels of performance. Too often, however, businesses become satisfied with the status quo and simply strive to maintain it. We've all heard the popular adage, *if it ain't broke, don't fix it*, and too many businesses adopt this mantra as

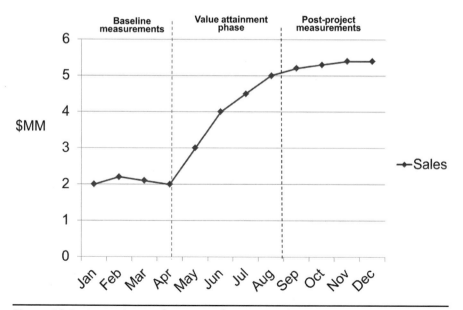

Figure 13.2   Increasing performance after project closure

their own. Many of the businesses that have adopted this mantra aren't around anymore! This adage may apply to some areas in life, but it certainly doesn't apply to today's competitive business environment. The adage that successful companies have adopted to remain competitive is, *if it ain't broke, fix it anyway*. When companies wait around for their products, processes, systems, or other essential areas to break, it's *much* more expensive to fix those breakages than it is to take small, simple measures to ensure that they don't break in the first place. When companies take proactive measures to continuously improve performance in all areas of their business, they become better positioned to maintain and increase that all-important competitive edge.

Businesses don't need to incorporate fancy, over-intellectualized management philosophies or techniques to ensure a culture of continuous improvement. We've seen some of the management philosophies and variations of those philosophies that have been introduced and re-introduced over the past century in Chapter 1. Organizations can embrace and implement any methodology or philosophy in which they are comfortable in order to instill a culture of continuous improvement. There are certainly merits to each and every one of the management approaches.

At the foundation of nearly all continuous improvement approaches and methodologies lies the popular, effective, and straightforward approach called the Deming cycle. For this reason, I strongly recommend leveraging this approach in structuring your continuous improvement activities. The Deming cycle is a continuous improvement methodology that focuses on four main stages, to include *Plan, Do, Check*, and *Act*. These four stages are repeated over time to ensure continuous learning and improvements in a product, process, or service. By leveraging the Deming cycle, companies achieve and maintain a culture of steady, ongoing improvement in practically all areas of their businesses. Figure 13.3 is a graphical depiction of the Deming cycle of continuous improvement. Placing this simple picture on your office door or wall can serve as a useful reminder that value attainment never stops and that continuous improvement must be an ongoing process.

When projects formally end, value attainment and continuous improvement efforts must not. By incorporating the Deming cycle into the operational aspects of business, companies can maintain a quantitative focus on business value and continually improve bottom-line results. Significant amounts of time, money, and resources are expended on project investments to achieve positive business results; it's an absolute shame when these results diminish on project closure. I'm sure you wouldn't like to see the financial returns of your personal investments dissipate after attaining all-time highs. Well, business leaders and shareholders certainly don't want to see the returns of their project investments diminish either. This is what happens, however, when businesses lose focus on maintaining and improving business results on project closure. The Deming cycle is a straightforward, proven approach that enables continuous

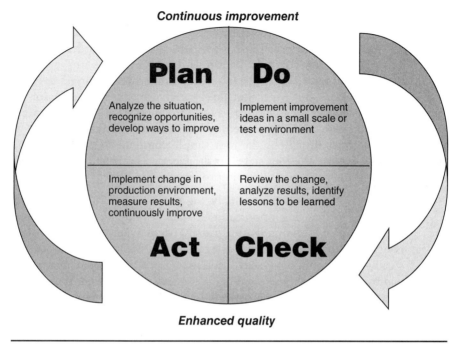

Figure 13.3   The Deming cycle

improvement and quality assurance. In leveraging the Deming cycle, organizations can employ quantitative measurement techniques and procedures to ensure that returns on project investments continue to trend favorably, keeping the shareholder investors satisfied with their returns.

A quick note on Deming. Dr. W. Edwards Deming was a pioneer in the field of quality and business management. His most notable achievement during his lifetime was the tremendous impact he had on the Japanese postwar industrial revival by teaching his quantitative approaches to quality management and continuous improvement. He taught that business processes and operational procedures should be constantly measured and evaluated to identify sources of variation that cause deviations from customer requirements. To ensure continuous improvement, he recommended that business processes be placed in a continuous feedback loop to allow business leaders to identify and modify the parts of the process that need improvements. In addition to the Deming cycle, he is also well known for other revolutionary approaches, such as the fourteen points, system of profound knowledge, and seven deadly diseases. There is a wealth of information out there covering this visionary's life and teachings. I highly recommend exploring some of his works. You won't be disappointed.

I was fortunate to have been a part of a Deming focus group early in my career where we studied the intricacies of his methods and philosophy. To this day I have not found an approach that is as straightforward, understandable, and effective as the Deming cycle with regard to continuous improvement and quality enhancement. That is not to say that other methods aren't as good, or even more effective, but I feel that the Deming cycle can be used universally across all businesses in all industries with the most ease. Of course, organizations should employ whatever method works for them, but at the core of any of these methods usually lie the four simple components of the Deming approach. Let's explore the four stages of the Deming cycle and see how they can be leveraged for your continuous improvement efforts:

1. **PLAN:** This stage involves analyzing the current situation, gathering data, recognizing opportunities, and developing ways to make improvements. These activities usually occur when a formal project is being executed, but once project deliverables are handed over to steady-state operations, they usually cease. Operational teams can and must perform these planning activities as part of their normal job functions. The operational goal is to continuously measure and improve on baseline performance metrics. Managers need to identify those areas that are not operating at peak capacity and devise solutions to rectify the problems. It's important for business units to focus intently on their respective *money makers* and not get too caught up *in the weeds*. Business leaders should focus primarily on those areas that produce the greatest business value and have the greatest impact on their organizations. There will always be low hanging fruit and it's good to achieve these quick hits, but concerted efforts should be taken continuously to improve those areas that most directly impact overall profitability.

2. **DO:** In this stage business professionals implement improvement ideas. It's advisable to implement changes in small-scale, testing or pilot environments to assess the effectiveness before deploying them to wider or production environments. Conflicts and glitches may arise during this stage that should be resolved before proceeding with the change or solution on a larger scale. The actions that are taken in the Do stage are usually operational procedures such as changing configuration parameters of a system, upgrading hardware revisions, automating process steps, or consolidating software platforms. These operational tasks may seem innocuous to some folks, but they can have adverse effects if they don't go as planned. For this reason, strict change and risk control procedures should always be followed.

3. **CHECK:** Business professionals should now review the changes, analyze the results, verify their effectiveness and identify lessons to be

learned so they can be applied when implementing the change to the wider or production environment. Remember, lessons learned is a continuous process and doesn't simply occur on project closure. Managers should verify that the desired results are being attained and that quality standards are also being achieved. Operational teams should also investigate any problems that result from the change and address them appropriately. Finally, the measurement reports should be presented to decision makers for analysis and approval.

4. **ACT:** Once the change has been verified and approved in the small scale environment, operations teams can now fully implement the changes into the production environment or to the wider audience, leveraging what was learned in the previous stages. Risk and change control procedures should again be strictly followed. Managers must continually measure and verify the results of the fully deployed solution until they are confident that the results are repeatable and sustainable.

Once all of the stages are successfully completed and business leaders are satisfied with the results, the improvements resulting from the changes are now standardized. The proverbial bar has been raised to a new level, and this level becomes the new and improved baseline. These new performance standards must be fully documented in all relevant documentation, such as OLAs, SLAs, and vendor contracts. The new performance standard is again subject to further improvement, given business requirements and timelines. The Deming cycle, thus, is repeated again and again continuously monitoring, measuring, and improving them, ensuring that companies don't become complacent.

For some companies, embracing philosophies of continuous improvement, constant learning, and unceasing focus on quality may require complete cultural transformations. But for most companies, the tenets of these philosophies already exist in some form or another, and it's usually simply a matter of focus and emphasis to ensure they are being followed. This strategic focus must begin at the top and must be filtered throughout the entire organization so that all business professionals are on board and are conducting appropriate continuous improvement activities. Projects may be officially closed out and core project teams disbanded, but the roles of senior managers, business owners, subject matter experts, and staff members certainly aren't going anywhere. When these key roles possess a perpetual focus on performance improvement, the financial returns and other business benefits resulting from project investments won't be wasted but will continue to trend favorably for the long haul. This is what it's all about.

Professional Development Game Plan for Success

1. Lessons learned sessions are tremendously valuable project activities when conducted thoroughly and with a quantitative, results-oriented focus. These sessions are useful for core project team members, stakeholders, extended team members, and even other project teams throughout the organization. What has your experience been with lessons learned? Have you learned from them? Do you leverage lessons learned from previous or other projects when embarking on a new project? Do you employ a quantitative, results-oriented focus? Is it a mandatory requirement to conduct, document, and post lessons learned on project completion? What about when embarking on a project? Is it a mandatory requirement to leverage lessons learned from a central repository to assist with planning efforts?

   Action Plan

   a. Pick two or three of the lessons learned sessions in which you've been involved over the years. Evaluate their effectiveness and usefulness. What did you learn from them? How did they enhance your professional development? What do you do differently as a result of them? How does your organization share lessons learned? What quantitative project aspects do they focus on? As a result of your analysis, write down five to eight activities you will do differently on your next project to ensure that lessons learned are not only conducted, but conducted in a way that is truly beneficial for the project team as well as other project teams throughout your organization. Think about some of the things you will do throughout all phases of the project and not just during project closeout. You may want to leverage any lessons learned templates and consider revising them, or perhaps you need to develop them from scratch. I'm sure you can think of many improvement areas. Start writing!

2. Continuous improvement initiatives ensure that the returns from project investments don't diminish on project closure but continue to improve long after these project milestones. How does your organization foster continuous improvement? What methodologies or approaches are followed to ensure continuous improvement? How long does your company measure and report on projects after closure?

   Action Plan

   a. Think about what happens after your project deliverables are submitted for approval, the project team disbands, and the project is officially closed. Does business as usual resume or do operations teams embrace the project outputs and use them to improve performance? Now think about several months to a year after project closure. Has performance improved, declined, or stayed steady? Revisit two or three of your prior projects that have been closed for at least a year and assess how your organization is currently performing as a result of those projects. What conclusions can you make? Record five to eight activities or processes that could have been done differently to improve overall performance. This includes what could have been done *during* the project, as well as *after* project closure. These can include transition activities, performance reporting, performance checkpoint meetings, operational tasks, improvement methodologies, or leadership practices. Be specific. Be sure to include anything that *you* could have done that would have improved performance over the last year or so.

b. Now write down what you will do or actions you will take on your current or future projects to ensure that performance parameters keep improving long after project closure. Record three to five continuous improvement actions that you will take or will influence. What will you do to maintain the momentum and ensure that the business results continually improve? How will you interact with operations teams? With management teams? What mechanisms or tools are in place or need to be in place for continuous improvement? How can you leverage these mechanisms or tools? Write them down!

Appendix

This appendix provides a template that can be leveraged for a departmental or operations business plan. Examples are inserted at various points throughout this template for illustrative purposes.

Business Plan Template

Introduction

Purpose of this document

Example

The purpose of this document is to provide a central source of information relating to the business focus for the Southeast operation for 2012. The business plan is also designed to communicate a vision and direction for the Southeast operation over the next 6 to 12 months as the organization continues to pursue increasing opportunities aggressively. The 2012 business plan should serve as a roadmap for the operation as it defines and implements the tactical and strategic steps needed to achieve its goals.

Executive Summary

Business overview

Examples

- Sales have been declining
- Competition has been increasing
- Economic conditions are turning around

Key findings

Examples

- Low morale
- Lack of in-depth industry expertise
- High attrition

Recommendations

Example

The Southeast operation defined challenging but attainable goals. In striving to achieve all of these goals, the operation determined specific strategic plans to be implemented and monitored over the next 6 to 12 months. A summary of these strategies is:

- Strategy 1: Reorganize business units along industry sectors
- Strategy 2: Retain top employees
- Strategy 3: Expand Vendor A partnership
- Strategy 4: Terminate Vendor B partnership
- Strategy 5: Implement process improvement initiatives
- Strategy 6: Increase international collaboration
- Strategy 7: Consolidate data centers
- Strategy 8: Revisit the business plan quarterly

Business Plan Methodology

Approach to Developing the Business Plan

Southeast operation sources of information

Examples

- Questionnaire responses
- Interview results
- Focus group results
- Sales collateral
- Performance reviews
- Sales reports
- Sales forecasts

Corporate sources of information

Examples

- Annual report
- Marketing information
- Financial reports
- Partnership documentation

External sources of information

Examples

- Industry benchmark reports
- Federal Reserve economic indicator reports
- Local economic reports
- Economic analyses from various websites
- Competitive analyses reports

Market Analysis

National economic trends

Examples

- Gross Domestic Product quarterly changes
- Dow Jones Industrial average trends
- Inflation trends
- Unemployment rates

Southeast economic trends

Examples

- Local unemployment rates
- New business openings
- Average salaries across industries

Industry-specific trends

Examples

- Manufacturing
- Financial services
- Information technology
- Food and agriculture

Southeast Current Operational State

Southeast operation mission statement

Primary product and service offerings
Geographic regions
Southeast management overview

Examples

- Organizational chart
- Average years of experience
- Average education levels

Southeast operational overview

Examples

- Organizational chart
- Average salaries
- Average years of service
- Average education levels

Southeast Operation SWOT Analysis

Strengths

Examples

- Mature management and sales teams
- Solid customer base
- Strong reputation

Weaknesses

Examples

- Lack of a vision
- Few employee incentives
- Low morale

Opportunities

Examples

- Increased sales through partnerships
- Merger potential with Company X
- Advanced employee leadership training

Threats

Examples

- Attrition
- Competition entering into the local market
- Local economic conditions

Southeast Vendor Partnership Analysis

Partnership 1

- Overview of the partnership
- Challenges
- Opportunities
- Plans for moving forward

Partnership 2

- Overview of the partnership
- Challenges
- Opportunities
- Plans for moving forward

Southeast Operation Financial Analysis

Financial overview

Examples

- Revenues
- Profit
- Expenses
- Accounts receivable

Financial Breakdown by Industry Sector

Financial trends

Examples

- Monthly
- Quarterly
- Yearly

Financial forecasts

Examples

- Sales/Profit
- By industry sector
- New customers
- Existing customers

Customer Analysis

Revenue by Customer

Top customers by vertical market

Sales pipeline

- Revenue potential
- Probability

Competitive analysis

Competitor 1 overview

- Competitive advantage
- Competitive disadvantage
- Conclusion and recommendations

Competitor 2 overview

- Competitive advantage
- Competitive disadvantage
- Conclusion and recommendations

Southeast operation goals

Examples

- Achieve revenue of $53.2 million
- Achieve net profit of 30%
- Achieve less than 10% attrition annually
- Increase partner business to 15% of total revenue
- Train 90% of all managers in advanced leadership techniques
- Increase business in the healthcare sector by 20%
- Consolidate manufacturing facilities
- Increase unit production by 5%

Southeast Strategies for Achieving Goals

Strategy 1: Reorganize business units along industry sectors

Challenge

- Example: We haven't been able to build deep industry knowledge because our employees are stretched too thin along too many various industries. Employees are not able to spend the appropriate time and energy in acquiring thorough and extensive industry knowledge for specific industries.

Strategy statement

- Example: Reorganize the business units along industry sectors to encourage and facilitate deep industry knowledge, skills enhancement, industry collaboration, and industry-specific brand recognition.

Action Plans

- Example: Deploy reorganizational task force to build out migration plan and oversee all reorganizational efforts.

Resources

- Example: All vice presidents and above meet weekly to review plans.

Timeframes

Examples

- Healthcare by Q2, 2012
- Financial services by Q3, 2012
- All others by end of year, 2012

Strategy 2: Retain top performers

- Challenge
- Strategy statement
- Action plans
- Resources
- Timeframes

Strategy 3: Expand Vendor A partnership

- Challenge
- Strategy statement
- Action plans
- Resources
- Timeframes

Threats and risks to achieving our goals

Examples

- Attrition due to salary freezes
- Low morale due to lack of outside training

- Economic instability
- Sales turnover due to start-up companies
- Aging equipment
- Local military base closure
- Government cutbacks

Business Plan Summary/Conclusion

Index